Praise for the first edition of *Biking Puget Sound*:

"This guide is a great resource."
—University Book Store Staff Favorites

"Biking Puget Sound *has something for everyone."*
—Seattle Magazine

"It's a decent wager that many bike riders—beginners to veterans—will find some sort of revelation in where to ride within the pages of Thorness's book."
—North Kitsap Herald

"Bill's creation is all someone would need in order to select an enjoyable route for a two-wheeled adventure anywhere between Thurston County and the San Juans."
—Washington State Grange News

"Thorness will steer you off the well-pedaled path with his new guidebook, which features clear, easy-to-follow maps and—equally important—elevation charts and time estimates for each ride."
—Seattle Weekly

BIKING
puget sound
2ND EDITION

*60 Rides from
Olympia to the
San Juans*

BILL THORNESS

MOUNTAINEERS
BOOKS

To my companion on and off the trails—
my wife, Susie Thorness—
without whose support and camaraderie this project
would have been work instead of play

Mountaineers Books is the nonprofit publishing division of
The Mountaineers, an organization founded in 1906 and
dedicated to the exploration, preservation, and enjoyment
of outdoor and wilderness areas.

MOUNTAINEERS
BOOKS

1001 SW Klickitat Way, Suite 201 • Seattle, WA 98134
800.553.4453 • www.mountaineersbooks.org

Copyright © October 2014 by Bill Thorness
All rights reserved. No part of this book may be reproduced or utilized in any form, or by
any electronic, mechanical, or other means, without the prior written permission of the
publisher.

Printed in the United States of America

Distributed in the United Kingdom by Cordee, www.cordee.co.uk

First edition 2007, second edition 2014

Copy editor: Kris Fulsaas
Design: Mountaineers Books
Layout: Emily Ford
Cartography and elevation profiles: Ben Pease, Pease Press
Cover photograph: Michael Hanson/Aurora Open/Corbis
All photographs by author unless noted otherwise

Frontispiece: *A cyclist crosses the Montlake Bridge in Seattle, part of the Lake Washington Loop.*
Back cover photograph: *Cattle Point Lighthouse*

Library of Congress Cataloging-in-Publication Data

Thorness, Bill, 1960–
Biking Puget Sound : 60 rides from Olympia to the San Juans / Bill Thorness.—Second
edition.
    pages cm.
  Includes bibliographical references and index.
  ISBN 978-1-59485-890-1 (pbk) — ISBN 978-1-59485-891-8 (ebook)
  1. Bicycle touring—Washington (State)—Guidebooks. 2. Bicycle trails—Washington
(State)—Guidebooks. 3. Washington (State)—Guidebooks.
  I. Title.
  GV1045.5.W2T56 2014
  796.6'4097977—dc23
                                    2014011600

 Printed on recycled paper

ISBN (paperback): 978-1-59485-890-1
ISBN (ebook): 978-1-59485-891-8

CONTENTS

THURSTON COUNTY

With your purchase of this book, you also get access to our easy-to-use, downloadable cue sheets:

» Go to our website: www.mountaineersbooks.org/PSQSheets
» Download a complete set of mileage cues for all 60 rides in this book.
» When you open the document on your computer, enter the code "sn0h0m1sh15" when prompted.

It's our way of thanking you for supporting Mountaineers Books and our mission of outdoor recreation and conservation.

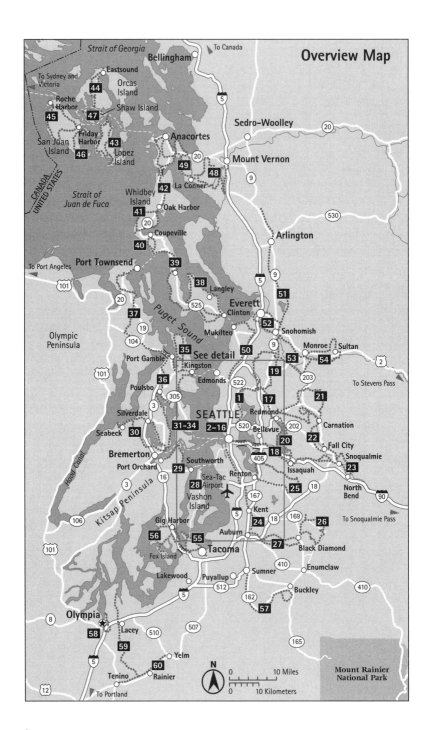

Overview Map

Strait of Georgia

To Canada

Bellingham

To Sydney and Victoria

Eastsound

Orcas Island

44

Roche Harbor

45

Shaw Island

47

San Juan Island

Friday Harbor

46

43

Lopez Island

Anacortes

Sedro-Woolley

20

5

Mount Vernon

9

49

48

20

CANADA UNITED STATES

Strait of Juan de Fuca

Whidbey Island

La Conner

42

Oak Harbor

41

Coupeville

20

530

Arlington

40

To Port Angeles

Port Townsend

39

101

20

Langley

38

5

9

Everett

51

525

Clinton

Olympic Peninsula

37

19

Mukilteo

52

Snohomish

104

Monroe

Sultan

Port Gamble

35

See detail

9

53

54

2

To Stevens Pass

101

Kingston

50

Poulsbo

36

Edmonds

522

19

203

To Stevens Pass

305

3

SEATTLE

Redmond

1

17

21

Silverdale

31-34

2-16

520

Bellevue

202

Carnation

Seabeck

30

Bremerton

Port Orchard

29

Southworth

Sea-Tac Airport

520

20

22

Fall City

18

405

Snoqualmie

23

Hood Canal

Kitsap Peninsula

16

28

Vashon Island

Renton

167

Issaquah

25

18

North Bend

90

3

Gig Harbor

5

Kent

24

18

169

26

To Snoqualmie Pass

106

56

55

Auburn

27

Black Diamond

101

Tacoma

Fox Island

Sumner

410

Enumclaw

Lakewood

Puyallup

512

162

57

Buckley

410

5

165

8

Olympia

Lacey

510

507

58

59

Yelm

12

60

Rainier

Tenino

To Portland

N

0   10 Miles

0   10 Kilometers

Mount Rainier National Park

8

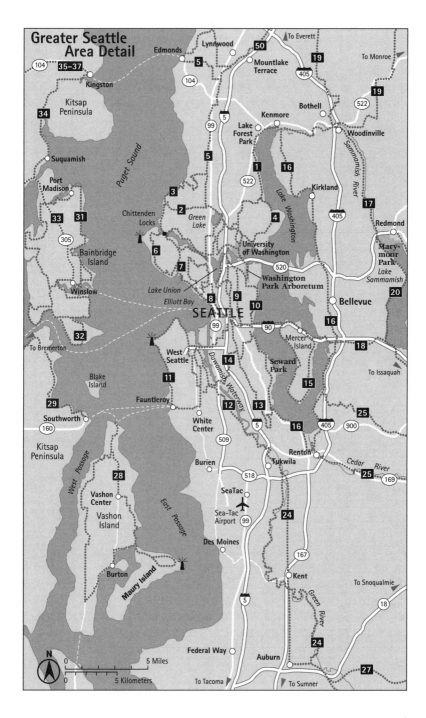

Greater Seattle
Area Detail

To Everett

104 35-37
Kingston

Edmonds 5
Lynnwood 50 To Monroe

104 Mountlake Terrace 19 19

Kitsap Peninsula 34

99 5 Lake Forest Park Kenmore Bothell 522 Woodinville

Suquamish

5 1 16 Sammamish River

Puget Sound

Port Madison 522 Kirkland

33 31 3 17 Redmond

Chittenden Locks 2 Green Lake 4 305

305 6 University of Washington Mary-moor Park Lake Sammamish

Bainbridge Island 7 520 Washington Park Arboretum 20

Winslow Lake Union Elliott Bay 8 9 Bellevue

SEATTLE 10 90 16

99 Mercer Island 18

32 West Seattle 14 Seward Park To Issaquah

To Bremerton Duwamish Waterway

Blake Island 11 15

29 Fauntleroy 12 13 405 900 25

Southworth White Center 5 16

160

Kitsap Peninsula 509

Burien Renton Tukwila Cedar River 25 169

28 518 25

Vashon Center SeaTac 24

Vashon Island Sea-Tac Airport 99

Des Moines 167

Burton Kent To Snoqualmie

Maury Island Green River 18

N 5

Federal Way Auburn 24

0 5 Miles 27

0 5 Kilometers

To Tacoma To Sumner

RIDES AT-A-GLANCE

Ride No.	Route	Difficulty	Distance in Miles	Elev. Gain in Feet	Time in Hours	Points of Interest
SEATTLE						
1	Burke-Gilman Trail	Easy	24.2	386	2.5	University of Washington, Magnuson Park, shopping district
2	Northwest Seattle	Easy	13.8	582	1.5	Golden Gardens Park, Chittenden Locks, shopping districts
3	Carkeek and Golden Gardens Parks	Moderate	19.6	1394	2.5	City parks, Chittenden Locks
4	Magnuson and Ravenna Parks	Easy	15.6	581	1.5	Ravenna ravine, Magnuson Park
5	Green Lake to Edmonds	Moderate	29.7	1382	3.5	Edmonds underwater park, ferry
6	Magnolia and Discovery Park	Easy	9.7	560	1.5	Olympics views, Discovery Park, Chittenden Locks
7	Queen Anne and Seattle Center	Moderate	9.2	541	1.5	Shopping district, Space Needle, SAM Olympic Sculpture Park
8	Downtown Seattle	Moderate	9.5	459	1.5	SAM Olympic Sculpture Park, International District, Seattle Public Library, Pike Place Market, Space Needle
9	UW, the Arboretum, and Central Seattle	Moderate	20.1	1447	3	UW, Washington Park Arboretum, Central Park Trail, Volunteer Park
10	Historic Seattle: Lake Union and Lake Washington Paths	Moderate	15.9	1116	2.5	South Lake Union Park, Cheshiahud Loop, Interlaken Park
11	West Seattle	Easy	15.1	750	2	Alki Beach, Lincoln Park, Seattle Chinese Garden
12	Duwamish Trail	Easy	25.6	251	3	Fort Dent Park, Duwamish access points
13	Chief Sealth Trail and Kubota Garden	Moderate	16.3	1214	2	Chief Sealth Trail, Kubota Garden, Mount Rainier views
14	South Seattle: Georgetown to Mount Baker	Moderate	20.3	1254	3	Hat and Boots historic buildings, shopping district, Beacon Food Forest
KING COUNTY						
15	Mercer Island Loop	Easy	13.9	712	1.5	Luther Burbank Park, winding lanes
16	Lake Washington Loop	Strenuous	48.9	1919	6	Multiple waterfront stops, parks
17	Sammamish River Trail	Easy	28.4	322	2.5	Marymoor Park, Velodrome, brewery, wineries

Ride No.	Route	Difficulty	Distance in Miles	Elev. Gain in Feet	Time in Hours	Points of Interest
18	Mountains to Sound Greenway	Challenging	37.3	2246	5.5	Mercer Slough, Issaquah cafés, Lake Sammamish State Park
19	Woodinville to Snohomish	Moderate	36.6	1870	4.5	Suburban trail, small-town cafés
20	Redmond to Issaquah and Preston	Challenging	49.4	2061	6	Issaquah shopping district, secluded Preston Trail
21	Redmond to Carnation and Duvall	Challenging	40.9	1967	5	Farms, Cascade mountain views
22	Snoqualmie Valley Farm Tour	Easy	35.6	587	3	Farms, rural roads
23	Snoqualmie Falls	Moderate	21.1	854	3	Mount Si views, Snoqualmie Falls overlook and trail
24	Green River and Interurban Trails	Moderate	39.3	398	4	Suburban parks
25	Cedar River Trail and May Valley	Moderate	28.1	1031	3	Rural roads, Lake Washington waterfront
26	Green River Gorge and Black Diamond	Moderate	26.5	1383	3	Rural roads, Gorge overlook, bakery
27	Auburn to Flaming Geyser State Park	Moderate	31.5	1009	3.5	Park, farms, bakery
28	Vashon and Maury Islands	Strenuous	37.4	2822	5	Farms, Point Robinson Lighthouse
KITSAP COUNTY						
29	Port Orchard	Easy	30.9	987	3	Coastline biking, Olympic views
30	Bremerton to Seabeck and Scenic Beach	Strenuous	37.1	2788	4.5	Scenic park, Olympic views
31	Bainbridge Island Loop	Challenging	33.9	2230	4	Olympic mountain views, Winslow shops and cafés
32	Winslow to Fort Ward	Moderate	19.7	1193	2.5	Military ruins, Olympic views
33	Bainbridge Ferry to Bremerton Ferry	Challenging	32	2234	4	Military museums, Poulsbo waterfront, Olympic views

Ride No.	Route	Difficulty	Distance in Miles	Elev. Gain in Feet	Time in Hours	Points of Interest
34	Bainbridge Ferry to Kingston Ferry	Moderate	21	1380	2.5	Chief Sealth's grave
35	Point No Point and Little Boston	Moderate	27.9	1529	3	Lighthouse, Native American community center
36	Port Gamble, Poulsbo, and Chief Sealth's Grave	Moderate	33.4	1789	3.5	Chief Sealth's grave, mill town, Scandinavian town
37	Kingston to Port Townsend	Challenging	41	1880	5	Hood Canal Bridge, country roads, farm stands, Victorian port town, rural trail
THE ISLANDS						
38	South Whidbey Island: Freeland and Langley	Challenging	34.1	2425	4.5	Artistic town, rural roads
39	Whidbey Ferries: Coupeville to Clinton	Moderate	34.9	2326	3.5	State park, agritourism, rural roads
40	Central Whidbey Island: Coupeville and Fort Casey	Easy	12.7	506	1.5	Coastal views, military ruins, farm roads
41	Central Whidbey Island: Oak Harbor and Fort Ebey	Easy	19.3	1309	3	Military ruins, farm roads
42	North Whidbey Island: Deception Pass and San Juan Islands Ferry	Challenging	47.4	2795	6	Deception Pass Bridge, rural roads, waterfront views
43	Lopez Island	Moderate	34.2	1865	4.5	Rural roads, waterfront views
44	Orcas Island	Moderate	21.8	1615	3	Farms, artistic town
45	San Juan Island: Lime Kiln and Roche Harbor	Moderate	31.8	2059	4	Coastal views, whale watching, historical park, marina
46	San Juan Island: Cattle Point	Moderate	26	1486	3	Historical park, coastal views
47	Shaw Island	Easy	13.4	886	2	Secluded roads, historic school

Ride No.	Route	Difficulty	Distance in Miles	Elev. Gain in Feet	Time in Hours	Points of Interest
SKAGIT COUNTY						
48	Skagit Flats and Tulip Fields	Moderate	35.7	227	4	Farm roads, tulip fields, artsy tourist town
49	La Conner to Anacortes	Challenging	38.8	2075	5	Rural roads, waterfront views, artistic towns
SNOHOMISH COUNTY						
50	Interurban Trail and Mukilteo	Challenging	44.3	2109	5	Urban exploration, ferry town
51	Centennial Trail	Challenging	65.6	1131	6.5	Rural, tree-lined trail
52	Snohomish to Everett	Moderate	21.8	793	2.5	Slough, river
53	Snohomish to Monroe	Moderate	30.9	815	3	Tourist town, farm roads
54	Monroe to Sultan	Moderate	24.7	965	2.5	Cascade mountain views
PIERCE COUNTY						
55	Downtown Tacoma, Point Defiance, and the Narrows	Moderate	23.8	1069	3	Museum of Glass, shady park ride
56	Gig Harbor and Fox Island	Challenging	33.2	2753	5	Quaint waterfront, shady park, big bridge, island bridge
57	Foothills Trail	Easy	29.8	402	2.5	Rural scenes, Mount Rainier views
THURSTON COUNTY						
58	State Capitol and Central Olympia	Easy	17.2	571	2.5	Capitol campus, parks
59	Chehalis Western and Woodard Bay Trails	Easy	28.8	512	3	Rural scenes, sculpture park
			16.5	236	1.5	
60	Yelm-Tenino Trail	Easy	27.3	527	3.5	Small towns, rural scenes

ACKNOWLEDGMENTS

Many thanks to cyclists across the Puget Sound region for pointing me in the right direction on my two-wheeled travels. Valuable guidance was provided by the Rides Committee and staff of the Cascade Bicycle Club in Seattle, and I've learned much from my fellow ride leaders at Cascade. Individuals from across the region providing particular assistance include Paul Ahart, Barbara Culp, Tom Fucoloro, Dave Gardiner, Jan Johnson, M. J. Kelly, Kristin Kinnamon, Pete Lagerwey, Darcy Patterson, Kent Peterson, John Pope, Jim Shedd, Jeff Smith, Kat Sweet, and Jim Taylor.

Thanks to John Lehman and the staff at R&E Cycles' great repair shop for keeping my wheels spinning during years of research and to the editorial and marketing staff at Mountaineers Books for keeping me on track during the writing. I'm especially appreciative of the guidance from Kate Rogers, the support and biking inspiration from Doug Canfield, and the stellar editing from Kris Fulsaas. Thanks also to the inspiration of Erin and Bill Woods and their well-loved book, *Bicycling the Backroads Around Puget Sound*, which was replaced by this title, and other influential biking authors whose books are listed in the Recommended Resources. May this book meet your standards. I hope it also would pass mettle with my inspirational late friend Karl Arne, who once rode from Seattle to San Francisco to attend a nonprofit board meeting. He was a principled environmentalist for whom the bike was an everyday instrument of good.

Finally, my deepest appreciation to the many friends who offered encouragement, support, and companionship on the trails, particularly Bill Alkofer, Chuck Ayers, Duane Brady, Steve Cardin, Sherri Cassuto, Matt Dunnahoe, Dempsey Dybdahl, Pam Emerson, Alison Evert, Tom Evert, Connie Fisher, Ted Fry, Andreé Hurley, Sylvia Kantor, Mike Kelly, Tai Lee, L. J. McAllister, Tim Olson, Rob Peterson, Neil Planert, Amy Reed, Pam Shea, Valerie Tims, Norm Tjaden, Jack Tomkinson, Cathy Tuttle, and Willie Weir.

Opposite: *A view of Mount Si*

INTRODUCTION

What are you doing this weekend? If you're like me, the answer probably involves escape. Get out of the office, off the telephone, away from cash registers, cubicles, customers, kids, or bosses. Get into a different mindset, which probably means a different physical setting. This book is for all those people who want to get away, do a little exploring, and get some fresh air into their lungs. My goal was to create a selection of cycling day tours that expose users to all our major bike trails and on-road bike routes. It's divided somewhat equally among urban, suburban, and rural settings. Because these 60 rides are sprinkled throughout the greater Seattle area, many people will find tours close to home. With a couple of exceptions, all rides are within an hour's drive of central Seattle.

We are fortunate to live in a cycling wonderland, with the beauty of nature found everywhere, from diverse city parks to agricultural valleys, from waterfront lanes to island coastlines to mountainous back roads. Climb a hill and be rewarded with a view of a sparkling cityscape, glittering blue bays, or towering snowy peaks. Pick blackberries by the side of a rural road, or take your comfort stop at a farm stand bursting with fresh produce. Our temperate climate allows for recreational biking nearly year-round, and an improving network of trails offers increased safety for beginners and families.

When you see a pack of cyclists whiz by in a "pace line" on sleek, high-tech bikes, you may think the sport of cycling sprouted recently to serve these athletes—but you'd be mistaken. Biking in Seattle has a history nearly as old as the city itself. The first bicycle was brought here in 1879, and by 1900—when the first automobile was spotted on our streets—the 55,000 residents of Seattle owned 10,000 bikes. (Seattle cyclists have been magnanimous in sharing our roads with cars ever since.) Also in 1900, an assistant city engineer, George Cotterill, created a bicycling map for residents that showed a 25-mile system of paths he had identified in his walks around the city. Those paths became some of the best cycling routes we still ride today, such as winding, tree-lined Lake Washington Boulevard.

Our enthusiasm for biking has grown along with our population, and the network of trails and street routes has greatly expanded to meet the need. Since the early 1970s, when cyclists advocated for building the Burke-Gilman Trail from Seattle's Lake Union to the northwest corner of Lake Washington, many trails have been created from

Opposite: *Vashon's celebrated* Bike in a Tree

Overlooking Nestlé's Carnation Regional Training Center

old railroad rights-of-way. This book uses nearly two dozen rail-trails, some of which comprise the major portion of the route. The rail-to-trail conversion still continues today; in 2013, Snohomish County extended the Centennial Trail to the Skagit County border, and Olympia broke ground for its third overpass that will connect its extensive network of former rail lines that are now paved bike trails.

One research firm recently declared finding a "bicycle renaissance" in America that is especially strong in western states, and our region's cities and counties are taking note of the increased interest. Today's smart road planners utilize "complete streets" designs, required by code in some municipalities, which includes accommodations for cyclists. In 2013 the City of Seattle updated its Bicycle Master Plan, which recommended expanding the miles of bicycle facilities (from bike lanes to protected-lane "cycletracks" to off-street trails) within the city from 135 miles today to more than 600 miles in 20 years.

Each year, thousands of people commute to work by bike, and a spring contest has teams competing for most miles biked during the month of May. A bicycle counter on Seattle's Fremont Bridge recorded nearly 1 million bike trips in 2013.

Recreational riding is booming too, with organized rides and tours more popular than ever. According to recent research, more adult Americans participate in bicycling than in any other outdoor sport.

Locally, free daily rides are led by volunteers from bike clubs—just check their website and show up! Charity rides help thousands of people raise money for good causes. Destination rides, such as the 10,000-rider two-day Seattle to Portland (STP), the lives-up-to-its-name Chilly Hilly in February, and the Ride Around Washington (RAW) are packing the roads. We love to get out on our bikes, and it shows. In 2013, the League of American Bicyclists named Washington the number-one bike-friendly state in the nation—for the sixth year in a row.

But you don't have to join group tours, ride an expensive bike, or wear high-tech clothes to enjoy the many benefits of cycling—although a properly fitted bike and specialized gear can enhance the experience. Simply choose a route that fits your abilities and interests, and give it a try. This book contains many rides that are suitable for those who haven't been on their bikes in a while; start with the flat, paved, off-street routes like the Foothills, Burke-Gilman, Sammamish River, Chehalis Western, and Centennial trails.

Commuters can search the maps for interesting ways to get to work. More challenge can be gained by navigating city and suburban streets or taking on a hillier, lengthier route. Many of the tours are designed to be linked, so that the experienced cyclist may find new challenges or different destinations. Pick a ride with a campsite destination, pack the essentials, and try a "bike overnight." To truly get away, load your bike with travel gear and try the five-day tour of the San Juan Islands included here.

This book is being augmented by a website, www.bikingpugetsound .com, providing updates on all the routes, club connections, events, and regional rides. Hopefully, with the enthusiasm and involvement of this book's readers, the rides in the book and on the website will grow and evolve, remaining current and accurate. Readers are invited to offer feedback and ideas via the website.

Researching this book has provided me with a deeper awareness about our region. You learn much more about getting around, interesting stops, and wonderful sights from the vantage point and the human-scale speed of bicycling than from any other form of transportation. One enjoyable exploration creates the desire to have another, so you can imagine what 60 such outings will do.

See you on the trails!

EQUIPPING FOR A RIDE

When you hop in your car for a trip, you probably don't think too much about safety or reliability. Most cars come with air bags and spare tires, and once you add a flashlight and an emergency kit, you can check it off your list.

But when you get on your bike for a ride, it helps to give a bit of thought to what you might need. Preparation can make the difference between a minor inconvenience and an unpleasant experience. Add a few amenities to increase your enjoyment.

Think about getting equipped for a ride in three basic categories: yourself, your bike, and your home bike-repair shop.

Yourself

Getting yourself ready for a ride involves health and comfort. First, choose a ride that matches your current physical abilities. Most people don't want to begin the season with a hilly, 50-mile ride.

Second, plan how to keep up your stamina. A full water bottle and some high-energy snacks will be welcome down the road. Many riders will "bonk" (suddenly find themselves sapped of energy) if they don't periodically fuel up.

Third, carry a small pack of first-aid supplies, including antibiotic ointment and bandages. Apply sunscreen before each ride.

Fourth, the proper clothing for the conditions is important. The most common advice for outdoor enthusiasts in the Northwest is to "layer": Wear layers of clothing that work together to keep you warm and dry but allow you to strip off some of them so you won't overheat. Start with padded bike shorts, which come in the clingy, form-fitting style or as loose shorts with a padded, suspended brief. To keep from chafing, don't wear additional underwear underneath. T-shirts or tops should be made of quick-drying, breathable material rather than cotton, which can stay wet with sweat and cause chills.

Tights or water-resistant biking pants are good for wet or chilly conditions, and fleece vests under waterproof shell jackets add warmth up top. In the winter, turtleneck-style shirts or pullover neck warmers hold in your body warmth. To warm your extremities, check out these specialty items: an ear-warming headband, a microfiber skull cap, a nose and chin mask, glove liners, socks that are a blend of wool and microfiber, and stretchy, water-resistant shoe covers.

Fifth, a helmet and gloves are safety necessities, and good shoes and eyewear are helpful. King County and many western Washington communities require helmets by law. The primary consideration with a helmet is how it fits, and any good bike retailer will help you choose. Some helmets have sun visors, and some have more vents than others for better air movement so you can keep a cool head.

Cycling gloves obviously offer warmth, but they also enhance safety by making sure you keep a good grip on handlebars and brake levers for steering and braking in wet conditions, and they have palm padding that protects the hand's tender nerves from bruising that can cause numbness on a long ride. Choose flexible biking gloves that provide good padding—fingerless for summer, full coverage for winter.

A solid pair of bike shoes will keep your feet happy. Most important is a stiff sole, so the pedal pressure is dispersed across the foot rather than localized in one spot. Equip your bike with clipless pedals and match them to shoes that allow you to clip onto your pedals. Although they take some getting used to, clip systems provide a more efficient pedal stroke so you'll expend less energy.

Finally, wraparound eyewear protects your eyes from sun, road grit, and rain and increases safe riding by keeping your eyes from watering or drying out. Sunglasses are an especially good precaution against the sun's rays when it's low on the horizon right before sunset, which can be quite blinding.

Your Bike

Bike design has become something of an art, and there are many styles available, offering a choice for each rider's individual needs and desires. The type of riding you intend to do—commuting, mountain biking, short tours, long tours—will dictate the type of bike that suits you. The best approach is to find a quality bike shop with knowledgeable staff who know how to fit a bike to each customer. Test-riding a number of different manufacturers' bikes will showcase the bikes' differences. If you already have a bike but didn't have it fit to you, consider having this done at a good shop.

What extras you put on your bike will also be dictated by your type of riding, but there are a few basics that everyone needs.

You must carry at least one water bottle; most of them fit in a cage mounted on the frame to be accessible while you're riding. For long rides, some cyclists wear a backpack "hydration pack."

Carry a lock; it provides peace of mind when you take breaks, and it is necessary if you need to leave your bike in an emergency, such as after a breakdown.

Speaking of breakdowns, distance riders should carry an extra inner tube, a tire patch kit, an air pump, tire wrenches, and a multitool for repairs. These might not be necessary if you're just riding to the corner store, but you'll want to avoid being stranded on a rural road or on the way to work.

Every rider should know how to do a few basic repairs: reattach the chain if it slips off; unhook the brakes and take off a wheel for repair; patch or replace an inner tube. More advanced repairs (which many people leave to their bike-shop mechanic) include tightening or replacing the chain, replacing a broken spoke, and adjusting the brakes or replacing brake pads.

On a day tour, carry an extra inner tube as a replacement in case the blowout is bad or if you don't want to hassle with a repair. Pack a rag to clean up after repairs. Consider taking a two- to three-hour course in basic bike repair, offered by most bike shops and bike clubs.

Basic maintenance includes airing up the tires at least weekly on a road bike. You should know how to clean and oil your chain and drivetrain components and complete this maintenance every month— or more often if you ride a lot or ride in sloppy weather conditions. Finally, to avoid major problems on the road, have professional service on the bike's mechanical systems done at least once every other year.

Your bike should have lights permanently mounted and in good working order. Washington State law requires a front white light and rear red reflector for bikes operated in hours of darkness. I believe every bike should have a rear red light that flashes brightly. Check the batteries on your lights regularly. Additionally, reflectors on the front and rear of the bike, on your clothing, on pedals, on the seat post, on wheels—on anything that might give you better visibility to the navigator of that moving ton of automobile steel—are well worth the investment.

To carry your lock, bike repair kit, extra clothes, food, cell phone, camera, extra batteries, or whatever else you might want on the trail,

Cycling on the Burke-Gilman Trail in Ballard takes you by two great attractions: the Chittenden Locks and Golden Gardens Park.

you'll need some sort of pack. Commuters often carry their basics in backpacks—especially the messenger-bag style—and keep their bikes very light. Many touring riders use a pack or saddlebags (commonly known by the French term *panniers*) mounted on a rack above the back wheel. A waterproof pannier or a pair of them offers the most cargo space. There are seat-post bags, handlebar bags, and front panniers as well. For just a few things, try a small, removable handlebar pack or seat-post bag big enough for a map, snacks, and a lock. Choose a pack combination that suits your riding style. A rear rack with a bungee cord will be useful for stowing some of those layered clothes when you aren't carrying a bag.

Comfort over a long ride will be dictated by the soreness of your rear end, so a specialized seat may be a welcome amenity. Many seats are padded with foam or gel, and higher-end models are anatomically designed for men or women. A good shop should let you try out the seat and bring it back in a reasonable time period if it's not the right fit.

Handlebars, too, can be upgraded for comfort. Choices include padded grips or added handlebar ends and "aero bars" that allow different hand positions.

Add a bell for safety, to be used when passing pedestrians or other cyclists. Another item that helps provide proper control and navigation is a rear-view mirror. These come in many styles, attaching to helmets, eyewear, or handlebars.

Add a bike computer, which also mounts on the handlebars, to keep track of your distance, the difficulty of the terrain, and the miles ridden. Knowing how far you've gone helps you chart your fitness and build a training program. It also provides stats to help you plan for routine maintenance and replacement of components such as tires and chain.

Your Shop

Most people park their bike in their garage, but a little planning and a couple of extra service items will keep it in better shape. Hang your bike on hooks or a rack between rides, especially if it's going to sit for a while, to keep it from getting banged up. A number of rack styles are available, and a good one doesn't have to be expensive.

A quality floor pump with a built-in, easy-to-read gauge is essential. Tires need to be pumped up every few days, so leave the pump out and ready for use.

Carve out a little space on nearby storage shelves for a bottle of chain oil, extra inner tubes, a set of tools, and a book on bike repairs. Use the oil on your chain regularly, scrubbing off the grit to keep the links limber.

If you plan to do your own maintenance and repairs, invest in a repair stand that will hold your bike off the ground while you work on it. To keep in shape for biking, buy a stationary trainer for use in the off-season. By hooking up your bike's rear axle to the trainer, you can train indoors and improve your stamina for the trail. Finally, for a quick getaway, keep a basket nearby that holds your helmet, gloves, lights, and packable items.

BASIC GEAR FOR BICYCLE TOURING

- Water and snacks
- First-aid kit and sunscreen
- Layered clothes
- Padded shorts
- Helmet
- Gloves
- Bike shoes
- Eyewear
- Lock
- Patch kit and pump
- Lights

CYCLING SAFELY

One of the primary concerns of new cyclists regarding road touring is the need to coexist with automotive vehicles on city streets and highways. Having had many near-misses and one direct hit, I can sympathize. But I also believe that, with proper understanding of the risks and safety precautions, riding on streets and roads doesn't have to be dangerous. Risks exist even on the off-street paved trails, but these too are manageable. It's mostly a matter of getting comfortable with situations that might arise.

Cyclists can greatly reduce their risk of accidents with vehicles, other cyclists, and pedestrians by using proper bike safety gear and observing safe riding practices. In many cases, following safety precautions also means following state and local laws.

Whether you're just out running a few errands or taking one of the tours in this book, cycling safely should always be your first goal. If you continually practice the basics—wear a helmet, carry and use the proper lighting, and follow traffic laws—safety will become second nature, making you increasingly comfortable in most traffic conditions.

Wear a Helmet

Protect yourself by always wearing a helmet when riding. Helmets are required throughout King County, including in Seattle and many other areas covered by tours in this book—and rightly so. When cars and bikes collide, the cyclist always gets the worst of it, and that could

Bicycling scarecrow in a San Juan garden

include injury or even death. Six hundred seventy-seven cyclists died in motor vehicle traffic crashes in the United States in 2011, and 48,000 were injured, according to the National Highway Traffic Safety Administration. While those numbers have been trending down, thankfully, in the last few years, studies have shown that such crashes are greatly underreported.

A review of bicycle helmet effectiveness studies by the Harborview Injury Prevention and Research Center concludes that helmets can cut the risk of head and brain injuries by 70 to 88 percent. The Washington State Department of Health says that 75 percent of all bicycle-related deaths involve severe head injury, and 20 percent of all head injuries in children ages 5 to 14 are caused by bike accidents. When shopping for a helmet, look for the American National Standards Institute (ANSI), Snell Foundation, or American Society for Testing and Materials (ASTM) symbols.

A helmet is effective only if it fits properly and is fastened snugly. Most bike shops can help you find the right helmet for your head and your riding needs. If the shop doesn't offer knowledgeable help with fitting, go somewhere else. If you're in charge of children, make sure their helmet straps are fastened and the straps are snug.

Some public-service campaigns offer helmets at reduced cost or free. Cascade Bicycle Club operates regular events to distribute free or low-cost helmets to low-income individuals, schoolchildren, and nonprofit groups. Health-care organizations, including Mary Bridge Children's Hospital in Tacoma, also offer such a service.

Light Your Ride

Bicycle lights are also governed by law. Washington State law mandates that a front light and rear reflector are to be used when riding during the hours of darkness. The front light must be white and visible from at least 500 feet away. The rear reflector must be red and make you visible from all distances 100 to 600 feet to the rear when the low beam of a vehicle's headlights hits you. The law also allows for the use of a red rear light visible from a distance of 500 feet.

Having your lights on for safety, even during cloudy or short days or when riding down lanes with intermittent shadows, is wise.

Most night cyclists install a battery-powered red light on the rear seat post or rack of their bikes. Many people also use a clip-on red light that can be attached to their clothing, backpack, or helmet. Front lights should be strong, but not blinding, and carefully aimed to be visible to other drivers but also to light the path ahead. Most red lights, and many headlights, offer a flashing mode as well as a steady-light mode, and the flashing mode seems to make a rider more visible. But flashers should not be used when you're riding in a group, as they can make it difficult for other cyclists to see, and cyclists with superbright light-emitting diode (LED) headlights should take care that their LEDs are not blinding—or angering—drivers of other vehicles too.

If you want to "go green," use rechargeable batteries or a generator that will eliminate the dead-battery problem. The drawback to generator systems is that they are heavy.

In addition to lights and reflectors, reflective tape can be used on the bike and on clothing to make you more visible. Add it to pedals, shoes, fenders, rims, jackets—anywhere that a car's headlights might shine. Also wear light-colored clothing for night riding. Visibility in all conditions should be your goal.

Follow Traffic Laws

A bicycle is considered a vehicle and is subject to the same laws as a car when you ride it on the roadway, which includes bike lanes and parking lanes. Simply following the same laws as motorists will cut the risks of bicycling by quite a bit.

USE HAND SIGNALS

Hand signals tell motorists what you intend to do. For turn signals, point in the direction of your turn. Signal as a matter of courtesy and safety and as required by law.

RIDE CONSISTENTLY

Ride as close as practical to the right. Exceptions: when traveling at the normal speed of traffic, avoiding hazardous conditions, preparing to make a left turn, or using a one-way street.

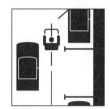

CHOOSE THE BEST WAY TO TURN LEFT

There are two ways to make a left turn: 1) Like an auto: look back, signal, move into the left lane, and turn left. 2) Like a pedestrian: ride straight to the far-side crosswalk, then walk your bike across, or queue up in the traffic lane.

USE CAUTION WHEN PASSING

Motorists may not see you on their right, so stay out of the driver's "blind spot." Be very careful when overtaking cars while in a bike lane; drivers don't always signal when turning. Some other smart things to be alert for: car doors opening and cars pulling out from side streets or driveways.

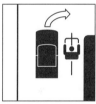

AVOID ROAD HAZARDS

Watch for sewer grates, slippery manhole covers, oily pavement, gravel, and ice. Cross railroad tracks at right angles. For better control as you move across bumps and other hazards, stand up on your pedals.

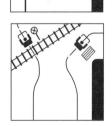

GO SLOW ON SIDEWALKS

Pedestrians have the right of way on walkways. You must give an audible warning when you pass. Cross driveways and intersections at a walker's pace and look carefully for traffic. In some communities, cycling on sidewalks is prohibited by law.

Source: City of Portland Office of Transportation, Portland, Oregon

Figure 1

Protected bike lanes, also known as cycletracks, began appearing in Seattle in 2013.

Traffic laws are primarily a set of standards to which everybody in society adheres. Such rules are the only way that we can reasonably be assured that another driver will act predictably. If we know the rules—and can be penalized for not following them—most of us will follow along with the crowd. For cyclists, the threat of a fine is often replaced by a much more painful penalty: the risk of getting physically injured. I believe that by following the same rules as a vehicle, we can be more predictable and thus less likely to be hit by another vehicle, which could be a car or another bike. I also believe that cyclists can only gain and keep respect as fellow road users if we follow the laws as we expect other vehicle drivers to do.

The most useful traffic rules are outlined in Figure 1. The graphics show the two best ways to execute a left turn, how to ride predictably between a traffic lane and a parking lane, and what hand signals to use when turning.

Cyclists should always assume that they are invisible to drivers of cars and trucks. That will cause you to be more cautious when you're in a bike lane and, due to these traffic conditions, must pass cars on the right (which should never be done otherwise). Be on the lookout for a driver turning right, directly in front of you (or left, if you are in a left bike lane on a one-way street). If you're riding on the sidewalk, slow to a pedestrian speed when crossing driveways and intersections.

Cars are not the cyclist's only road worries. Stay alert for potholes, railroad tracks, and pavement or steel utility covers that are slippery with rain or oil. Watch for pedestrians entering a crosswalk or jaywalking in your path. Animals, such as dogs protecting their territories or deer dashing across a rural road, can be quite a surprise. Unseen hazards can cause a startle reaction, which may not be a big deal if you're alone on a road but could be quite a problem if you jerk your handlebars just as a car is passing you. Practice remaining calm and steering consistently when in difficult conditions. Stand up on your pedals to reduce the jolt of an uneven road. Whenever possible, ride in the direction of car traffic when crossing bridges on walkways to avoid perilous collisions with oncoming bikes.

Verbal notice or hand signals will help avoid a crash with another cyclist. If you're slowing or stopping and you know there are cyclists behind you, extend your left arm downward with your open palm facing back. If you're overtaking another cyclist and going to pass, use your bell or call out "Bike on your left" as a warning. Make sure you can be seen and heard under the conditions of the road.

Other signals may help fellow cyclists ride more safely. If you're behind others in a group of bikes and a car approaches from the rear, yell "Car back!" to inform the riders in front. If you are leading other riders and come upon a hazard on the road, such as broken glass, extend either arm down and point to the hazard with a sweeping motion. When crossing railroad tracks, signal their presence by sweeping either arm at an angle behind you.

Many of these laws and rules apply equally to a paved bike trail as they do to a road. You might want to signal riders behind you when you come upon a small child on her first bike ride or see some debris on the trail. You might want to keep your speed down on paved trails that get heavy use, especially by families and dog walkers. A crash with another cyclist can be very damaging to bike, body, and spirit, so do your best to ride safely.

Safely Use Transit and Ferries

In the Puget Sound region, most buses have bike racks. There is no extra charge for the bus to carry your bike.

It's a simple procedure to pull down the bike rack, set your bike's wheels into the tracks, and pull the retaining bar over the front wheel. But always get the bus driver's attention *before* you approach the rack, and when you're getting off, let the driver know that you'll be removing your bike from the rack. Note that buses do not allow bikes with gas motors to use the bike rack, but electric-powered bikes are OK.

The two drawbacks to this system are limitations on the number of bikes any bus can carry and the difficulty of taking your bike off the bus in certain areas. Unloading in a high-traffic city center may be challenging from a safety standpoint because so many buses stack up at downtown stops. If you're heading downtown, plan ahead and exit the bus before the congested area. If you're waiting for a bus and it arrives at your stop with a full bike rack, you are stuck waiting for the next bus; bikes are not allowed inside buses. However, you might consider either taking another route that drops you somewhere near your destination and simply riding the rest of the way or putting your bike in a secure locker and walking on the bus.

Light-rail, commuter trains, and streetcars also take bikes. Look for the bike hooks or designated spots for bikes in each car; again, you might be challenged by limited available spaces.

Washington State Ferries are commonly used by cyclists, and there are a few tricks to safely boarding and disembarking a ferry.

Enter the ferry dock along with the car traffic and pay at the vehicle toll plaza, unless instructed otherwise. There is a small surcharge for bikes, although cyclists should lobby the state to remove this as a measure to support the environment and citizen health.

First-time ferry riders should follow the lead of other riders waiting at the loading ramp. Bikes queue up in front of the cars in a signed waiting area and receive a verbal signal from dock workers when it's time to board. On some ferries, cyclists are required to walk up the ramp. Once onboard, follow crew instructions, take your bike to the bow of the ferry, and tie up with the provided ropes attached to eyebolts along the rails. If you leave the car deck, remember that exposed bike-shoe cleats are not allowed on the passenger deck; riders with those cleats need covers or a change of shoes.

When exiting the ferry, again wait for the ferry workers' verbal signal. If you're uncertain about riding on and off the ramps, it is acceptable to walk your bike—but stay off to one side, out of the way of riders. Also, it's a good idea to gear down when entering the ferry, because the exit ramp at many ferry docks gets somewhat steep at low tide, and the road departing the ferry often quickly turns uphill. Cyclists should move to the right off the ferry ramp, because motorcycles and cars will soon be coming behind. You'll be happier and safer if you let the cars zoom by and the exhaust clear before setting off.

COMMUTING BY BIKE

Thousands of people in the Seattle area have discovered the benefits of commuting to work by bicycle, and bike commuting numbers seem to grow with every traffic backup or spike in gas prices. Each year, participation in the May "Bike to Work Day" rises, and an analysis of US Census data shows bike commuting in Seattle spiked to 3.6 percent of our population (more than 20,000 people) in 2010, almost doubling since 2000. With a bit of preparation, you can reap the many advantages of bicycle commuting and suffer minimal risks.

One of the major benefits will be to your health. Bike commuting allows you to integrate a daily workout into a busy schedule. The exertion provides a natural way to arrive at work more alert, so you may experience less reliance on caffeine. By leaving your car at home, you'll contribute to the overall air quality of our area.

Keeping control of your schedule is another plus. How many times have you been stuck in traffic and arrived late to work? When you bike, you can say goodbye to transit schedules, traffic reports, freeway backups, and parking hassles. King County published some interesting statistics on its bike commuting web pages a few years ago. It estimated that driving time from the University District to Pike Place Market would be 15 minutes in light traffic or 35 minutes in heavy traffic. By bike at a moderate pace, the trip would take 30 minutes. How often does "light traffic" describe rush hour in Seattle? Score another one for bikes.

If you're thinking about bike commuting, some important considerations include route planning, proper equipment, personal safety, mass transit interaction, bike security, and workplace amenities.

Route Planning

The shortest distance between two points may be over the top of a big hill, which is probably not the kind of sweat-inducing exertion you want to go through before arriving at work. Therefore, your criteria for the best route to work may include finding one that is as flat as possible. Or it may be a combination of shortest and flattest, allowing for a little hill climbing if it means saving 15 minutes of commute time.

In 2013 the City of Seattle bicycle network included 47 miles of multiuse trails; 78 miles of on-street, striped bike lanes; 92 miles of shared-lane pavement markings; 6 miles of neighborhood greenways; and about 128 miles of signed bike routes. Other area cities and suburban communities contribute many more miles, and some of the routes even link up. Many of those paths and routes are used in this book, so chances are good that some leg of your commute can be part of a recreational tour.

Next, get yourself some city and county bike maps; see the Recommended Resources at the back of this book. The maps show bike trails, striped-and-signed bike lanes on city streets, and neighborhood "greenways" with less traffic.

Finally, test your route on a pleasure ride before using it for work. Time yourself, check road and traffic conditions, and look for possible amenities you'll need, such as a bike shop or bus stop. Many people commute partway by bike and partway by bus, or they use the bus if the weather turns bad. After you've become familiar with your route, you might enjoy adding length to it after work to increase the level of exercise.

EMPLOYER SUPPORT OF BIKE COMMUTING

Bike commuters who want to lobby their employers for parking facilities and work amenities can get help from Washington Bikes, a nonprofit organization that supports bike safety and commuting (see Recommended Resources). These are a few creative ideas to support bike commuting:

Loaner Cars. Make loaner cars available to bicyclists for use in case of emergencies or personal errands that require a car while at work.

Health-Care Coverage. Reward bicyclists with better health-care coverage. This might include extended benefits, lower rates, or a lower deductible. Similar programs are offered for nonsmokers.

Employee Awards. Reward outstanding employees, customers, students, etc., with a new bicycle or other bicycle-related items. A reflective vest, safety lights, a mirror, or a helmet with the person's name and the organization's insignia are awards that convey support for bicycling and concern for a person's safety.

Bike Lease Program. Lend or lease bikes for an established period of time— say, 30 to 90 days. This allows people to try bicycling without having to buy a bike. This program could be structured as an offer to lend or lease with an option to purchase. Purchase price could be discounted.

Stranded Bicyclists. Implement a program to assist bicyclists who become stranded when their bike breaks down on the way to work.

Recruitment Awards. Reward employees who recruit new bike commuters.

Enhancing Your Safety

Commuters often face the issues of riding in the dark, navigating in heavy traffic, and riding in the rain. You can enhance your safety under these difficult conditions, and for general riding, by adhering to a few safety precautions.

First rule: You can never be too visible to cars. Many commuters use two rear flashing red lights, one mounted on the seat post or rack on their bike and a second on their jacket, backpack, or helmet. Use an

Crossing the Interstate 90 floating bridge

LED headlight to be more visible to traffic you'll meet at intersections and to more easily spot potholes or other road obstructions.

Some cyclists use lights in rainy weather during the daytime as well as after dusk. Many wear lighter-colored clothes in winter. Reflective, water-resistant green or yellow bike jackets are the most common clothing item among bike commuters.

Second rule: Assume that drivers don't see you. Navigating in traffic is a challenge not to be taken lightly. Watch for cars changing lanes, stopping suddenly to grab a parking spot, or turning in front of you.

For instance, people who've just parked their car often don't check the bike lane before opening their car door. Give yourself 4 feet of space to avoid being "doored" by people getting out of parked cars. Stay in a traffic lane if no bike lane is available, and don't weave into the parking lane just because there's an opening between parked cars— maintain a straight, predictable course.

A note about sidewalk riding: You may think it is safer, because you're away from the traffic, but it carries its own hazards. Consider the driveways and intersections you must cross. Most drivers are not expecting bikes on the sidewalks, and if you arrive in a crosswalk at the last second, don't be surprised if a driver doesn't see you. Also, because of the width of sidewalks and the many obstructions on them, you're more likely to fall over, hit another biker, or hit a pedestrian.

Seattle does not prohibit biking on sidewalks, although it is illegal in some communities. The city law says that when a bike is in the roadway, it is to be treated as a vehicle, but a cyclist riding on the sidewalk is to be treated as a pedestrian. Moving at pedestrian speed on a sidewalk is wise.

Speaking of laws, it's in everyone's best interests for all bike commuters to obey traffic laws, especially stop signs and signals. Do it primarily because an oncoming car with the right-of-way will definitely not be expecting a cyclist to pop out against the light. Often, drivers speed up to catch a yellow light or beat a red one, making it even more dangerous for a biker hoping to get a jump-start when a light is about to turn green.

Second, stay legal for the sake of your fellow bikers: For every scofflaw cyclist, there's a motorist shaking his head and assuming all cyclists act the same way. That attitude will make the streets more dangerous for all of us, because a motorist with that opinion is less likely to share the road. Consider the bottom line: How much time is really saved by jumping a red light or illegally cutting through traffic? Relax, be safe, and help boost the safety of your cycling community.

One final note on traffic signals: You as a biker can make them change, and you don't have to go to the curb and push the pedestrian walk button. Look for a "magnetic loop" cut into the pavement in the driving lane or bike lane. In Seattle, they're often marked with a T; in Bellevue, they're marked with an X. Positioning yourself on top of this loop engages a sensor that triggers the signal as though you were a car. Thank you, technology wizards!

Third rule: Get used to getting a little wet. If you commute year-round in the Puget Sound area, you're bound to be riding in the rain. Especially in the winter, riding in the rain is unavoidable, and lower temperatures make it easy to get chilled. But often even winter days contain dry spells, and many rainy days accumulate relatively little rainfall. The best approach to riding in the rain combines caution, preparation, and common sense.

Good raingear is your best defense. If you're a damn-the-torpedoes rider, shop for waterproof outer clothing; if you ride only when there's a light mist, perhaps water-resistant gear will suffice. The drawback to waterproof gear is that it is generally not breathable, so you can really heat up in it. However, you might be surprised how fast rain soaks through water-resistant outerwear. Err on the side of staying drier. Buy gear with zipper vents to relieve the steam within.

Shoe covers will keep your feet drier, and a helmet cover will do the same for your head. Keep a dry towel on hand to clean your eyewear. Carry a plastic bag and rubber bands to cover your bike seat if you need to leave your bike out in the rain. Take an extra pair of socks and gloves to use for the ride home in case yours haven't dried by then.

Riding safely in the rain entails making yourself more visible and knowing the limitations caused by a wet bike. Use extra lights, and make sure your raingear has reflective patches or strips. Leave more space for braking, and proceed a little slower down hills. Assume that other riders aren't being as cautious as you, and give them wider berth.

If you get caught in a really nasty squall, there's no shame in pulling over and opting out; a warm and dry bus seat awaits.

Mass Transit Interactions

Transit systems are getting savvy about bike commuting and have a number of programs to support it. It's sometimes easier to bike one direction and take transit the other. It's a quick backup to riding if you run out of energy or the weather turns nasty. For procedural and safety information about using transit systems, such as buses or ferries, see the Safely Use Transit and Ferries section earlier in this introduction.

If you participate in a vanpool, you can also take your bike. Many King County Metro vans have racks, and the agency will install bike racks on vanpool vans upon request.

Bike Security

More bus-system park-and-ride lots are installing bike lockers for use by commuters, so you can bike from your home to the park-and-ride, store your bike safely and out of the elements, then catch the bus into work. The ferry dock on Bainbridge Island has an expansive "bike barn" for use by commuters.

Those not using bike lockers at park-and-ride lots need to safely secure their bikes for the day at their workplace. Enlightened employers provide dry bike parking in garages or their buildings. If this is not

A group in training for the Arthritis Foundation's People's Coast Classic heads south on a bridge over the Green River.

available where you work, consider lobbying management for some facilities. It's worth the effort to avoid chaining your bike to a sidewalk rack for the day, exposed to weather and possible theft.

Workplace Amenities

Arriving at work all hot and sweaty or soaking wet after your bike commute is usually not a good idea. In fact, it can be downright off-putting to coworkers and bosses. Bike commuters have many ways to handle this situation. At the most basic level, some bring their own towels and take a quick sponge bath in the restroom. Others join a health club near work and make that their first stop.

Again, enlightened employers support the efforts of their healthy, nonpolluting bike-commuting employees by installing locker rooms with showers. Locker rooms serve not just bike commuters but also runners or others who like to exercise at lunchtime. The lockers should be large enough to hold suits or dresses at night and bicycle bags, shoes, and a helmet during the day. They absolutely need to be in a heated, ventilated space, because no cyclist wants to put on the morning's damp bike clothes before the ride home.

A good tip for making the bike commute easier is to drive or take the bus to work one day a week and leave a supply of work clothes in your locker. It makes for a quicker, lighter ride in the morning; the clothes won't get wrinkled; and it allows storage of garments such as suits or jackets that don't easily fit in a bike bag.

～～～～～～～～～～～～～～～～～～～～～～～～～～～～～～～～

BIKING TO SCHOOL

The idea of commuting conjures up images of adults heading to work, but it can also be applied to children going to school. The nonprofit Washington Bikes operates a program called "Safe Routes to School" that encourages kids to ride their bikes or walk to school.

The effort, funded by the Washington State Traffic Commission, gives children more exercise and cuts down on the traffic generated by parents shuttling their kids to school by car. See the contact information in the Recommended Resources section at the back of this book.

～～～～～～～～～～～～～～～～～～～～～～～～～～～～～～～～

RIDING WITH CHILDREN

Almost every community covered in this book has a route or two that is safe for taking small children on their first public rides on their own bikes. I most often see preteens riding with their parents on dedicated trails, such as the Burke-Gilman. These trails seem like the safest places for new riders—children or adults—to enjoy the outdoors from atop a bike.

In her excellent book *Bicycling with Children*, Trudy Bell delves expertly into all the issues parents must tackle when getting their children on the bike trail, from toting toddlers to reining in teens. She even offers a detailed system for teaching your child to ride a bike. I recommend her book to any parent wanting complete instructions, but here I also present a few of her ideas that are germane to taking children on day rides on trails in this book.

First, a child needs to know how to balance, steer, pedal, and stop before riding in public. I have seen children on bike trails who weave from side to side or who react with a wobbly turn when overtaken by a rider coming up from behind. These situations are dangerous when children are in the presence of adults who are riding fast or commuters who are locked into their daily routine. Of course, when adult riders see small children ahead, they should be on their best, most careful behavior. Bell advises that when an adult is riding with a child, the adult ride behind and slightly to the left to coach the child and warn of oncoming vehicles.

Bell suggests that beginning riders should choose locations that are relatively free of distractions (including joggers, in-line skaters, and dog walkers). That would eliminate most of the Seattle area's dedicated, paved bike trails. If you're riding with a child who's just learning trail etiquette, try using those trails at nonpeak times, such as weekday afternoons or early weekend mornings. Or practice in an empty parking lot, setting out cones or using lined spaces to teach your children steering control.

Bell notes that a bicycle is not a toy—it is a child's first vehicle; hence, children should be taught the rules of the road. Some useful road rules relating to bike trails are these:

- Look before entering a trail.
- Go with the flow of traffic, and always ride on the right side of the road or trail.
- Stop only in a safe, visible place, out of the way of other trail users.
- Obey traffic signs.
- Use hand signals to communicate turning or stopping.
- At stop signs and driveways, stop, put a foot down, look both left and right, then left again. If it's safe, then go.
- To keep from swerving, practice "no noodle arms" and look ahead on the trail.
- Use voice or bell when passing.

Valuable practice can be gained by older children and teens if they are taken on lightly trafficked roads, such as a flat, rural farm road. Graduating to those outings can give a parent a chance to assess the child's skill level, too, and such rides may provide more confidence for a child when he or she is allowed to bicycle without the parents.

On all outings with children, it's advisable to carry extra water, snacks, and clothes for the child. Before riding, do a helmet check and make sure shoelaces are tucked in and pant legs rolled up or secured. Also, be sure to have repair tools to avoid having a breakdown turn into an ordeal.

Trails Suitable for Young Children

GREEN LAKE
Location: northwest Seattle. The 2.9-mile trail circling Green Lake is flat, smooth, and scenic, with separate lanes for wheels and feet. Heavy use, especially during weekends, is the only drawback. See Tour 2, Northwest Seattle, for details.

SEWARD PARK
Location: southeast Seattle. A 2.4-mile bike and walking trail circles a center hill on the Bailey Peninsula, a thumb of land that sticks out into Lake

Family riding at Green Lake

Washington at this popular park. The trail can be very busy at times, and it contains some uneven and unpaved patches. But it is a beautiful location with kid-friendly attractions, including an Environmental Learning Center and swimming beaches. See Tour 16, Lake Washington Loop, for details.

LAKE WASHINGTON BOULEVARD ON BIKE-ONLY WEEKENDS
Location: southeast Seattle. Let your child start practicing road riding on summer weekends when a 4-mile stretch of Lake Washington Boulevard is closed to car traffic. The street is car-free from Seward Park north to Mount Baker Beach. Check with Seattle Parks and Recreation for current bike-only weekend dates. See Tour 16, Lake Washington Loop, for details.

SAMMAMISH RIVER TRAIL
Location: Bothell to Redmond, east King County. Sections of this 28.4-mile trail are among the most widely used by Eastside families. See Tour 17 for details.

GREEN RIVER TRAIL
Location: Tukwila to Kent, south King County. You see a lot of children on this winding trail, which runs more than 11 miles along the Green

River, because stretches of it take you right behind suburban town-homes. It is less traveled than the city trails but does not offer as many amenities. See Tour 24, Green River and Interurban Trails, for details.

CEDAR RIVER TRAIL
Location: Renton to Maple Valley, south King County. This 10-mile trail is flat and has very few street crossings. However, it also runs right next to a very loud highway. See Tour 25, Cedar River Trail and May Valley, for details.

CENTENNIAL TRAIL
Location: Snohomish to Arlington, Snohomish County. Recently extended to stretch 30-plus miles into very rural farmlands, this trail is less used than ones closer to Seattle, and it has one of the smoothest surfaces of any trail. See Tour 51 for details.

FOOTHILLS TRAIL
Location: south of Puyallup, east Pierce County. One of the most rural trails, this 15-mile path also has the benefit of great Mount Rainier views. The most services are found in Orting. See Tour 57 for details.

CHEHALIS WESTERN TRAIL
Location: Olympia, Thurston County. Combine a ride on this 22.6-mile trail with a road trip to the state capitol. See Tour 59, Chehalis Western and Woodard Bay Trails, for details.

YELM–TENINO TRAIL
Location: southeast Thurston County. The 13.6-mile trail runs through three small towns. See Tour 60 for details.

Trails and Routes Suitable for Older Children

BURKE-GILMAN TRAIL
Location: northeast Seattle. The granddaddy of Seattle's rail-trails, this flat trail winds 18.8 miles through the city and King County from Golden Gardens Park on Shilshole Bay to Kenmore at the northwest end of Lake Washington, passing other beaches and parks en route. The trail, heavily used by commuters and college students on weekdays, is also very busy on weekends. The trail has a gap in Ballard, requiring riding on busy city streets, and in other areas it is necessary to cross some city streets,

although the crossings are well marked. In places, tree roots have caused the asphalt to heave and crack. With children, ride east from Gas Works Park. See Tour 1 for details.

ALKI TRAIL
Location: West Seattle. Another busy city trail, this 3-mile path offers many attractions for children, such as the beach and ice cream stands. The trail truly has shared use: Part is on a sidewalk, and part is on a wide striped shoulder next to the auto traffic. See Tour 11, West Seattle, for details.

CHIEF SEALTH TRAIL
Location: southeast Seattle. This 4-mile trail runs under electric powerlines across Beacon Hill. Its hills should be fun and challenging for children with more skills. See Tour 13, Chief Sealth Trail and Kubota Garden, for details.

Rural Roads Suitable for More Experienced Riders

SNOQUALMIE VALLEY
Location: Carnation, east King County. State Route 202 is a farm road, but it does see some traffic, and if you want to ride to Fall City, you must ride a mile or so on a busy road. The rural part of it, however, provides great exposure to farmland. Access is excellent from the park in Carnation. See Tour 22, Snoqualmie Valley Farm Tour, for details.

PORT ORCHARD
Location: southeast Kitsap Peninsula. Access this tour via a ferry from West Seattle, then ride the flat suburban roads that hug the Puget Sound shoreline to Port Orchard. There's some traffic and sections of road with no shoulder, but the center section is mostly flat and very scenic. See Tour 29 for details.

SKAGIT FLATS
Location: Mount Vernon or La Conner, southwest Skagit County. This route can be broken up in many ways, all of them flat but with some traffic. Start in Mount Vernon and ride through the riverine delta of Fir Island (least traffic), or start in La Conner and ride through the tulip fields (more traffic). Caution: there is some farm-truck traffic and, during tulip season, much tourist traffic. See Tour 48, Skagit Flats and Tulip Fields, for details.

HOW TO USE THIS GUIDE

Each tour begins with an information block summarizing the ride's difficulty, suggested time, riding distance, and elevation gain, followed by driving directions and both GPS coordinates and transit options to get to the starting point. Each tour includes a narrative description, route connections, a mileage log, a route map, and an elevation profile. Below is an explanation of each of these components.

Each ride's **difficulty** rating is based on its combination of distance, elevation gain, and traffic exposure. A flat, 25-mile trail-only ride would be rated as easy, whereas the same distance on city streets or highways might be rated as moderate. Similarly, a long, flat ride might be rated as easy or moderate, but a shorter hilly ride might be rated as challenging or strenuous. It's best to try one or two rides at the level where you'd rate your abilities, then determine whether this book's ratings are similar to your own. Use the difficulty rating in combination with the elevation profiles to get a full picture of each tour's challenges. Below is a general description of each difficulty level.

Easy: predominately flat terrain; tour distance can be ridden within two hours; a lesser amount of interaction with vehicle traffic. Try these rides if you're a new cyclist or if you're getting back in shape at the beginning of the season.

Moderate: terrain of rolling hills; some road riding in city traffic or on highways with good shoulders or bike lanes; distances can be ridden in three to four hours. Take these tours if you are comfortable on long, off-street trail rides or are an occasional bike commuter.

Challenging: rolling terrain, with possibly a couple of big climbs; intermittent heavy traffic or highway crossings; routes may take four to five hours to complete. Ride these if you're in training for long rides or want to push yourself to the next level.

Strenuous: some challenging hill climbs; roads with heavy traffic or no shoulders; may be longer than five hours of saddle time. These tours are for more experienced cyclists who can comfortably climb hills and switch lanes in vehicle traffic and have built up endurance for longer rides.

The suggested **time** to allow for each ride assumes a moderate riding speed of 10 to 12 miles per hour and a half hour of breaks for every two to three hours of riding time. On tours where special activities are suggested, such as whale watching, museum visits, or picnicking, extra time has been added. Ferry crossings are not included in tour times. On all tours, it's advisable to start as early in the day as possible to enjoy the tour without worrying about ferry schedules or approaching darkness.

ROUTES MAP LEGEND

——	Featured route	⑤	Start
----	Route on bike path	⑥	Finish (if different from start)
······	Route variation	■	Point of interest
- - - -	Other bike path	○	Town or city
⟶	Route direction	⁓)(	Bridge, underpass, or tunnel
		▲	Peak
⑨⓪	Interstate highway	⚠	Campground
②	US highway	⚐	Lighthouse
⑨⑨	State highway		Body of water
═══	Freeway or expressway	⁓⁓	Stream
───	Highway or major road	⊣⊢	Waterfall
───	Secondary road		Park/public land
+─+	Railroad or light rail line	─··─	Boundary
▭▭▭	Ferry route		

Total **distance** in miles and total **elevation gain** in feet for each tour were charted using the latest Garmin cyclometer.

Driving directions are based on use of major roads, although there may be many possible routes.

GPS coordinates were determined using online mapping services.

Transit information is based on online route planning from transit agencies. *Transit note:* As this book was going to press, King County Metro was in the process of making extensive cuts to its bus routes due to budget problems. Please be sure to check Metro's website, http://metro .kingcounty.gov, for the latest route information.

Route descriptions begin with a general overview of what the ride is like, then a short narrative describing the highlights and challenges en route. At the end of each ride description, **route connections** are provided that help you to link to other tours in the book. This feature allows for making extended training rides or linking routes together to avoid having to use other transportation to get to a distant route. Study the map for the connecting tour to find the intersecting point; in some cases, a more detailed map may be required to accurately follow connecting streets.

Mileage logs were compiled by cycling the routes using the Garmin cyclometer. Parks and locations en route with services such as restrooms are noted in the mileage logs and on the maps, with the assumption that these locations also have potable water; only when drinking water is scarce on a route is its availability also noted. Restrooms and drinking water are not indicated at Washington State Ferries docks, either in the text or on the maps, because every ferry dock—and every ferry— has these facilities.

Elevation profiles were supplemented and verified by using online mapping services.

Routes and **route maps** for each tour in this book were created through personal research and route planning. Although I have ridden each tour—in many cases, multiple times—changes in roads or trails may have occurred by publication time. Therefore, it is advisable to carry a bicycle map or road map of the area on all tours. I will endeavor to include all route changes in subsequent editions of this book.

A NOTE ABOUT SAFETY

Safety is an important concern in all outdoor activities. No guidebook can alert you to every hazard or anticipate the limitations of every reader. Therefore, the descriptions of roads, trails, routes, and natural features in this book are not representations that a particular place or excursion will be safe for your party. When you follow any of the routes described in this book, you assume responsibility for your own safety. Under normal conditions, such excursions require the usual attention to traffic, road and trail conditions, weather, terrain, the capabilities of your party, and other factors. Keeping informed on current conditions and exercising common sense are the keys to a safe, enjoyable outing.

—*Mountaineers Books*

Opposite: *Gas Works Park offers great views of downtown Seattle across Lake Union.* (Photo by L. J. McAllister)

SEATTLE

1   Burke-Gilman Trail

DIFFICULTY: easy
TIME: allow 2.5 hours
DISTANCE: 24.2 miles
ELEVATION GAIN: 386 feet

Getting There: Take I-5 to exit 169, N. 45th/N. 50th Sts., and turn west onto N. 45th St.; proceed 1 mile. Turn left onto Stone Wy. N. and proceed south to N. 34th St. Cross 34th, and road becomes N. Northlake Wy.; proceed east. Gas Works Park is on the right in 0.3 mile; park here.

  GPS Coordinates: N47 38 48 W122 20 04

  Transit: King County Metro 26

Like a number of the region's flat, broad, off-road paved trails, the "B-G" was originally created as a way to move large numbers of goods. Thomas Burke, Daniel Gilman, and 10 other investors created the Seattle, Lake Shore, and Eastern Railroad in 1885 in a bid to put the city on the map by connecting their railroad to the Canadian Transcontinental Line for shipping Northwest goods to larger markets. Although the line never got past Arlington, it created a valuable link to logging communities east of Seattle in its youth. The railroad operated until 1963 and was abandoned for rail use in 1971, at which time a citizens' effort led to acquisition of the line as a recreational trail. The conversion of this trail, which opened in 1978, marked a renaissance of bicycling in Seattle that had not been seen since the turn of the 20th century (for a historical ride on Seattle's first bike trail, see Tour 10).

Some days, riding this rail-trail can seem like a mass-transit experience, and finding that open stretch for locomotion is sometimes impossible. A steady stream of bikers, walkers, runners, and skaters traverse the trail, especially from Gas Works Park through the University District. But whether you're riding a quiet, shady stretch or weaving through trail traffic on a sunny summer afternoon, the B-G provides access to and views of the best of Seattle.

200'
0'
0 miles   5   Magnuson Park   10   Log Boom Park   15   20   24.2

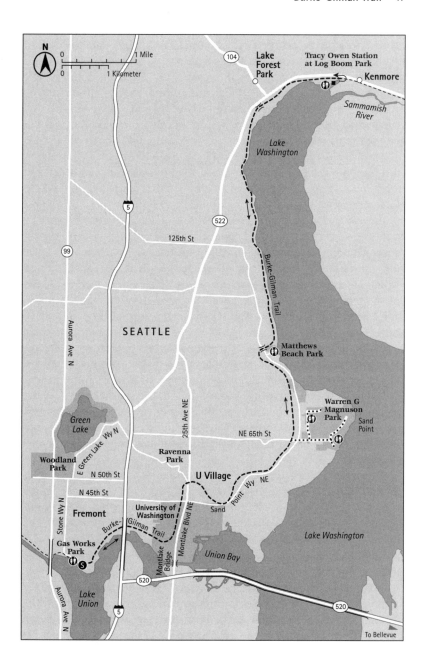

Gas Works Park, at the north end of Lake Union in the Wallingford neighborhood, is a logical starting point for this tour, although the trail can be accessed at many streets crossing its 12-plus-mile route. The free parking at Gas Works Park has a time limit, so use street parking or a paid lot if you're planning a full-day excursion.

Because the trail extends in two directions from Gas Works, there are really two tours to be taken to fully see the B-G: The original 12.1-mile trail goes east and north to the north end of Lake Washington (the tour described here); the other 6-mile segment goes west and north to Shilshole Bay on Puget Sound (that route is part of Tour 2, Northwest Seattle).

Most Seattle-area cyclists know the B-G, and it's a great starting route for visitors or people beginning to bike in the area. The pipe maze of the old gasworks is worth a visit, too, as are the park's stunning views of the city across glittering Lake Union, which is lined with houseboats and marinas and often dotted with sailboats and commercial vessels.

Heading east from Gas Works Park, first climb slightly to a ridge above Lake Union's east passage to Portage Bay. Overhead looms the massive Interstate 5 bridge and more human-scale University Bridge. Under the freeway, on the south side of the trail at 0.8 mile, you'll see the Wall of Death, a sculpture commemorating carnival motorcycle acts.

A series of street crossings takes you onto the southern edge of the University of Washington campus. Just east of University Avenue, look up to the side of UW's engineering building to see a spiderlike sundial grasping the brick walls, raising the question, does time pass on a cloudy day?

Soon after you pass the high-concept clock comes the university's horticultural greenhouses at the UW Farm, a good place for a warming walk on a chilly day or a self-guided tour of the student-planted grounds and the professionally curated Medicinal Herb Garden beyond. The trail then curves north at Montlake Boulevard NE at 2.1 miles, just north of the Montlake Bridge. East are the Husky Stadium and the university's intramural playfields. (A Link light-rail station is being constructed near here as well.) Curve east again at University Village shopping center. Often in summer there's a fruit vendor selling fresh cherries or peaches trailside at the busy 25th Avenue NE intersection north of the shopping center. At the east edge of the shopping center is another busy crossing, at NE Blakeley Street.

If you're thinking about packing a picnic, University Village is a good place to stop for supplies. To access the shopping center's grocery and cafés, turn right off the trail at Blakeley and proceed a half block to a right turn.

A nice break from the trail comes at just over 5 miles. Turn right off the trail onto the protected "cycletrack" on NE 65th Street and coast down the hill two blocks to the massive Warren G. Magnuson Park. It's about a mile to the boat launch at Lake Washington, and another half mile past the sports fields to a community garden and off-leash dog run. The old buildings of this former US Navy installation now house many nonprofit organizations, including the Cascade Bicycle Club and the Mountaineers. If you're thinking about a public beach, exit the B-G at 7.5 miles as the trail bridges Sand Point Way, then skirts the edge of smaller Matthews Beach Park. Either stop makes a great turnaround point for a shorter tour.

The last 5 miles of trail winding behind large lakeside homes afford only peeks at the blue water; occasional park benches

Burke-Gilman Trail in lower Wallingford (Photo by L. J. McAllister)

are the trail's only amenities along this stretch. At 11.4 miles, cross McAleer Creek at Lake Forest Park, and you are close to the end of the B-G. The shopping center across the road here has a large bookstore, a bakery, and coffee shops that make it a popular stop for cyclists. At 12.1 miles you reach Tracy Owen Station, also known as Log Boom Park; this small green space adjacent to a private marina is a great place for a picnic lunch before turning back. For picnic provisions, ride another half mile beyond the park to a shopping area.

Route Connections: Instead of turning around here, you can continue east to the connection with the Sammamish River Trail (Tour 17), which takes you another 10 miles east into the suburbs, ending at

Marymoor Park in Redmond—or hang a right in Kenmore and make an entire loop around Lake Washington (Tour 16). You can also loop through north Seattle neighborhoods (Tours 2, 3, or 4), turn north on Stone Way to Green Lake to connect with the Edmonds ride (Tour 5), or cross the Chittenden Locks and loop Magnolia (Tour 6).

MILEAGE LOG

0.0 From Gas Works Park (restrooms), cross N. Northlake Wy. to access trail, turn right, and ride east with I-5 bridge ahead.

1.3 Cross University Ave.

2.9 Cross 25th Ave. NE.

3.1 Cross NE Blakeley St. Caution: high-traffic area.

5.3 Cross NE 65th St. For a detour to Warren G. Magnuson Park (restrooms), turn right.

7.5 Cross Sand Point Wy. NE on an overpass. Matthews Beach Park (restrooms) on the right.

11.4 Cross McAleer Creek at Lake Forest Park town center.

12.1 Right turn into Log Boom Park, aka Tracy Owen Station (restrooms). Retrace route to return.

18.9 Cross NE 65th St.

24.2 Return to Gas Works Park to end tour.

2   Northwest Seattle

DIFFICULTY: easy
TIME: allow 1.5 hours
DISTANCE: 13.8 miles
ELEVATION GAIN: 582 feet

Getting There: From I-5 northbound, take exit 170, NE 65th St./ Ravenna. Turn left onto NE Ravenna Blvd. toward Green Lake, continuing north onto E. Green Lake Dr. N. Green Lake Park community center and parking on left at Latona Ave. NE. Additional parking on E. Green Lake Wy. N. along east side of lake.

The Aurora Bridge soars over the Burke-Gilman Trail in Fremont.

From I-5 southbound, take exit 171, NE 74th St. Turn right onto 74th, left onto 5th Ave. NE, then right onto NE 71st St., then right onto E. Green Lake Dr. N. Green Lake Park community center and parking on left at Latona Ave. NE.

GPS Coordinates: N47 40 54 W122 19 39
Transit: King County Metro 16, 26, 48, 82, 316

Many bicycle tours in Seattle take the rider to landmarks, through parks, and in front of stupendous views. Here's a ride to take when you just want to poke around neighborhoods, discover the best biking streets, and do a little shopping. In its quick 14 miles, you ride through six unique areas where small shops abound.

Departing from the northeast side of Green Lake, ride along the lake's north shore and climb a bit to the Greenwood neighborhood. You'll see the city's green bike route signs as you cross Fremont Avenue North, because turning right here would take you north to the Interurban Trail that connects to Shoreline and Edmonds. Greenwood also offers a detour

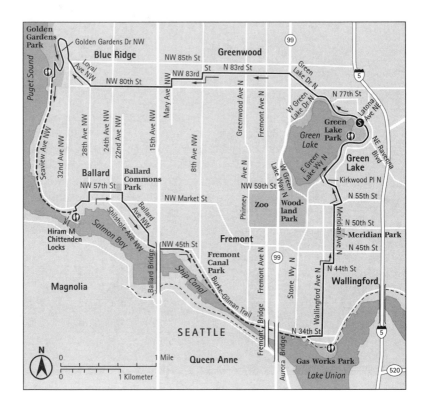

for some entertaining browsing. As you cross Greenwood Avenue at North 83rd Street, one block north is the Greenwood Space Travel Supply Company, the storefront effort of nonprofit 826 Seattle, a literacy drop-in center for youth. You won't find a better place to spend a few bucks on a book or a quirky gift for your space-traveling friends.

Back on the route, continue west on residential side streets into north Ballard. Make your way to the intersection on the bluff above Golden Gardens Park, then enjoy the quick descent on the winding, shady lane that takes you down to the waterfront park. At the bottom of the hill, ride north through the parking lots to where the pavement ends at North Beach. Attractions at this popular park include sand, surf, sailboats, a waterfowl marsh, and kite flying.

Ride south along the water on the recently extended Burke-Gilman Trail that parallels Seaview Avenue NW toward Shilshole Bay. Golden Gardens Park is the western terminus for the B-G, the granddaddy of our rail-trails, which has one unfinished section in this booming neighborhood. Pass by (or dismount and visit) the Hiram M. Chittenden Locks, then navigate through Ballard's retail core, necessary because of the trail's "missing link." The route takes you by the Ballard Commons Park with its skateboard bowl, then the attractive Seattle Public Library branch with its Viking ship design and green roof, and finally down the area's old shopping street, Ballard Avenue NW, which delights with funky, small shops in two-story brick buildings.

Pick up the Burke-Gilman Trail again as you leave Ballard behind and approach Fremont. After riding through Canal Park, you can either stay along the canal as the B-G takes you under the Fremont Bridge or turn onto North 34th Street in Fremont and make a stop in "the center of the universe," as this neighborhood playfully calls itself. Healthy snacks can be had at the PCC Natural Market on 34th, and one block north you can watch the universe slowly expand from a perch under a huge statue of Soviet leader V. I. Lenin.

Continue east on the B-G to reach Gas Works Park. The gasworks may be rusty, but the park's big green hill offers stunning views of Lake Union and downtown Seattle. Ride north through the residential streets of Wallingford to its shopping street, North 45th. Side trips on this street take you to a wonderful teahouse (half block left) and two old-style movie theaters (half block right), while the few blocks to the west are filled with small cafés in old houses.

Ride north on Meridian Avenue North past Wallingford Playground to North 50th Street, where sits the artistic stone entrance to Meridian Park and the Good Shepherd Center, home to Seattle Tilth. Their organic demonstration gardens offer a quiet, welcoming respite from the retail scene. But just north on Meridian, you have one last chance to exercise your wallet as you ride through the Meridian shopping area at 55th. To celebrate the neighborhood tour, quaff a fresh brew at the Tangletown pub or pop a relatively healthy doughnut at Mighty-O.

Dropping back down to East Green Lake Way North, circle around the lake's east shore to return to parking. To work off the doughnut or ale, try a dozen or so loops on the 2.9-mile trail around the lake before racking the bike.

Route Connections: Continue east on the Burke-Gilman Trail (Tour 1), continue north to Edmonds (Tour 5), or cross the Chittenden Locks and loop Magnolia (Tour 6).

MILEAGE LOG

0.0 Left out of Green Lake Park community center (restrooms) parking lot onto E. Green Lake Dr. N.

0.7 After business district, right to stay on Green Lake Dr. N.

1.1 Cross SR 99/Aurora Ave. at N. 83rd St.

1.3 Cross Fremont Ave. N.

1.6 Cross Greenwood Ave. N. at N. 83rd St.
2.2 Left onto 8th Ave. NW, then immediately jog right to continue on 83rd.
2.5 Left onto Mary Ave. NW.
2.7 Right onto NW 80th St.
3.5 Right onto Loyal Ave. NW.
3.9 Forward at stop sign onto 32nd Ave. NW, which becomes Golden Gardens Dr. NW.
4.9 Arrive at Golden Gardens Park (restrooms). Left to join Burke-Gilman Trail on east side of Seaview Ave. NW.
6.4 Cross Seaview Ave. NW at light. Caution: busy intersection.
7.1 Arrive at Hiram M. Chittenden Locks (restrooms). Continue forward on NW 54th St. as trail ends.
7.3 Left onto 28th Ave. NW.
7.4 Right onto NW 57th St.
7.7 Pass Ballard Commons Park, then right onto 22nd Ave. NW.
7.8 Cross NW Market St. at Bergen Place.
7.9 Left onto Ballard Ave. NW.
8.3 Right onto 17th Ave. NW for a block, then left onto Shilshole Ave. NW. Caution: busy intersection.
8.4 At Y where arterial street curves left, stay right to ride under Ballard Bridge and join NW 45th St.
8.8 Cross four-way-stop intersection by Fred Meyer and rejoin Burke-Gilman Trail.
9.6 Arrive at Fremont Canal Park.
9.9 At N. 34th St. stay on trail to go under Fremont Bridge and along canal; for side trip to visit Fremont's shopping area, exit trail onto 34th. If visiting Fremont, cross Fremont Ave. N. and continue east on bike lane on N. 34th St.
10.6 Cross Stone Wy. N. and continue east on N. 34th St. For side trip to Gas Works Park (restrooms), take trail on right.
10.9 Left onto Wallingford Ave. N. Caution: busy intersection.
11.8 Right onto N. 44th St.
11.9 Left onto Meridian Ave. N.
12.5 Right onto N. 55th St.
12.6 Left onto Kirkwood Pl. N.
12.8 Left to stay on Kirkwood Pl. N. as arterial curves right.
12.9 Right onto E. Green Lake Wy. N.
13.6 Left onto E. Green Lake Dr. N. Caution: busy intersection.
13.8 Left at Latona Ave. NE. into Green Lake Park community center parking lot to end tour.

3   Carkeek and Golden Gardens Parks

DIFFICULTY: moderate
TIME: allow 2.5 hours
DISTANCE: 19.6 miles
ELEVATION GAIN: 1394 feet

Getting There: From I-5 northbound, take exit 170, NE 65th St./ Ravenna. Turn left onto NE Ravenna Blvd. toward Green Lake, continuing north onto E. Green Lake Dr. N. Green Lake Park community center and parking on left at Latona Ave. NE. There is additional parking on E. Green Lake Wy. N. along east side of lake.

From I-5 southbound, take exit 171, NE 74th St. Turn right onto 74th, left onto 5th Ave. NE, right onto NE 71st St., then right onto E. Green Lake Dr. N. Green Lake Park community center and parking on left at Latona Ave. NE.

GPS Coordinates: N47 40 54 W122 19 39
Transit: King County Metro 16, 26, 48, 82, 316

At some of our magic places where streams meet Puget Sound, city parks have kept development at bay, just as devoted volunteers now keep the wetlands and banks free of invasive species. It's being done to support the return journey of oceangoing salmon. Keep the salmon in mind as you ride this tour. Each species carries its own struggle: The leisure world of humans seeking health and strong legs through biking might be a bit less essential than the salmon's upstream spawning cycle, but no less noble.

Begin your journey by cycling along Green Lake's north shore and then north through Greenwood's residential streets before turning west to Carkeek Park. This gem is somewhat of a well-kept secret, tucked away in a neighborhood far from freeways or even major arterial roads. It's really a series of ravines bisecting surrounding neighborhoods. Numerous hiking trails are open to walkers. To a biker, it's a down-and-back proposition. At the parking lot, a grassy knoll looks across railroad

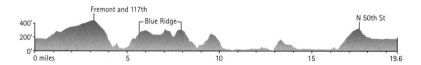

The beach at Golden Gardens Park

tracks to the shore. Park and lock your bike, then use the over-tracks walkway to reach the beach.

Resume your two-wheeled effort by rising out of the saltwater air back through Carkeek and up into the winding, hilly Blue Ridge area. All the best view spots along the ridge have long ago been taken by large, glassy-eyed homes, so bikers must crest a road for an expansive view, drop into the valleys between, then emerge again. Do this a few times, and you may sense the genetic imperative of the salmon.

You'll also wend your way south, eventually coming out on the upper reaches of Golden Gardens Drive NW, just above yet another spot where you can dip your fingers into the salmon's watery world. A shady lane takes you quickly down to Shilshole Bay, bisecting Golden Gardens Park. Turn right and coast to the end of the parking lot, then go a bit farther north on the walking path to North Beach. Common sights here include windsurfers, kites, and gatherings of the posse around campfires.

Follow Shilshole Bay south along Seaview Avenue NW on the Burke-Gilman Trail. At the Chittenden Locks, continue your meditation on the migration of species with a stop at the fish ladder, on the south side of the locks, which provides a salmon's-eye view of the journey.

From the south side of the locks, climb into the Magnolia neighborhood, traversing a clattering but safe railroad trestle before coming out onto West Government Way. Take its broad bike lane down to the ship canal bike trail along Nickerson, which skirts Queen Anne's north edge, to the Fremont Bridge, then cross north into Fremont and take residential streets north to get back to Green Lake's well-used bike lanes.

Slip your toes into the lake and consider the challenges you encountered on your course from salt water to freshwater, along major and minor tributaries, past locks and ladders, from park to park to park.

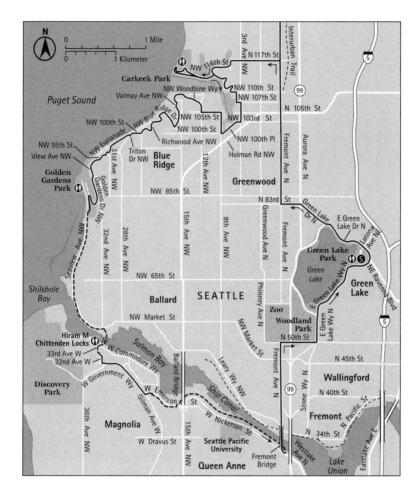

Route Connections: Continue east on the Burke-Gilman Trail (Tour 1), connect with the Interurban Trail at NW 107th Street to Edmonds (Tour 5), or loop Magnolia after crossing the Chittenden Locks (Tour 6).

MILEAGE LOG

0.0 Left out of Green Lake community center (restrooms) parking lot onto E. Green Lake Dr. N.

0.7 After business district, right to stay on Green Lake Dr. N.

1.1 Cross SR 99/Aurora Ave. N. at N. 83rd St.

1.3 Right onto Fremont Ave. N.

3.1 Left onto N. 117th St.

3.2 Cross Greenwood Ave. N. at light.

3.4 Cross 3rd Ave. NW and proceed downhill to Carkeek Park; 117th curves left and becomes 6th Ave. NW, which in 1 block becomes NW 116th St. Caution: steep grade.

4.0 Right into Carkeek Park (restrooms) at stop sign.

4.6 Reach pedestrian overpass to beach. Continue on one-way road to exit park.

5.2 Right to exit park, onto NW Carkeek Park Rd.

5.8 Right onto 4th Ave. NW.

6.0 Curve left as 4th dead-ends, then right onto 3rd Ave. NW.

6.3 Right onto NW 103rd St., which becomes NW 100th Pl.

6.6 Right onto 8th Ave. NW.

6.8 Left onto NW 105th St.

7.1 Right onto 12th Ave. NW.

7.2 In 1 block, left at Y onto NW Woodbine Wy. at sign for Blue Ridge.

7.3 Left at Y with NW Norcross Wy. to stay on NW Woodbine Wy.

7.6 Right onto Valmay Ave. NW.

7.9 Right onto NW Blue Ridge Dr.

8.4 Left at Y onto Richwood Ave. NW.

8.6 Right onto NW 100th St.

8.7 Left at T at Blue Ridge Club onto Triton Dr. NW. In ½ block, right onto NW Esplanade.

9.1 Left at Y onto 31st Ave. NW.

9.2 Right onto NW 95th St.

9.3 Straight onto View Ave. NW.

9.6 Right onto Golden Gardens Dr. NW. Caution: fast-moving traffic on curving descent.

10.4 Arrive at Golden Gardens Park (restrooms). Left to join Burke-Gilman Trail on east side of Seaview Ave. NW.

11.9 Cross Seaview Ave. at light. Caution: busy intersection.

12.5 Arrive at Hiram M. Chittenden Locks (restrooms). Walk bike through locks to Magnolia exit.

13.0 Exit locks onto W. Commodore Wy., jog right 10 yards, then left onto 33rd Ave. W. Caution: steep uphill grade. Trail begins on railroad bridge at street end.

13.2 Curve left off trail onto 32nd Ave. W.

13.4 Left onto W. Fort St. briefly, then left at stop sign onto W. Government Wy., which becomes Gilman Ave. W.

14.0 Left onto W. Emerson Pl., which becomes W. Emerson St.

14.3 At 21st Ave. W., join Ship Canal Trail on the right.

14.6 Cross under Ballard Bridge on trail, which then runs next to canal parallel to W. Nickerson St.

15.3 Pass Seattle Pacific University.

16.0 Continue under Fremont Bridge on trail, then take first right in 100 yards onto access road and right onto sidewalk trail at top of climb.

16.2 Continue forward onto Fremont Bridge; merge into turning lanes or use crosswalks to enter bridge walkway-bikeway. Caution: high-traffic, complex intersection.

16.4 Continue forward on Fremont Ave. N. at N. 34th St. on north side of bridge. Climb long grade out of Fremont.

17.6 Right onto N. 50th St. to SR 99 underpass.

17.7 Continue forward at stop sign to stay on N. 50th St.

18.0 Merge to left-turn bike lane between vehicle lanes to turn left onto E. Green Lake Wy. N.

19.4 Left onto Green Lake Dr. N. Caution: busy intersection.

19.6 Left at Latona Ave. NE into Green Lake community center parking lot to end tour.

4 Magnuson and Ravenna Parks

DIFFICULTY: easy
TIME: allow 1.5 hours
DISTANCE: 15.6 miles
ELEVATION GAIN: 581 feet

Getting There: From I-5 northbound, take exit 170, NE 65th St./ Ravenna. Turn left onto NE Ravenna Blvd. toward Green Lake, continuing north onto E. Green Lake Dr. N. Green Lake Park community center and parking on left at Latona Ave. NE. Additional parking on E. Green Lake Wy. N. along east side of lake.

From I-5 southbound, take exit 171, NE 74th St. Turn right onto 74th, left onto 5th Ave. NE, right onto NE 71st St., then right onto E. Green Lake Dr. N. Green Lake Park community center and parking on left at Latona Ave. NE.

GPS Coordinates: N47 40 54 W122 19 39
Transit: King County Metro 16, 26, 48, 82, 316

Northeast Seattle provides a relaxing excursion on a summer afternoon. This short tour connects two of the city's most popular parks on a gentle route between Green Lake and Lake Washington and reveals a third park that is a hidden gem.

Begin and end the tour at Green Lake, one of the favorite fitness spots for Seattleites. Cross onto the most luxurious, if brief, bike lane in Seattle: NE Ravenna Boulevard. Bikes get equal space with cars here, and for a half-dozen blocks you're cycling under a broad tree canopy with room to spare.

Jogging north in the University District, the route continues on a brief gravelly trail above Ravenna Park. A stop on the pedestrian-bike bridge at 20th Avenue NE provides a sneak peek at the hidden haven below: Ravenna Park's ravine. A hard-packed dirt trail runs its length.

The Ravenna neighborhood holds another unique Seattle landmark: the Picardo Farm P-Patch. It is the oldest and largest of Seattle's community gardens. From a street-side view of its sunken garden north of University Prep, you can see back-to-the-land types tending vegetables and plucking weeds from the fertile soil.

From Ravenna, climb north into the Wedgwood neighborhood and then descend in a winding downhill loop east to the Burke-Gilman Trail.

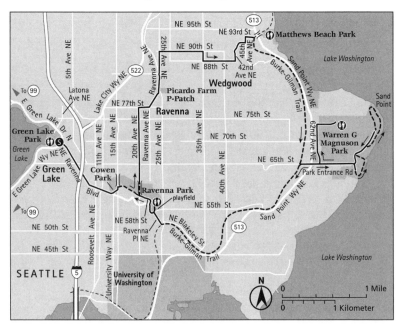

Ravenna ravine

Heading south on the B-G, you'll soon be at your midtour break. Exit the trail at NE 65th Street and drop down to Warren G. Magnuson Park.

Previously a US Navy base, this sprawling complex is now a city park and possibly the zenith of the "multiuse" concept. Ride past the short-term transitional housing for homeless families and the offices and performance spaces for nonprofit organizations. The former brig, now a community center, sits in front of a community garden and an off-leash dog park. Past the dog park are trails to the Lake Washington waterfront. You'll also find playfields, a boat ramp, an amphitheater, meadows with walking trails, and large sculptures.

Cyclists might opt for reclining on the grass or lounging along the off-leash area fence to watch the canines frolicking. When your break is over, ride south again on the B-G, pass University Village shopping center, then depart the trail to cut northwest along Ravenna Park.

On a warm day, savor a noticeable drop in temperature as you visit this verdant urban canyon. A recently daylighted creek babbles alongside much of the trail. Visible among the dense greenery above are the bridges of the streets you traveled earlier. Walking trails angle up the ravine on each side, and a broad main path is lined by large Douglas firs and western red cedars.

After a visit to the ravine, ride back along its upper rim, then emerge at the edge of Cowen Park, across which begins the wide thoroughfare that brought you from Green Lake and will take you back there again.

Route Connections: Continue north or west on the Burke-Gilman Trail (Tour 1), turn south through the University of Washington to tour Central Seattle (Tour 9), or connect with the Lake Washington Loop (Tour 16).

MILEAGE LOG

0.0 Right out of Green Lake community center (restrooms) parking lot onto E. Green Lake Dr. N.

0.3 Merge to left lane and continue through intersection at NE 71st St. onto bike lane on NE Ravenna Blvd.

1.1 Left onto University Ave. NE, which becomes Cowen Pl. NE near Cowen Park.

1.2 Left onto 15th Ave. NE, then immediate right onto a trail just south of the bridge.

1.5 Left onto 20th Ave. NE, on the bike and pedestrian bridge.

2.5 Right onto NE 77th St.

2.6 Left onto Ravenna Ave. NE.

2.8 Left onto 25th Ave. NE, which in 1 block becomes Ravenna Ave. NE. Picardo Farm P-Patch on the right.

2.9 Left to continue on Ravenna Ave. NE.

3.0 Right onto 25th Ave. NE.

3.3 Right onto NE 90th St.

3.8 Right onto 35th Ave. NE.

3.9 Left onto NE 88th St.

4.2 Left onto 42nd Ave. NE. Caution: narrow road, limited visibility.

4.5 Left onto 45th Ave. NE.

4.6 Right onto NE 93rd St.

4.7 As road curves left, go right on brief trail connecting with Burke-Gilman Trail, visible through trees; turn right onto B-G. Matthews Beach Park (restrooms) to left on B-G in 0.25 mile.

6.4 Left onto NE 65th St.

6.6 Cross Sand Point Wy. NE onto Park Entrance Rd. in Warren G. Magnuson Park (restrooms).

7.1 Curve right to enter parking area.

7.2 Continue forward through bollards onto trail.

7.3 Rejoin parking and continue forward along lake.

7.4 Forward through bollards at northeast corner of parking onto trail.

8.5 Left at off-leash dog area onto brief unpaved section. Continue forward as trail forks. Right unpaved section climbs to north playfields.

8.6 Rejoin road by parking.

9.2 Right onto Sportsfield Dr. NE.

9.7 Arrive at north complex. Right onto NE 74th St. to community center, amphitheater, community garden, and off-leash area.

9.9 Road ends at off-leash area. Retrace route.

10.1 Left onto Sportsfield Dr. NE to retrace route through park.

10.5 Right onto NE 65th St. to exit park.

10.7 Cross Sand Point Wy. NE onto cycletrack on NE 65th St.

10.9 Left onto Burke-Gilman Trail.

12.9 Cross NE Blakeley St. Caution: high-traffic area.

13.2 Cross 25th Ave. NE, then immediately exit trail to the right and turn left onto Ravenna Pl. NE. Caution: busy intersection.

13.3 Right onto NE 55th St. In ½ block, turn left into Ravenna Park. Creek and ravine trail are adjacent to playfield (restrooms).

13.5 Exit park back onto 55th; turn right.

13.6 In 1 block, curve right onto NE Ravenna Blvd.

13.7 As Ravenna curves left, stay straight into alley next to park.

14.1 Cross 20th Ave. NE and continue on NE 58th St., then angle right to brief unpaved trail next to ravine.

14.4 Exit trail at 15th Ave. NE. Cross 15th and angle left onto Cowen Pl. NE near Cowen Park.

14.5 Right onto NE Ravenna Blvd., merge to left bike lane.

15.4 Proceed straight through intersection at NE 71st St. onto E. Green Lake Dr. N.

15.6 Left at Latona Ave. NE into Green Lake community center parking lot to end tour.

5 Green Lake to Edmonds

DIFFICULTY: moderate
TIME: allow 3.5 hours
DISTANCE: 29.7 miles
ELEVATION GAIN: 1382 feet

Getting There: From I-5 northbound, take exit 170, NE 65th St./Ravenna. Turn left onto NE Ravenna Blvd. toward Green Lake, continuing onto E. Green Lake Dr. N. Green Lake Park community center and parking on left at Latona Ave. NE. Additional parking on E. Green Lake Wy. N. along east side of lake.

From I-5 southbound, take exit 171, NE 74th St. Turn right onto 74th, left onto 5th Ave. NE, right onto NE 71st St., then right onto E. Green Lake Dr. N. Green Lake Park community center and parking on left at Latona Ave. NE.

GPS Coordinates: N47 40 54 W122 19 39
Transit: King County Metro 16, 26, 48, 82, 316

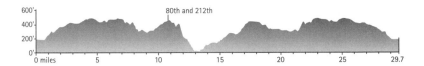

Edmonds is a well-loved Seattle suburb because of its homey down-town, wonderful views across Puget Sound, and easy access by ferry to Kitsap Peninsula. On top of that, it's a great ride from Green Lake.

Heading north, the route barrels through the neighborhoods of Greenwood, Bitter Lake, and Shoreline. For a taste of officially sanctioned kitsch, make a stop at the Viewlands Hoffman Receiving Station, a Seattle City Light power substation at Fremont and North 107th. The northwest corner of the industrial enclosure contains a curious set of handmade wind sculptures made from kitchen items. It's a tribute to the quirky pastime of Emil Gehrke of Grand Coulee, who created and maintained the rusting art.

The way north is a combination of city streets and yet-to-be-connected sections of the Interurban Trail. At the Aurora Village Transit Center, where you cross into Snohomish County, bike lanes take you into Edmonds, past busy bus-laden streets near the Lynnwood mall.

Enter downtown Edmonds by pedaling past a plethora of Main Street shops to a roundabout formed by a brick fountain. Just to the north are the local historical museum and, on summer Saturdays, a vibrant farmers market.

A favorite way to enjoy Edmonds is to pop into the bakery or one of the cafés and grab a bit of food and drink to go, then coast down to the

A well-designed water fountain along the Interurban Trail allows cyclists to easily fill water bottles.

water's edge. North of the ferry dock is the extensive Brackett's Landing Park with sandy beaches, rocky outcroppings . . . and underwater trails. You'd need a bit more than an average cyclist's lung capacity to visit

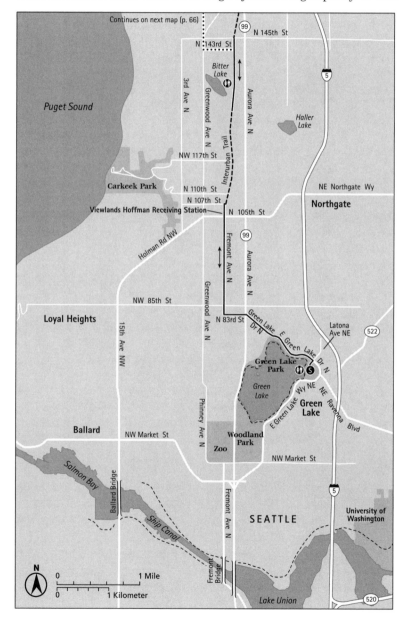

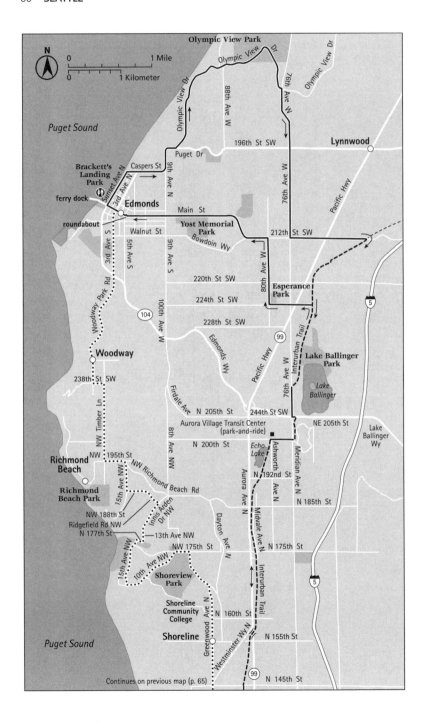

Continues on previous map (p. 65)

these trails without scuba gear, though you can watch others come and go on their watery "hikes" in full wet suits and loaded down with air tanks, flippers, and lights. From the shore, review a map of the park, which is marked on the surface with colored buoys. Benches, restrooms, and a well-kept stretch of sand make it easy to spend an hour or two waterside.

There are many choices for the route home. The easiest ride is to retrace the trip you took on the way north; a more challenging way is to head south along the water to explore the hilly neighborhoods of Woodway, Innis Arden, and Shoreline. However, this tour's route travels north through a bit more of Edmonds and east to the Lynnwood city line, then picks up the Interurban trail to retrace the route back to Seattle.

Cycle north out of downtown Edmonds along stunning Sunset Avenue North, then pick up Olympic View Drive, which winds above the shore for a bit, with more views west beyond the homes, then heads east and snakes through large, shady Olympic View Park. Turn south and then east to cross State Route 99 again before picking up the Interurban Trail and continuing south through Shoreline and back into Seattle.

Route Connections: Loop northwest Seattle (Tour 2), ride east to Magnuson and Ravenna parks (Tour 4), or continue north on the Interurban Trail to Mukilteo (Tour 50).

MILEAGE LOG

0.0 Left out of Green Lake Park community center (restrooms) parking lot onto E. Green Lake Dr. N.

0.7 After business district, keep right to stay on Green Lake Dr. N.

1.1 Cross SR 99/Aurora Ave. N. at N. 83rd St.

1.4 Right onto Fremont Ave. N.

2.9 At 107th St., merge right onto Interurban Trail.

3.9 Merge onto cycletrack at Linden Ave. N. at N. 128th St. Bitter Lake Playground on the left (restrooms).

4.3 Cross N. 145th St. at Seattle city limits and rejoin Interurban Trail.

4.8 Cross N. 155th St. and then SR 99/Aurora Ave. N. on two bike-pedestrian overpasses.

6.3 Cross N. 175th St.; trail continues on near (west) sidewalk on Midvale Ave. N.

6.8 Turn right on sidewalk at N. 185th St. at Gateway shopping center. In 1 block, left on near (west) sidewalk at Midvale to continue on trail.

7.6 Right onto N. 200th St. at Aurora Village Transit Center.

7.9 Cross Meridian Ave. N.; turn left onto Interurban Trail in 100 yards.

8.3 Cross 244th St. SW/Lake Ballinger Wy./SR 104 and continue north into Snohomish County, where Meridian becomes 76th Ave. W.

8.6 Right onto Interurban Trail at Ballinger Park Station.

9.6 Left onto 224th St. SW, unsigned—but parking for dental lab on right.

9.8 Cross SR 99/Aurora Ave. N. at light. Caution: traffic.

10.1 Right onto 80th Ave. W. at Esperance Park.

10.9 Left onto 212th St. SW.

11.1 Soft right at 5-way intersection onto Main St.

12.7 Arrive at fountain roundabout at 5th Ave.; continue forward on Main St. to waterfront.

12.9 Arrive at ferry dock and park. Depart waterfront back onto Main, and in ½ block left onto Sunset Ave. N.

13.4 Sunset curves and becomes Caspers St.

13.5 Left onto 3rd Ave. N.

13.8 Curve left as road becomes 9th Ave. N.

14.1 Curve right onto Puget Dr./SR 524.

14.2 Left onto Olympic View Dr. Caution: traffic. Pass Olympic View Park.

16.6 Right onto 76th Ave. W.

18.3 Left onto 212th St. SW. Caution: traffic.

19.1 Right onto the Interurban Trail.

20.2 Cross 224th St. SW.

21.2 Left onto 76th St. SW at Ballinger Park Station as trail intersects road.

21.8 Right onto N. 200th St.

22.1 Left at intersection with Ashworth Ave. N. to enter trail at Echo Lake.

22.9 Cross N. 185th St. at light, then right onto sidewalk to pick up Interurban Trail.

24.3 Cross bridges again over SR 99. Continue south on trail.

25.1 Exit trail onto cycletrack at N. 145th St.

25.8 Merge back onto trail at N. 128th St. near Bitter Lake (restrooms).

26.8 Exit trail right onto 107th. Left in ½ block onto Fremont Ave. N.

28.3 Left onto N. 83rd St.

28.7 Cross SR 99/Aurora Ave. N. and make a soft right onto Green Lake Dr. N.

29.1 Left to stay on E. Green Lake Dr. N.

29.7 Right at Latona Ave. NE into Green Lake Park community center parking lot to end tour.

6   Magnolia and Discovery Park

DIFFICULTY: easy
TIME: allow 1.5 hours
DISTANCE: 9.7 miles
ELEVATION GAIN: 560 feet

Getting There: Take I-5 to exit 169, 45th/50th Sts., and turn west onto N. 45th St. Proceed west as 45th becomes 46th, then NW Market St. Turn left onto 15th Ave. W. and cross over Ballard Bridge. As 15th becomes Elliott Ave. W. just south of Magnolia Bridge, turn left onto overpass at W. Galer St. to Terminals 90/91. Proceed 1 block, turn right to go under bridge, then right again to dead-end at 16th Ave. W. Parking is trailside on 16th.

GPS Coordinates: N47 37 53 W122 22 39

Transit: King County Metro D line, 19, 24, 32, 33

This short tour skirts the edges of hilly Magnolia and stops for a visit at the ship canal locks and an exploration of the grand open spaces of Discovery Park. Aside from some climbing, it's an easy ride on low-traffic neighborhood streets. This route can be ridden in either direction, though the clockwise route outlined here spreads out the climbing just a bit and makes it more pleasant. But if you try it in the other direction, the views will be completely different, and it will be a good workout too!

Start and end the tour at the Terminal 91 Bike Path parking area, conveniently located on Elliott Bay between Magnolia and Queen Anne. The bike path is a paved trail that runs between the Interbay train tracks and a large Port of Seattle terminal. Smell the creosote and listen for the huffing of the locomotives as you ride this 1-mile stretch north. Watch for oncoming cyclists at two points where the trail narrows and at one spot where it climbs up over the tracks.

Coming off the trail at the rail yards, curve left one block and then climb a bit to Thorndyke Avenue West. Here you take a left and continue north on a long, gradual uphill course in a wide, well-marked bike lane.

Magnolia's bike route is one of the best-signed in the city, so follow the signs through the well-manicured neighborhood of stately view

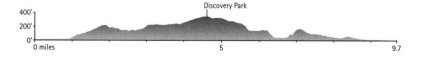

Fall is a great time to visit the Hiram Chittenden Locks and find salmon in the adjacent fish ladder.

homes, and in a few minutes you arrive at Magnolia Park, which sports restrooms in a chalet-style building adjacent to the road.

The tour turns at West Howe Street, but if you went straight here you'd have a good half-mile climb to the neighborhood's town center. Stay on the arterial, and prepare to be stunned again as you turn onto wide-open Magnolia Boulevard West, which offers more great views of the city and Elliott Bay along a gradual climb.

This route takes you up to the southwest corner of Discovery Park, at 534 acres, Seattle's largest park. Discovery contains large open meadows, wooded trails down to Puget Sound, and stunning views of the Olympic Mountains and area waterways.

A ride through the park is a relaxing tour of closed roads dating from when this was a bustling military base. Today there's still a small cadre of military families occupying some of the old Fort Lawton housing, and a massive golfball-shaped radar installation still exists. On the edge of the grand meadow, the main road (unsigned, but Oregon Avenue) forks, with the left branch going down to the bluffs that overlook Puget Sound. Continue on the middle branch, and then make a left past the second house in a row of large homes from the Fort Lawton days. A side road connects you to Discovery Park Boulevard, which heads down to the beach in front of the West Point Water Treatment Plant. Stay on this road only briefly, making the first right, onto the loop trail that leads out of the park after a glorious, tree-lined downhill glide.

Departing the park, continue downhill on 40th Avenue West, then on West Commodore Way until you arrive at the Hiram M. Chittenden Locks. The locks, operated by the US Army Corps of Engineers, let boat traffic through from Puget Sound to Lakes Union and Washington.

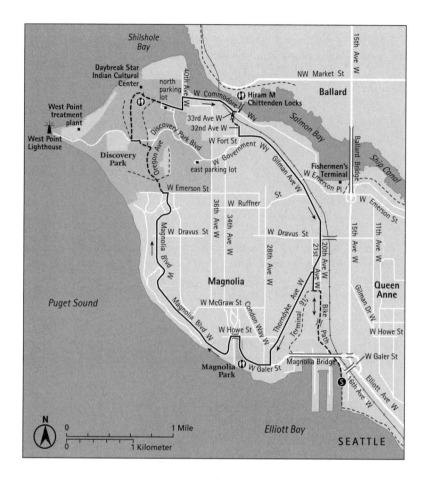

The locks create an essential connection between Magnolia and Ballard. The Magnolia side features a grassy, terraced hillside that is a great place to kickstand-back and watch the frothy water shoot forth from the spillway adjacent to the fish ladder, which salmon must navigate during spawning season (varies by type of fish). The fish ladder is worth a visit when the salmon are jumping. Its subterranean viewing area is marked by a series of six-foot shiny metal waves set onto the concrete plaza.

You can ride down to the locks, but not through them. Bikers are required to dismount and walk through the busy, touristy site. Don't push your luck: cyclists are regularly ticketed for ignoring the rule. This tour continues on the Magnolia side of the locks, crossing over West Government Way at the locks entrance, then climbing the steep fragment of 33rd Avenue West. At the end of the street, ride across a clacking wooden (but quite safe) pedestrian-bike trestle that spans railroad tracks and the Kiwanis Ravine and connects to 32nd Avenue West. In a couple of blocks, make a left onto a long downhill around the eastern edge of the neighborhood. A side tour can be taken at West Emerson Place to Fishermen's Terminal, two blocks east. You can purchase seafood from those who caught it, right off the back of their boats.

Just after West Dravus Street, turn left onto 20th Avenue West and cycle along Burlington Northern Santa Fe Railway's Balmer Yard, where you'll often see hulking train engines idling on their tracks at the road's edge as casually as a pizza delivery car while their operators visit the yard's office. This connects to the Terminal 91 Bike Path, which takes you back to parking.

Route Connections: Cross the Chittenden Locks to ride the Burke Gilman Trail (Tour 1), loop northwest Seattle (Tour 2), or tour Carkeek and Golden Gardens (Tour 3). Or you can ride south through the waterfront parks to connect to Queen Anne (Tour 7) and downtown Seattle (Tour 8).

MILEAGE LOG

0.0   From parking, turn right and ride north on Terminal 91 Bike Path.

0.2   Cross entrance to Terminal 91. Caution: truck traffic. Continue on rail-yard bike path.

0.8   Left as trail intersects with street.

0.9   Right onto 21st Ave. W.

1.0   Left onto Thorndyke Ave. W.

1.9   Left to stay on Thorndyke at intersection with Hayes.

2.0   Right onto W. Galer St. Pass Magnolia Park (restrooms) on left.

2.5   Left onto W. Howe St., cross bridge, then curve left onto Magnolia Blvd. W.

4.5   Left onto W. Emerson St. In ½ block, right into Discovery Park. Proceed forward through bollards onto paved park trail.

4.6   At Y, stay right on main park road.

5.0   Left onto side road after first two houses.

5.2   Left onto Discovery Park Blvd.

5.3   Right at stop sign onto loop trail; go straight through bollards; follow signage for north parking lot.

6.0   Straight at intersection with Daybreak Star turnoff (restrooms to right).

6.1   Left onto 40th Ave. W.

6.4   Right onto W. Commodore Wy.

6.8 Left to visit Hiram M. Chittenden Locks (restrooms) if desired. Across from entrance to locks on W. Commodore Wy., tour continues on short spur of 33rd Ave. W. Caution: steep uphill grade. Trail begins on railroad bridge at street end.

6.9 Exit bridge and curve left off trail onto 32nd Ave. W.

7.1 Left onto W. Fort St. briefly, then left at stop sign onto W. Government Wy., which becomes Gilman Ave. W.

7.9 Cross W. Emerson Pl. (Fishermen's Terminal and start of ship canal trail to left.)

8.4 Cross W. Dravus St. (Left here gets you to Queen Anne in 0.5 mile.)

8.6 Left onto 20th Ave. W. at Thorndyke; follow "To Downtown" bike trail signs.

8.9 Left at street end to rejoin Terminal 91 Bike Path.

9.4 Cross entrance to Terminal 91.

9.7 Arrive at parking to end tour.

7 Queen Anne and Seattle Center

DIFFICULTY: moderate
TIME: allow 1.5 hours
DISTANCE: 9.2 miles
ELEVATION GAIN: 541 feet

Getting There: Take I-5 to exit 169, 45th/50th Sts., and turn west onto N. 45th St. Proceed west as 45th becomes 46th, then NW Market St. Turn left onto 15th Ave. W. and cross over Ballard Bridge. As 15th becomes Elliott Ave. W. just south of Magnolia Bridge, turn left onto overpass at W. Galer St. to Terminals 90/91. Proceed 1 block, turn right to go under bridge, then right again to dead-end at 16th Ave. W. Parking is trailside on 16th.

GPS Coordinates: N47 37 53 W122 22 39
Transit: King County Metro D line, 19, 24, 32, 33

Queen Anne is another short loop like the Magnolia ride (Tour 6), climbing up and around one of Seattle's many populated hills. On this

brief ride, you'll find tree-lined neighborhoods, a vibrant shopping street, and the tourist haven of Seattle Center. Access to Queen Anne was made much more pleasant with the addition in 2012 of the Thomas Street Overpass, which connects the waterfront parks to lower Queen Anne a few blocks west of Seattle Center.

Ride south through the parks and onto the overpass, and then prepare for climbing a few steep streets to get to a broad arterial that curves around the west edge of the hill. You'll shortly be northbound on 10th Avenue West, which becomes West Fulton Street, then curves around the south side of Mount Pleasant Cemetery. Through a half-dozen twists and turns, you'll find it's easiest to ignore the tree-obscured street signs and just stay on the arterial. It delivers you to West McGraw Street.

Turn south onto Second Avenue West through this comfortable neighborhood of modest-looking homes. Queen Anne is well known as

The Thomas Street Overpass takes cyclists from the waterfront Centennial Park to lower Queen Anne.

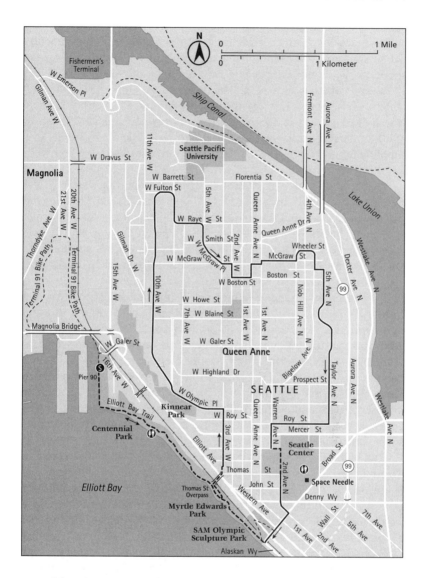

one of the city's priciest close-in neighborhoods, and this tour takes you past homes that are grand and spacious, on streets where the valuable lots are tightly packed together. Along the way, you'll notice a growing number of remodels that plop a boxy modern home in the midst of century-old Craftsman styles.

In a few blocks you arrive at Queen Anne Avenue North, the hilltop shopping street. Where Boston Street meets Queen Anne, the recent coffee craze for a time created a ridiculous sight: three competing coffee shops on this corner, with the fourth corner occupied by a tea shop. It's been toned down a bit today. South on this avenue you'll find shops and cafés for a dozen blocks, followed by "the counterbalance," which heads very swiftly down to Seattle Center. The counterbalance is so named because of the trolleys that once conquered the 20 percent grade of Queen Anne Avenue, using two cars linked by a cable; one was filled with concrete, the other used for passengers. As one went up, the other went down.

This tour skips that screaming downhill for one that's slightly less steep, along the hill's eastern edge. Ride north on Queen Anne to continue your loop around the east side of the hill, spotting views between apartment buildings east across Lake Union to Capitol Hill. A ride down to the Seattle Center area of lower Queen Anne is a fast experience. Turn west onto Roy Street, which has a generous bike lane that takes you past the north side of Seattle Center.

For a side trip through Seattle Center, head left on Warren Avenue North to enter the park and ride the wide lane between Key Arena and the sparkling International Fountain, then exit at Thomas Street. Lock up the bike at this entrance to the center, between the renovated plazas of the Fisher Pavilion and stylish Seattle Children's Theatre, to explore the grounds. The busy park contains the Space Needle, the Experience Music Project, and live theater, opera, and ballet, as well as facilities to host festivals and events. With the many arts organizations, there's always something interesting going on. In the renovated Armory, cafés serve coffee and snacks.

One of the few structures in Seattle Center that has not received an external remodel—and has not needed it—is the graceful, often-imitated Space Needle. Over the years, it's only required a name change: it was originally called the Space Cage. Recline on the well-kept grass for a daydream on the city of the future evoked by the Jetsons-like needle before leaving Seattle Center to wrap up this tour.

From the Thomas Street exit, continue south down Second Avenue North, which carries you to Broad Street. Turn right and ride west toward the waterfront, past the Seattle Art Museum Olympic Sculpture Park and into the bayside parks—Myrtle Edwards and Centennial— whose trails lead north back to the starting point.

Route Connections: Ride north to loop Magnolia (Tour 6), south through downtown Seattle (Tour 8), or east from Lake Union to the Historic Seattle ride (Tour 10).

MILEAGE LOG

0.0 From parking, ride south on Terminal 91 Bike Path.

0.3 Enter Port of Seattle's Centennial Park (restrooms).

1.2 Right onto Thomas Street Overpass after passing under it. Follow trail sign "Uptown" and "Seattle Center."

1.4 Exit trail at corner of Thomas St. and 3rd Ave. W. Continue north on 3rd.

1.8 Left onto W. Olympic Pl.

2.1 Pass Kinnear Park on left. As road splits, take center fork, Olympic Wy. W.

2.4 Road becomes 10th Ave. W.

2.7 Cross W. Howe St.

3.4 Stay on arterial as 10th curves right into W. Fulton St., then curves again onto 8th Ave. W., then W. Raye St., then 5th Ave. W., and finally W. McGraw Pl.

4.2 Left onto W. McGraw St.; cross 3rd Ave. W. In 1 block, right onto 2nd Ave. W.

4.3 Left onto W. Boston St.

4.4 Left onto Queen Anne Ave. N.

4.5 Right onto McGraw St. In 1 block, left onto 1st Ave. N., then in ½ block, right to return to McGraw.

4.8 Soft left onto Nob Hill Ave. N., then soft right onto Wheeler St.

4.9 Right onto Bigelow Ave. N.

5.0 Left onto W. Lynn St.

5.1 Right onto 5th Ave. N.

5.4 Stay left on arterial at the Y, curving onto Taylor Ave. N.

6.1 Right onto Roy St.

6.2 Cross 5th Ave. N. and continue west in bike lane on Roy St.

6.4 Merge into left lane, then left onto Warren Ave. N. In 1 block, cross Mercer St. Caution: traffic.

6.6 Left onto Seattle Center campus at intersection with Republican St. Park road is signed August Wilson Wy. In 1 block, right to stay on asphalt between International Fountain and Key Arena.

6.8 Exit Seattle Center campus through bollards at Thomas St. Continue forward onto 2nd Ave. N. Cross Denny Wy. as street becomes 2nd Ave. Caution: busy intersection.

7.1 Right onto Broad St.

7.3 Right onto Elliott Bay Trail past SAM Olympic Sculpture Park.

7.5 Ride through Myrtle Edwards Park (restrooms).

8.1 Ride through Centennial Park (restrooms).

8.9 Arrive at parking to end tour.

8 Downtown Seattle

DIFFICULTY: moderate
TIME: allow 1.5 hours
DISTANCE: 9.5 miles
ELEVATION GAIN: 459 feet

Getting There: Take I-5 to exit 169, 45th/50th Sts., and turn west onto N. 45th St. Proceed west as 45th becomes 46th, then NW Market St. Turn left onto 15th Ave. W. and cross over Ballard Bridge. As 15th becomes Elliott Ave. W. just south of Magnolia Bridge, turn left onto overpass at W. Galer St. to Terminals 90/91. Proceed 1 block, turn right to go under bridge, then right again to dead-end at 16th Ave. W. Parking is trailside on 16th.

GPS Coordinates: N47 37 53 W122 22 39
Transit: King County Metro D line, 19, 24, 32, 33

Some people get great enjoyment from being a tourist in their own town, but for longtime locals who work in downtown Seattle, a bike tour through the city center may seem like the last thing they would want to do on a day away from the office. However, this short ride is designed to hit many high spots a tourist might enjoy, so you can either play visitor or grit your teeth and use the tour to entertain out-of-town guests.

This modest 9.5-mile spin would take about an hour if you rode it straight through, and it has only one gradual incline, stretching from the Chinatown/International District to the downtown Seattle Public Library, so it should be within the abilities of even the occasional rider. The difficulty comes from street traffic, which can be significant during workdays or on game days in the stadium area, so this tour is best done on a weekend, fit in around game schedules at the professional sports stadia and ridden by people comfortable riding in traffic.

Head south on the Elliott Bay Trail through Centennial Park, Myrtle Edwards Park, and the Seattle Art Museum Olympic Sculpture Park. Take an early break here and walk your bike through the free exhibits, many of which are visible from the trail. The downtown waterfront is undergoing years of renovation with the building of a new seawall and

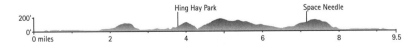

Trailside sculptures greet cyclists at the popular Seattle Art Museum Olympic Sculpture Park.

destruction of an old elevated highway, so this ride skips Alaskan Way and instead heads south on Elliott and Western avenues.

The benefit of this route is reached next, as you ride right by one of Seattle's most beloved landmarks, the Pike Place Market. Here's another chance to lock up your bike and take a stroll past the first Starbucks store, fish and produce vendors, and many cafés, craft stalls, and shops.

Continue south past the market toward Pioneer Square, where a left turn at Yesler Way takes you into Pioneer Square. In two blocks, cross First Avenue and pass the neighborhood's famous totem pole and pergola on the left.

Turn right and head to Occidental Square. On the brick-lined, tree-covered square, you will find more historic statues between Washington and Main streets. A detour left at Main for one block provides a delightful side trip to Waterfall Park, a small enclosed park that marks the original location of United Parcel Service. Cross Main and chain up your bike to stroll through galleries that line the pedestrian mall. Depart the square by turning left onto South Jackson Street.

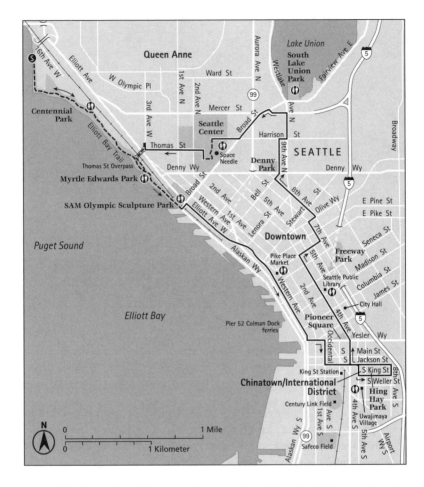

Cycling into the Chinatown/International District takes you by the evolving transit stations for Amtrak and regional rail and bus service. Both Union Station and the regional rail hub of King Street Station have been renovated, restoring architectural grandeur.

Turn right onto Fifth Avenue South, ride between the old buildings of the Chinatown/International District and the modern new office towers, and then pass under the Chong Wa Gate to enter Seattle's urban Asian neighborhood. To the right one block is the fascinating Uwajimaya Village development. The expansive Asian supermarket created a new focal point in this busy neighborhood. Tour the store to marvel at, sample, and shop for unique imported food and snack at the Asian food court.

Two blocks farther on the route is Hing Hay Park, which sports a colorful pagoda and a dragon mural on the wall of an adjacent building. All around this park, at South King Street and Maynard Avenue South, you'll find small Asian shops and cafés.

Loop up to Eighth and back down Jackson for a few more views of the neighborhood, then cycle north on Fourth Avenue into Seattle's business district, stopping for a view of the new City Hall building at James Street. The building's unusual glass awnings, an environmental feature that keeps the building cooler in the summer, overhang the tan stone facade, and the paved plaza sports a series of water channels. A few blocks beyond is the Rem Koolhaas–designed Seattle Public Library at Madison Street, whose angular glass shape launched a thousand architectural reviews.

Continue north on Fourth to Westlake Park, then turn right on Pike Street and angle out of the shopping district north toward the hip South Lake Union area. Make a stop at South Lake Union Park before heading west through another neighborhood that will be years in development as a new car tunnel is dug under downtown to replace the Alaskan Way Viaduct.

Cut back to Seattle Center, and approach the center grounds at the colorful Frank Gehry–designed Experience Music Project, to the right of the Space Needle. It's easy to tarry at Seattle Center, grabbing a coffee or snack and watching the parade of visitors from a park bench or strolling around the International Fountain.

Head back to the waterfront via the Thomas Street Overpass and finish the tour with a ride back through the two adjoining waterfront parks on the Elliott Bay Trail.

Route Connections: From the starting point, connect with the Magnolia (Tour 6) and Queen Anne (Tour 7) routes, turn east at Lake Union to the Historic Seattle ride (Tour 10), or turn east on Pine Street and connect with the Central Seattle route (Tour 9) at Cal Anderson Park. Or from the ferry terminal at Colman Dock, you could connect to many fun bicycling adventures across Elliott Bay (Tours 30, 31, 32, 33, and 34).

MILEAGE LOG

0.0 From parking, ride south (left) on Terminal 91 Bike Path. As it curves left, it becomes the Elliott Bay Trail through Centennial (restrooms) and Myrtle Edwards parks (restrooms).

1.7 Left on near sidewalk when exiting SAM Olympic Sculpture Park (restrooms). In 1 block, right onto Elliott Ave. W. Merge carefully to left bike lane.

2.1 Soft left onto Western Ave. at viaduct on-ramp.

2.4 Pass entrance to Pike Place Market (restrooms) at Victor Steinbrueck Park.

3.0 Pass Madison St. (access Colman ferry dock by turning right here).

3.1 Left onto Yesler Wy.

3.2 Right onto Occidental Ave. S. In 1 block, straight through bollards into Occidental Park. Go through 2 blocks of the park.

3.4 Left onto S. Jackson St.

3.6 Right onto 5th Ave. S.

3.7 Left onto S. King St. and under Chinatown gate.

3.8 Pass Hing Hay Park on left.

3.9 Left onto 8th Ave. S. In 1 block, left onto S. Jackson St.

4.3 Right onto 4th Ave. S. Merge carefully into left bike lane. Caution: heavy bus traffic; use crosswalk to bike lane if necessary.

4.6 Pass City Hall at James St.

4.8 Pass Seattle Public Library Central Library (restrooms).

5.3 Right onto Pike St. Caution: heavy traffic; merge right carefully or use crosswalk at stoplight.

5.4 Left onto 7th Ave.

5.5 Right onto Olive Wy. Caution: heavy traffic; merge carefully to left lane.

5.6 Left onto 8th Ave.

5.9 Right onto Bell St. In 1 block, cross Denny onto 9th Ave. N. in bike lane. Pass Denny Park on left.

6.3 Right onto Harrison St. In 1 block, left onto Westlake Ave. N.

6.5 Left onto Mercer St. at South Lake Union Park (restrooms).

6.7 Merge right onto Broad St.

7.0 Right onto N. Harrison St. Straight across 5th Ave. N. into Seattle Center on right edge of EMP museum. Continue through bollards onto Center grounds.

7.1 First left between EMP and Armory (formerly Center House; restrooms). In 1 block, jog left, then right to continue between Space Needle and Chihuly Garden and Glass Museum.

7.4 Right at Pacific Science Center. In 1 block, left at Seattle Children's Theatre before Fisher Pavilion.

7.6 Exit Seattle Center grounds through bollards at Thomas St. Continue forward on Thomas.

7.7 Cross 1st Ave. N. In 1 block, cross Queen Anne Ave. N. Caution: fast one-way traffic on each street.

7.9 Right onto 3rd Ave. W, then immediately left onto sidewalk under Thomas Street Overpass ramp. Make U-turn to loop up onto overpass.

8.2 Left off overpass onto Elliott Bay Trail in Myrtle Edwards Park (restrooms); pass through Centennial Park (restrooms).

9.5 Arrive at parking to end tour.

9 UW, the Arboretum, and Central Seattle

DIFFICULTY: moderate
TIME: allow 3 hours
DISTANCE: 20.1 miles
ELEVATION GAIN: 1447 feet

Getting There: From I-5 northbound, take exit 170, NE 65th St./ Ravenna. Turn left onto NE Ravenna Blvd. toward Green Lake, continuing onto E. Green Lake Dr. N. Green Lake Park community center and parking lot on left at Latona Ave. NE. Additional parking on E. Green Lake Wy. N. along east side of lake.

From I-5 southbound, take exit 171, NE 74th St. Turn right onto 74th, left onto 5th Ave. NE, right onto NE 71st St., then right onto E. Green Lake Dr. N. Green Lake Park community center and parking lot on left at Latona Ave. NE.

GPS Coordinates: N47 40 54 W122 19 39
Transit: King County Metro 16, 26, 48, 82, 316

When you want to explore a few bustling city neighborhoods and take in some tree-lined, shady lanes, this route is for you. It's long on scenery, whether you're biking over bridges or along some of Seattle's many paved bicycle trails.

Begin the tour at Green Lake, the watery gem of northwest Seattle. Your first shady lane awaits, as you take to the broad bike lane on Ravenna Boulevard, then detour north a bit to traverse your first bridge, the one-lane-wide 20th Avenue bike-pedestrian bridge that spans the Ravenna Park ravine.

Connect to fraternity row, which leads into the University of Washington campus, then cycle the "U-Dub's" main roads to the Husky

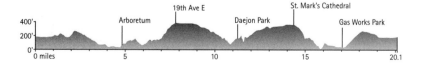

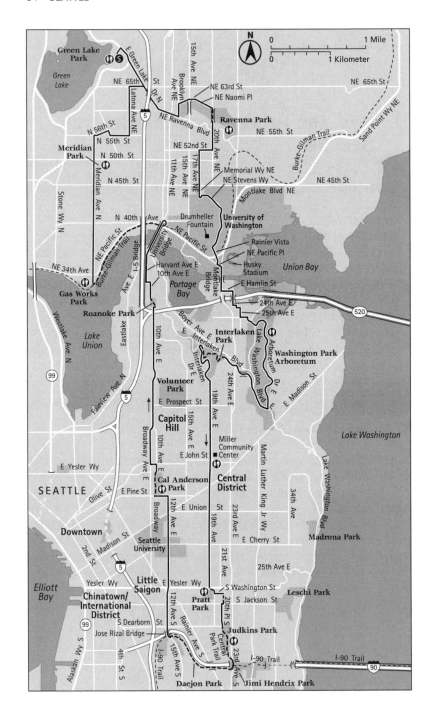

Stadium area. The ride takes you past the Burke Museum of Natural History and Culture, just inside the campus at NE 45th Street. Check out some old and new architecture at your first turn onto Stevens Way. On your immediate right is the gleaming, business-focused PACCAR Hall, circa 2013, while just beyond it is the oldest building on campus, Denny Hall, erected in 1895 of Tenino sandstone and named for a city founder. Pass the Husky Union Building (HUB), which reopened in 2013 with a great expansion, then slow down to look for four free-standing white pillars on the right, just beyond the Paul G. Allen Center for Computer Science and Engineering. That modern building shades the columns, which are even older than Denny Hall, as they came from UW's first campus in downtown Seattle. When the university's first building was to be demolished, the columns were saved and transported out to the new campus. They now form the backdrop for a small outdoor amphitheater.

Next to the columns is Rainier Vista, a broad, tree-lined promenade that stretches southeast from Drumheller Fountain. On a clear day, the area lives up to its name, offering stunning views of the big mountain. Depart the campus by turning left and riding a short trail on the near edge of the Vista to cut across the Burke-Gilman Trail, past Husky Stadium, and into the Montlake neighborhood.

After navigating the stately old bridge and the neighborhood back roads, enter the verdant Washington Park Arboretum, a treasure trove of interesting landscapes maintained by the University of Washington. You get a good sampling from Arboretum Drive: azaleas and rhododendrons burst with color in spring, a small grove of giant sequoia trees commands a majestic corner, and a roadside Pacific Connections garden showcases plants of New Zealand.

After picking up Lake Washington Boulevard East for a short ride north among the serious traffic, angle left onto the biking haven of East Interlaken Boulevard. Again you'll find a one-lane bridge, but watch out for cars on this one. West of busy 24th Avenue East, the street becomes a trail. Wend your way up into north Capitol Hill surrounded by large trees lording over steep ravines where downed logs nurse ferns and moss. Dappled sunlight filters through it all. After a steady climb, you emerge into a neighborhood of stately old homes on tree-lined streets.

Ride south on 19th Avenue East, where apartment density is beginning to merge with single-family living, and it's bringing more retail energy to arterial streets like this one. Cross East Denny Way (there's that founder again) and make a left at East Yesler Way (another pioneer Seattleite) to pick up a string of bikeways through parks known as

A horizontal tree sculpture marks the paths at Pratt Park.

the Central Park Trail. This three-quarter-mile trail, dedicated in 1998, linked a number of existing bike-ped routes through Pratt and Judkins parks and along the west edge of Washington Middle School. At the south end, it connects at the Northwest African American Museum to the I-90 Trail, also known as the Mountains to Sound Greenway (Tour 18).

Ride the I-90 Trail to its western terminus at the north end of Beacon Hill, then bike north over the Jose Rizal Bridge into the east addition of the Chinatown/International District, known locally as Little Saigon. That name might inspire you to stop at one of the many small stands or cafés—who can resist a bubble tea?

Continue north into the Capitol Hill neighborhood, first on bustling 12th Avenue. Ride past Seattle University campus, which has the renowned Chapel of St. Ignatius near the corner of Spring Street that is worth a visit. Continuing north on 12th, cross the nightclub-filled Pike-Pine corridor, then spin past Cal Anderson Park, a pleasant green lid placed atop a city water reservoir, and briefly tour the vibrant Broadway shopping street.

Beyond Broadway, pass the venerable, if understated, St. Mark's Cathedral on the left. The massive square box, which can be seen from Elliott Bay, was to be built in a grand church style, with spires and ornamentation. But the Great Depression intervened, and the building opened in 1931 in its scaled-down form.

Continue on the arterial north to Roanoke Park and then down to the University Bridge, where you cross and loop down to the Burke-Gilman Trail. To finish the tour, ride a long, moderate climb north through the side streets of the Wallingford and Green Lake neighborhoods to return to the community center.

Route Connections: From Green Lake, connect with the Edmonds (Tour 5) or Magnuson and Ravenna Parks (Tour 4) rides, link up with the Lake Washington Loop (Tour 16) at Husky Stadium, or continue on the Mountains to Sound Greenway (Tour 18) via the I-90 Trail.

MILEAGE LOG

0.0 Right out of Green Lake Park community center parking lot onto E. Green Lake Dr. N. In 35 yards, cross 5-way intersection at NE 71st St. and go forward into bike lane on NE Ravenna Blvd.

1.0 Left onto Brooklyn Ave. NE.

1.2 Right onto NE 63rd St. In 1 block, cross 15th Ave. NE. Caution: fast traffic.

1.4 At traffic circle, soft right onto NE Naomi Pl.

1.6 Right onto 20th Ave. NE.

1.8 Forward through bollards onto bike-ped bridge over Ravenna Park ravine.

1.9 Forward into bike lane onto 20th Ave. NE.

2.0 Right onto NE 52nd St.

2.2 Left onto 17th Ave. NE.

2.6 Forward across NE 45th St. onto Memorial Wy. NE to enter UW campus.

2.7 Left onto NE Stevens Wy.

3.4 Left onto first path immediately past Mason Rd., at Rainier Vista promenade.

3.5 Cross Burke-Gilman Trail and NE Pacific Pl. in front of Husky Stadium to continue on designated bike route across Montlake Blvd.

3.6 Proceed south on Montlake Blvd. sidewalk, following Lake Washington Loop signage.

3.7 Cross Montlake Bridge, also on sidewalk.

3.9 Left onto E. Hamlin St.

4.0 Right as street Ts, then through bollards onto 24th Ave. E. over SR 520.

4.2 Left at T into paved alley. Right in 1 block, then left in ½ block onto E. Roanoke St., then right in ½ block onto 25th Ave. E.

4.4 Left onto E. Miller St. In 1 block, right onto Lake Washington Blvd. E. Caution: traffic.

4.5 As road curves right, merge left and turn left at stop sign onto E. Foster Island Rd.

4.7 Right onto Arboretum Dr. E. Pass Graham Visitor Center (restrooms).

5.7 Right onto Lake Washington Blvd. E.

5.9 Left onto E. Interlaken Blvd. Caution: traffic.

6.2 Cross one-lane bridge. Below is 25th Ave. E., which continues the Lake Washington Loop route.

6.3 Cross 24th Ave. E. to stay on Interlaken. Caution: if traffic is heavy, go right 1 block and use stoplight and sidewalks at Boyer Ave. E.

6.5 As road curves left and becomes 21st Ave. E., go straight through bollards onto trail through Interlaken Park.

6.8 Exit trail through bollards and proceed straight onto E. Interlaken Blvd. In 1 block, left at Y to continue uphill on Interlaken Dr. E.

7.3 As Interlaken ends at 5-way stop sign, choose middle way and proceed forward onto 19th Ave. E.

8.1 Pass Miller Community Center (restrooms).

9.5 Left onto E. Yesler Wy., then in 1 block, right at 20th Ave. S. around Pratt Park (restrooms). Or ride southeast through park trails.

9.6 Left onto S. Washington St.

9.7 Right onto Central Park Trail at street end; follow sign south toward Judkins Park.

9.8 Cross S. Jackson St. and continue on trail on right (west) edge of Washington Middle School.

9.9 At S. Weller St., continue forward on sidewalk to right of parking.

10.0 At S. Dearborn St., curve left to stay on trail next to playfields.

10.4 Cross S. Judkins St. and continue on trail in park (restrooms). In ½ block, left as trail Ys at skate park; follow sign to I-90 Trail. In ½ block, trail curves right and continues on sidewalk along 23rd Ave. S.

10.5 Right to ride west on trail next to I-90.

10.9 Right as trail intersects with a greenway that goes to Beacon Hill and Jefferson Park.

11.1 Pass Daejon Park.

11.3 Left at Y in trail, signed International District.

11.4 Right onto 12th Ave. S. over Jose Rizal Bridge through Little Saigon.

12.5 Pass Seattle University campus on left.

12.9 Left onto E. Pine St. Caution: traffic.

13.0 Right onto Nagle Pl. next to tennis courts.

13.1 Curve right onto packed gravel path in Cal Anderson Park (restrooms). Continue north, parallel to Nagle.

13.3 Straight to exit park onto 10th Ave. E., then left onto E. John St.

13.4 Right onto Broadway Ave. E., which then curves and becomes 10th Ave. E.

14.0 Cross E. Prospect St. (a right here would take you to Volunteer Park in 5 blocks).

14.2 Pass St. Mark's Cathedral.

15.0 At E. Roanoke St., get in right lane but go straight at light onto sidewalk trail in Roanoke Park. Angle diagonally left through park toward northwest corner.

15.2 Exit park at corner of E. Edgar St. and Broadway Ave. E. Proceed forward onto Broadway through curb cut.

15.3 Left on E. Shelby St. In 1 block, right onto Harvard Ave. E.

15.7 Forward onto University Bridge.

16.0 Right at first curving exit off bridge, and continue right on a Burke-Gilman Trail connector under bridge ramp.

16.2 Merge left at stop sign to join Burke-Gilman Trail and head west.

17.1 Right onto Meridian Ave. N. as trail meets Gas Works Park (restrooms). In 1 block, cross N. 34th St. Caution: fast-moving traffic on a curve.

17.8 Cross N. 40th St. Caution: fast traffic.

18.1 Cross N. 44th St., the neighborhood greenway. In 1 block, cross N. 45th St. at light.

18.4 Cross N. 50th St. Meridian Park (restrooms) is on right.

18.6 Right onto N. 56th St. In 3 blocks, jog right 1 block, then left onto N. 55th St.

19.0 Left onto Latona Ave. NE.

19.5 Right onto NE 65th St.

19.6 Left onto NE Ravenna Blvd. Caution: busy intersection.

19.9 Forward through 5-way intersection onto E. Green Lake Dr. N.

20.1 Return to Green Lake Park community center parking lot to end tour.

10 Historic Seattle: Lake Union and Lake Washington Paths

DIFFICULTY: moderate
TIME: allow 2.5 hours
DISTANCE: 15.9 miles
ELEVATION GAIN: 1116 feet

Getting There: From I-5 southbound, take exit 166, Stewart St./Denny Wy., and proceed west on Denny Wy. to Denny Park. From I-5 northbound, take exit 166, Olive Wy., turn left on Melrose Ave., then left on Denny Wy. and proceed 0.6 mile west to Denny Park. The park borders Denny Wy. between 9th Ave. N. and Dexter Ave. N., a few blocks east of the Space Needle. Plentiful paid street parking with four-hour limit.

GPS Coordinates: N47 37 11 W122 20 24
Transit: King County Metro 8, 26, 28, 40, 62, 98

Before there were cars in Seattle, there were bikes. Cycling became a craze in the 1890s, and as Seattle was expanding north from downtown toward Lake Union, bike trails were created so that riders could visit the wild lakeshores of Lake Union and Lake Washington. Cabled streetcars took residents of the expanding city out to the new University of Washington campus and neighborhoods at Madison Park and Leschi, crisscrossing Capitol Hill.

It was not until the 1890s that Seattle saw any paved streets, and prior to that time, cycling in Seattle was a perilous effort. In fact, assistant city engineer George Cotterill, who later became mayor, mapped many of the early bike routes and told of the woeful roads. Cotterill was quoted in the May 1982 edition of the *Wheelmen* magazine, which published a history of Seattle's Queen City Bicycle Club and discovered an article by the engineer in Seattle's *Argus* newspaper written on December 17, 1898, about street conditions: "The main thoroughfares of the City were strewn with wrecks of old planking which had survived from five to ten years of traffic. Spikes, splinters, and holes were the principal features which distinguished the remains. An occasional lonely cyclist might be seen picking out a tortuous course among such difficulties, and the general public

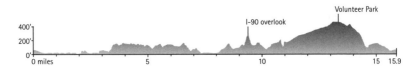

naturally and properly wondered where the fun came in." The city began paving downtown streets with bricks in 1893, primarily due to the clamor for better bicycling surfaces. But the short runs were evidently not satisfying to cyclists wishing to get some distance under their wheels, so a series of cinder bicycle paths was created: around Lake Union, up to the military post Fort Lawton (now Discovery Park) on Magnolia, between Ballard and Fremont, and out to Lake Washington.

On September 19, 1896, nearly 200 cyclists paraded with lanterns on their bikes to celebrate the opening of the Lake Union Path. It stretched 2.5 miles up the lake's

Cyclists ride the original path between Lake Union and Lake Washington along the wooded ravine of Interlaken Park.

east shore and consisted of sidewalks, streets, bridges, and a dedicated bike path. Later, it was connected with a half-mile path on the north side and other links to form a 10-mile route around the lake. The next year, the route was extended, and on June 19, 1897, a 10-mile path to Lake Washington was opened. It ran along what are now Lakeview and Interlaken boulevards.

Today, a number of streets exist that evolved from sections of early bike routes, but the combined Lake Union–Lake Washington path provides the only historic route that can be substantially ridden by present-day cyclists.

The path started at Eighth Avenue and Pine Street in downtown Seattle, but to avoid today's traffic, this route begins a bit north of the city center. It starts at Denny Park, Seattle's first public park, which was given to the city by the founding Denny family in 1864 and opened as a park in 1884. The small park is graced by large trees, with a formal design of intersecting paths coming in from the corners to a central circle.

Depart the northeast corner of the park into the urban renewal of the South Lake Union neighborhood. In a half mile you'll be riding along the south edge of South Lake Union Park, looking at yachts and floatplanes beyond the Museum of History and Industry and the Center for Wooden Boats. Farther east, pass a row of upscale restaurants. Curve around the east side of the lake and ride north, passing

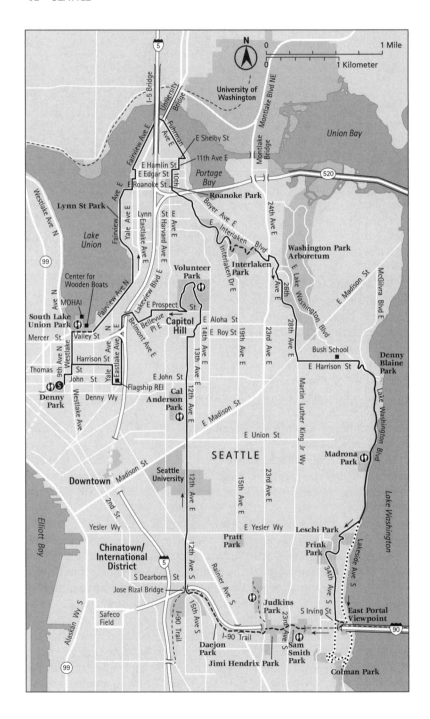

N

0   1 Mile

0   1 Kilometer

University of
Washington

I-5 Bridge

University Bridge

Montlake Blvd NE

Union Bay

E Shelby St

Fuhrman Ave E

Fairview Ave E

11th Ave E

E Hamlin St

E Edgar St

Portage
Bay

Montlake Bridge

520

E Roanoke St

10th Ave E

Roanoke Park

Lynn St Park

Boyer Ave E

24th Ave E

Fairview Ave E

Yale Ave E

Lynn St E

Eastlake Ave E

Harvard Ave E

Ave E

E Interlaken Blvd

Lake
Union

Washington Park
Arboretum

99

Center for
Wooden Boats

Fairview Ave N

Lakeview Blvd E

Interlaken Dr E

Volunteer
Park

Interlaken
Park

E Lake Washington Blvd

26th Ave E

E Madison St

McGilvra Blvd E

MOHAI

South Lake
Union Park

Belmont Ave E

Bellevue Pl E

E Prospect St

Capitol
Hill

E Aloha St

14th Ave E

19th Ave E

23rd Ave E

28th Ave E

Bush School

Denny
Blaine
Park

Mercer St

Valley St

E Roy St

Harrison St

13th Ave E

E Harrison St

Lake Washington Blvd

Thomas St

9th Ave N

Westlake

Eastlake Ave E

John St

Yale

E John St

Flagship REI

Cal
Anderson
Park

12th Ave E

Denny
Park

Denny Wy

Westlake Ave

E Madison St

SEATTLE

E Union St

15th Ave E

23rd Ave E

Madrona
Park

Martin Luther King Jr Wy

Downtown

Madison St

Seattle
University

2nd St

12th Ave E

Lake Washington

Elliott Bay

Yesler Wy

E Yesler Wy

15th Ave E

23rd Ave E

Leschi Park

Lakeside Ave S

Pratt
Park

Frink
Park

Chinatown/
International
District

5

12th Ave S

34th Ave S

S Dearborn St

Jose Rizal Bridge

Rainier Ave S

Judkins
Park

S Irving St

East Portal
Viewpoint

Safeco
Field

I-90 Trail

15th Ave S

23rd Ave S

Sam
Smith
Park

90

Alaskan Wy S

Daejon
Park

I-90 Trail

Jimi Hendrix Park

Colman Park

99

a floatplane company and industrial docks before coming to a floating residential neighborhood. Colorful houseboats are dressed up with rooftop gardens and berthed kayaks.

At the heart of the floating-home neighborhood is Lynn Street Park, across from Pete's Supermarket, where you can stop and see the homes from its gaily tiled lakeside benches. The park has an interesting bit of history. Pete the grocer led an effort to build it, but the community had to come together to rebuild it after a driverless delivery truck barreled down steep Lynn Street, caromed through its tiny space, and crashed into the lake in 1995.

There's not a continuous road or bike path along the lake, so you must jog up and ride through a couple of alleys before dropping back down to lakeside. It's well signed; this section of the tour is on the Cheshiahud Loop, a 10-mile city-sponsored route around Lake Union. Look for the blue loop signs. It was named for a Duwamish chief whose family was the last of the tribe to live on the lake. Their home was at the foot of Shelby Street.

At the north edge of this neighborhood, climb east one block to Eastlake Avenue, where you reach the intersection with the University Bridge. Continue riding east into the Portage Bay neighborhood, then tackle one of two significant climbs on the tour, up to the north edge of Capitol Hill. Here you'll pass Roanoke Park, whose land also was originally owned by a member of the Denny family. It was acquired by the city in 1908 to be used as a resting place for cyclists and hikers making the long trek to Lake Washington.

But the prime cycling respite lay a bit beyond the park, in the wilds of Interlaken. The route continues along the side of a heavily wooded ravine, and for a mile you are riding through a verdant landscape that must look much the same today as it did to cyclists more than a century ago. Along this route, lost but not forgotten, was the "Halfway House," which served as a breakfast and lunch café and rest stop for cycling tourists. It was most likely located a bit below street level, west and north of the intersection of East Interlaken Boulevard and Interlaken Drive East. Today, a short section of East Interlaken Boulevard is closed to all vehicles except bicycles, so riders can truly say they are on the city's original bike path.

Back on the streets, drop down to the well-marked Lake Washington Loop bike route that parallels the Washington Park Arboretum. As you cross East Madison Street, imagine early cyclists meeting the streetcar line here and sharing a wooden trestle over the swampy lowlands of Madison Valley.

Ride by the Bush School, then join Lake Washington Boulevard and wind down to the lake, passing Denny Blaine and Madrona parks before cutting away from the lake at Leschi. The small shopping district here makes for a good "halfway house" on this short tour. There's a branch of Seattle's most famous coffee chain, a grocery store, and a family deli in the two blocks of businesses.

Depart Leschi by staying on Lake Washington Boulevard and climbing through Leschi and Frink parks to the edge of the hill above the Interstate 90 tunnel. An alternate route: continue forward through Leschi on Lakeside Avenue South to Colman Park, then climb through the park and ride north a few blocks on Lake Washington Boulevard to this ride's next turn at the Interstate 90 overlook and tunnel-bridge entrance.

The overlook above the tunnel entrance provides another bit of history: the newer of the two broad floating-bridge freeways was named after Homer Hadley, a pioneering Seattle engineer who designed and proposed the first concrete floating bridge in 1920. He saw the first of these bridges built in 1940. Today, Homer's bridge includes a grade-separated bike-pedestrian lane often used by commuter and recreational cyclists to get to our eastern suburbs.

On this ride, though, turn west instead of east and enter the tunnel under the Mount Baker neighborhood to ride toward downtown Seattle. Although the route is a bit south of the historic bike path, it's today's best bet for getting comfortably back into town. You're riding the western end of the Mountains to Sound Greenway (Tour 18), which takes you along another bit of Interstate 90 to the north edge of Beacon Hill. From there, with stunning views of the sports stadia and downtown Seattle, head north through the bustling Asian shopping district known as Little Saigon.

Our historic route continues north on 12th Avenue, past Seattle University's Logan Field, where one of Seattle's first bicycle racetracks was built. The Triangle Bicycle Club, organized by the YMCA, opened a track in 1895 between East Cherry and Jefferson streets that presumably thrilled residents with track racing under electric lights. Two other such tracks, on Third Avenue downtown and up north at Woodland Park, operated in Seattle at the turn of the 20th century, feeding the craze for all things bicycle. They would often host traveling bicycle racers competing in "Six-Day Races," in which teams rode the banked oval tracks continually around the clock.

Another early municipal park, Volunteer Park, is our next stop. The land was purchased in 1876, but was much improved by the end of the century. Early in the 1900s, a reservoir and water tower were added, and formal plans for the grounds were drawn up by the Olmsted

Brothers, famous landscape designers. Today, it hosts the Seattle Asian Art Museum, the glass-walled Conservatory (which dates from 1912), and an iconic picture spot for visitors: a massive black truck-tire-shaped sculpture called *Black Sun,* created by Isamu Noguchi. The sculpture's center hole serves as a perfect frame for the Space Needle. If you climb the stairs in the old brick water tower, you'll find a permanent exhibit on early bicycling in Seattle.

Depart the park with a downhill spin (mind your brakes) to the western edge of Capitol Hill at Lakeview Boulevard. Here, as you cross over Interstate 5, is a great view of Lake Union and Queen Anne Hill beyond. Drop down to Eastlake Avenue East and ride past, or to, the flagship REI outdoor equipment store. From there, it's a bit more downhill through the morphing South Lake Union neighborhood to return to Denny Park and end the tour.

In this tour's short 16 miles, you've visited three of Seattle's earliest parks and viewed some of the city's historic infrastructure. Now, don't you feel closer to those pioneer cyclists?

Route Connections: Connect with Queen Anne (Tour 7) at South Lake Union Park, the Lake Washington Loop (Tour 16) at Washington Park Arboretum, or the Mountains to Sound Greenway (Tour 18) or Central Seattle (Tour 9) at Interstate 90.

MILEAGE LOG

0.0 At corner of John St. in Denny Park, left onto 9th Ave. N.

0.1 Right onto Thomas St.

0.2 Left onto Westlake Ave. N.

0.5 Cross Valley St. at crosswalk into South Lake Union Park (restrooms). Turn right onto South Lake Union Trail, on the sidewalk next to streetcar tracks. Caution: cross-traffic into parking lots for next 0.5 mile.

0.6 Valley St. becomes Fairview Ave. N. Continue on sidewalk.

1.1 As sidewalk ends at a boat dock, curve right onto protected pedestrian-bikeway on the street. Caution: oncoming bike traffic at east end.

1.2 Left onto Fairview Ave. E.

1.9 Pass Lynn Street Park.

2.0 Road curves right and becomes Roanoke St.

2.1 Left onto tiny Yale Ave. E.

2.2 Right onto E. Edgar St., then left into alley in 100 yards. Follow blue bike-route signs that say "Cheshiahud Loop." As alley ends, left onto E. Hamlin St.

2.3 Right onto Fairview Ave. E.

2.8 Right onto Fuhrman Ave. E.

2.9   Cross Eastlake Ave. E. at light and continue on Fuhrman.

3.3   Right on E. Shelby St. In 1 block, left onto 11th Ave. E.

3.4   Right onto E. Hamlin St. for a steep, block-long climb. In 1 block, left onto 10th Ave. E. Pass Roanoke Park on right.

3.6   Left onto E. Roanoke St.

3.8   Right onto E. Interlaken Blvd. after crossing over SR 520. Caution: limited sight distance.

4.4   Stay left (downhill) at a curving Y joining Interlaken Dr. E. In ½ block, continue straight through bollards to enter off-street trail in Interlaken Park.

4.9   Continue forward to return to E. Interlaken Blvd.

5.0   Left onto 24th Ave. E. Caution: fast traffic. If necessary, ride nearside sidewalk downhill 1 block to stoplight. Right onto Boyer Ave. E.

5.2   Right onto 26th Ave. E.; follow bike-route signs for Lake Washington Loop.

5.3   Left onto E. Galer St., which becomes 28th Ave. E.

6.0   After crossing E. Madison St., left onto E. Harrison St. Caution: busy arterial.

6.5   Soft right onto Lake Washington Blvd. at intersection with 37th Ave. E. In 1 block, stay right as road curves downhill.

6.7   Continue straight at intersection with 39th Ave. E. to stay on Lake Washington Blvd. In 1 block, stay right at roundabout to continue on Lake Washington Blvd.

8.1   Right to continue on Lake Washington Blvd. Pass Denny Blaine Park on left, then Madrona Park (restrooms) on left.

8.5   Arrive at Leschi neighborhood business district. At intersection with Lakeside Ave., right to stay on Lake Washington Blvd. and climb away from the lake (for alternate route through Colman Park, continue straight on Lakeside Ave. S., then right from Lake Washington Blvd. S. up through the park and north to rejoin route by turning right onto S. Irving St.).

9.2   Left onto S. Irving St. above I-90 bridge, then right in ¼ block, past bollards. Stay right to enter tunnel.

9.5   Exit tunnel into Sam Smith Park. Continue forward as I-90 Trail crosses Martin Luther King Jr. Wy. S. at stoplight.

9.9   Cross 23rd Ave. S. at stoplight (Judkins Park is 2 blocks north; restrooms), then left on sidewalk and, in 100 yards, right to continue on I-90 Trail.

10.5 Pass Daejon Park.

10.7 Left at Y in trail to curve uphill.

10.8 Right onto Golf Dr. S., which becomes 12th Ave. S. Caution: traffic.

11.3 Cross Boren Ave., then Yesler Wy. to continue north on 12th.

11.6 Pass playfields at Seattle University.

12.3 Cross E. Madison St., then E. Pine St. (Cal Anderson Park is 1 block left; restrooms).

12.9 Right onto E. Roy St., a nearly hidden alley-size street 1 block north of E. Mercer St. In 1 short block, left onto 13th Ave. E.

13.0 Right onto E. Aloha St. Caution: traffic.

13.1 Left onto 14th Ave. E.

13.3 Entrance to Volunteer Park (restrooms). Ride north through park, past Seattle Asian Art Museum. Left at Conservatory, and proceed downhill.

13.6 Right through bollards onto E. Prospect St. heading west.

13.8 Cross 10th Ave. E.

13.9 Left onto Boylston Ave. E. In 1 block, right onto Bellevue Pl. E.

14.3 Curve downhill, then right onto Belmont Ave. E. Caution: traffic, steep downhill grade.

14.4 Straight onto Lakeview Blvd. E. at stop sign.

14.7 Left onto Eastlake Ave. E. Caution: traffic.

15.0 Right onto John St. In 1 block, right onto Yale Ave. N.

15.3 Left onto Harrison St. in 2 blocks. Caution: streetcar tracks in road.

15.7 Left onto 9th Ave. N.

15.9 Arrive back at Denny Park to end tour.

11 West Seattle

DIFFICULTY: easy
TIME: allow 2 hours
DISTANCE: 15.3 miles
ELEVATION GAIN: 743 feet

Getting There: Travel west on West Seattle Bridge, just south of downtown Seattle. Take Harbor Ave./Avalon Wy. exit. Turn right onto Harbor Ave. SW, travel 0.9 mile to a right turn into Jack Block Park, then another 0.2 mile to parking.

GPS Coordinates: N47 34 58 W122 22 19

Transit: King County Metro 37 (weekday commute hours only)

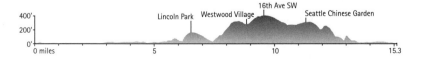

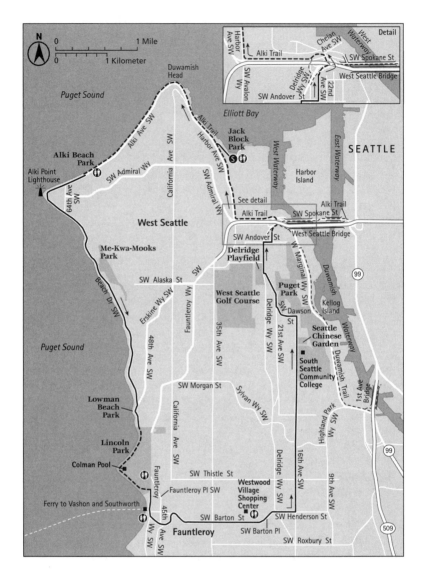

Visitors to Seattle are often wowed by the views, which can be spectacular, especially from the edge of the city's downtown waterfront. But how many of them know that just around the south end of Elliott Bay lies another perspective on the city that is even more stunning? That's one of the high points of this tour, which also connects to the Fauntleroy ferry terminal.

The wide Alki Trail consists of a broad sidewalk path and generous bike lane, all with stunning downtown Seattle views.

Begin at Jack Block Park, just west of Harbor Island. This Port of Seattle facility offers free parking, restrooms, and a great look at the container shipping operations on nearby Harbor Island. Join the trail heading north then west along Alki, and you will find numerous options for sticking your toes in the sand or stopping for snacks and drinks. The entire waterfront is public space, with green grass or sandy beach. Rows of white condos face Elliott Bay above Alki Avenue SW, and the street is bordered by an array of coffee joints, making it a popular terminus for bike groups looping here from Green Lake.

Here on the beach sits a small statue that will look familiar: a scale replica of the Statue of Liberty. It's on the beach rather than in the harbor; it's about 8 feet tall rather than 151; and it is a replacement of one donated by a local Boy Scout troop in 1952, rather than the big one given by the people of France in 1886. However, its symbolism is strong, and it has become a gathering place for commemorations. After the original was vandalized in 2005, local residents replaced it in 2007.

Alki Beach has a much longer history than the statue, though. It stretches back to Seattle's beginnings. On November 13, 1851, the 24-member Denny Party came ashore here and, presumably not finding a Starbucks nearby, "the ladys sat down on the loggs and took A Big Cry," according to historical writings on the excellent website www .historylink.org. You shouldn't have that problem, but some still mourn the loss of Luna Park, a saltwater swimming pool (or natatorium) built on Alki in 1907. The park offered "warm and cold saltwater tanks, dancing, and good eats," according to a plaque that now marks the site. The park burned down in 1931, and the remains of the structure were replaced with a fish-friendly pier in 2004. If you want to keep this outing short and flat, make the Luna Park memorial or the Birthplace of Seattle monument your turnaround point.

Depart the waterfront and ride west alongside beachfront apartments and small homes holding against the tide of condominiums. Swing south around the corner of Alki Point by the historic lighthouse, open for visitors on summer weekends. It marks the southern point of Elliott Bay.

Beach Drive SW takes you past Me-Kwa-Mooks Park, where Vashon Island seems close enough to touch, and south toward Lincoln Park, which offers nature trails and an outdoor saltwater swimming pool. Pass by the ferry terminal, where ferries depart for Vashon and Southworth, then climb the curving streets east to West Seattle's interior.

Close the loop on this tour by riding north on 16th Avenue SW, which provides an opportunity for one more interesting stop on the way back. At South Seattle Community College, turn into the north parking area to find the Seattle Chinese Garden. Years in the planning and fund-raising stages, the six-acre site has begun to take shape, with demonstration gardens and a wonderful pavilion. Above a wooded gorge, the garden boasts enviable city and mountain views.

Twisting streets take you down to Delridge Way SW. From here it's a quick jog across a five-way intersection on Harbor Island to the trail back to the park.

Route Connections: From either the starting point or 16th Avenue SW near this tour's southernmost route, you can connect with the Duwamish Trail (Tour 12) and South Seattle ride (Tour 14).

MILEAGE LOG

0.0 Depart Jack Block Park (restrooms) north to join Alki Trail.

0.2 Right onto trail out of parking.

0.6 Pass Elliott Bay Water Taxi pier.

1.3 Trailside sign commemorating Luna Park.

2.9 Trailside monument commemorating birthplace of Seattle in Alki Beach Park (restrooms off-trail on beach).

3.1 Continue west on Alki Ave. SW.

3.2 Continue on Alki Ave. SW as it curves left at Point Pl. SW.

3.6 Left onto Beach Dr. SW.

6.1 At Lowman Beach Park, continue on Beach Dr. SW to dead-end.

6.4 Pass through bollards onto waterfront trail in Lincoln Park.

6.9 Pass Colman Pool, continue on trail to exit park. Restrooms at left.

7.4 Right onto Fauntleroy Wy. SW.

7.6 Pass Fauntleroy ferry dock.

7.7 Curve left onto SW Wildwood Pl.

7.9 Left onto SW Brace Pt. Dr., which becomes SW Barton St., then SW Barton Pl., then SW Henderson St.

9.1 Pass Westwood Village Shopping Center (coffee shop, restrooms).
9.6 Left onto 16th Ave. SW.
11.5 Arrive at north entrance of South Seattle Community College and Seattle Chinese Garden.
11.9 Stay on 16th as arterial curves left into SW Dawson St., which becomes 21st Ave. SW, then curves left again and becomes 22nd Ave. SW, then 23rd Ave. SW, then SW Oregon St.
12.7 Right onto Delridge Wy. SW.
13.1 Right onto SW Andover St.
13.2 Left onto 22nd Ave. SW.
13.3 Forward onto trail at street end.
13.5 Left at trail intersection with Duwamish Trail and Marginal Pl. SW.
13.6 Follow bike symbols and arrows on crosswalks to cross SW Spokane St. and W. Marginal Wy. SW at 5-way intersection, rejoining trail at plaza on intersection's northwest corner, marked by marine-style bollards across sidewalk.
14.1 Right onto Harbor Ave. SW and Alki Trail.
15.1 Right into Jack Block Park.
15.3 Arrive at parking to end tour.

12 Duwamish Trail

DIFFICULTY: easy
TIME: allow 3 hours
DISTANCE: 25.6 miles
ELEVATION GAIN: 251 feet

Getting There: Travel west on West Seattle Bridge, just south of downtown Seattle. Take Harbor Ave./Avalon Wy. exit. Turn right onto Harbor Ave. SW, travel 0.9 mile to a right turn into Jack Block Park, then another 0.2 mile to parking.

GPS Coordinates: N47 34 58 W122 22 19

Transit: King County Metro 37 (weekday commute hours only)

This tour skirts one of Seattle's major industrial regions and stumbles upon historical connections to the living and trading patterns of Native

100'
0'
0 miles   5   10   15   20   25.6

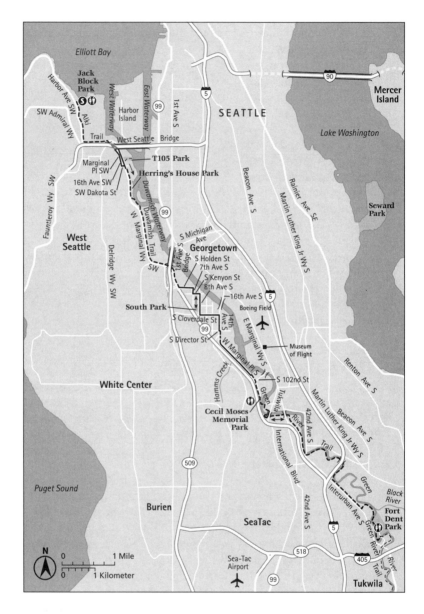

Americans and settlers. Although this route runs past manufacturing areas and warehouses, it provides a vital link to riding the wonderful south King County routes. Thankfully, it's possible—amid the power-lines and bridge ramps—to find some interesting stops along the journey.

This Kellogg Island overlook enhances birdwatching from a trailside park.

Start the tour at the Port of Seattle's Jack Block Park and head south across the challenging intersection at SW Spokane Street and West Marginal Way SW to pick up the short trail. The route takes you through the warehouseland of South Park, where you'll see the occasional well-kept small house and interesting metal sculpture among the machine shops. If you were to crest the South Park Bridge, you would see Boeing Field, and a short side trip would take you to the airplane maker's Museum of Flight. Instead, continue south next to State Route 99.

Pass by Seattle City Light's Ham Creek Watershed, a vacant area among the warehouses where ospreys sometimes nest on the platforms atop tall utility poles. At this point you join the Green River Trail, which heads south through Tukwila to Kent. Traverse a quiet, scenic section, cross a quaint pedestrian-bike bridge, then travel behind office parks and alongside Interstate 5 before riding alongside Tukwila's busy Interurban Avenue.

Next to the river is the site of the Foster Homestead, the destination of flat-bottomed boats that brought provisions for settlers up the Duwamish River from the Green and Black rivers. The Black River, which was lost when the level of Lake Washington was lowered, previously joined the Green at Fort Dent. Fort Dent Park, once a winter community for the Duwamish tribe and then a military outpost, is now a bustling recreation center. Take a break and then turn around here.

On the return trip, stop at a couple more public access areas along our waterways. Herring's House Park is one of the "Duwamish Public Access" points, where you can watch shipping traffic and bird activity along the river. This roadside park also includes greenery and some delightful Native American plaques and sculptures that give you a hint of cultures here before shipping terminals took over. A brief stop is also warranted at T105 Park, a smaller public access area carved out between industrial sites. The entrance to T105 is just north of SW Dakota Street. From Dakota, it's a quick jaunt to meet up with connecting trails under the West Seattle Bridge.

Route Connections: From the starting point, head north to the flat, scenic Alki Trail (Tour 11), head south on a climb into West Seattle via Delridge Way or the South Seattle ride (Tour 14), or turn east to ride across Harbor Island toward downtown Seattle (Tour 8). From Fort Dent Park, connect with the Green River ride (Tour 24).

MILEAGE LOG

0.0 Depart parking at Jack Block Park (restrooms).

0.2 Turn left (south) on Alki Trail.

1.2 Turn left at Harbor Ave. SW on near-side sidewalk to stay on trail.

1.7 Follow bike symbols and arrows on crosswalks to cross W. Marginal Wy. SW and SW Spokane St. at 5-way intersection, rejoining trail as it climbs under bridge's on-ramp.

1.8 Forward at intersection with Duwamish Trail onto Marginal Pl. SW.

1.9 At intersection with 17th Ave. SW, veer right onto 17th, then left onto 16th Ave. SW.

2.2 Left onto SW Dakota St. In ½ block, right onto W. Marginal Wy. SW.

2.4 Cross W. Marginal Wy. SW to rejoin trail on east side of street.

2.7 Arrive at Herring's House Park.

4.5 Cross under 1st Ave. S. Bridge on left sidewalk as trail ends. Continue on sidewalk along W. Marginal Wy.

4.9 Left onto S. Holden St.

5.2 Right onto 7th Ave. S.

5.3 Left onto S. Kenyon St.

5.5 Right onto 8th Ave. S.

5.8 Left onto S. Cloverdale St.

6.2 Right onto 14th Ave. S.

6.5 Left at S. Director St., then immediately right onto sidewalk trail next to 14th Ave. S.

6.7 Curve left at Y to continue south on W. Marginal Pl. S.

7.7 Cross S. 102nd St. and join Green River Trail to continue southbound.

8.1 Pass Cecil Moses Memorial Park (restrooms), then cross pedestrian bridge.

8.5 Exit trail and turn right onto Tukwila International Blvd. bridge.

8.6 Turn right at end of bridge to rejoin Green River Trail.

10.5 Trail exits into parking lot, then resumes at far edge of parking.

12.8 Cross into Fort Dent Park (restrooms, water). Reverse route to return.

15.1 Trail exits into parking lot, then resumes at far edge of parking.

17.0 Loop under bridge at Tukwila International Blvd., cross bridge, and rejoin trail.

17.4 Cross pedestrian bridge.

17.9 At intersection with S. 102nd St., cross 102nd and continue north on W. Marginal Pl. S. as Green River Trail ends.

19.0 Curve right onto 14th Ave. S.

19.4 Left onto S. Cloverdale St.

19.8 Right onto 8th Ave. S.

20.1 Left onto S. Kenyon St.

20.4 Right onto 7th Ave. S.

20.5 Left onto S. Holden St.

20.7 Right onto sidewalk at W. Marginal Wy.

21.1 Approaching 1st Ave. S. Bridge, transfer to north sidewalk to ride under bridge ramp on W. Marginal Wy. to join Duwamish Trail.

21.5 Right at W. Marginal Wy. SW to stay on trail.

22.9 Pass Herring's House Park.

23.2 Continue north on W. Marginal Wy. SW as trail ends.

23.5 Left onto SW Dakota St. Caution: busy street. In ½ block, right onto 16th Ave. SW.

23.7 Soft left onto Marginal Pl. SW.

24.1 Forward at intersection with Duwamish Trail to rejoin Alki Trail.

24.2 Cross 5-way intersection to continue on trail.

24.4 Right onto Harbor Ave. SW and Alki Trail.

25.4 Right into Jack Block Park.

25.6 Arrive at parking to end tour.

13 Chief Sealth Trail and Kubota Garden

DIFFICULTY: moderate
TIME: allow 2 hours
DISTANCE: 16.3 miles
ELEVATION GAIN: 1214 feet

Getting There: From I-5, take exit 163, Columbian Wy. Take Columbian Wy. south and turn left on S. Spokane St., then right on Beacon Ave. S. Turn right into parking at Jefferson Park Community Center in 0.2 mile.
GPS Coordinates: N47 34 11 W122 18 28
Transit: King County Metro 36, 50, 60

Southeast Seattle holds many charms for a nice summer day: a long stretch of Lake Washington waterfront, multiple swimming beaches, and verdant Seward Park are the highlights. But on a city tour around this quadrant, you also will discover stunning views of Mount Rainier, a colorful pavilion donated by an Asian sister city, and a charming park that was the vision of an expert Japanese gardener.

Begin this short loop tour at Jefferson Park, atop north Beacon Hill. Continue south, pass Jefferson Park Golf Course, and join one of Seattle's scenic bike trails, the Chief Sealth Trail, which opened in 2007 as an offshoot of the light rail being installed along Martin Luther King Jr. Way. Contractors building Sound Transit's light rail moved many tons of excavated soil into the corridor to grade the trail. It snakes under powerlines and provides hilltop connections for this sprawling neighborhood. The trail rises and falls under the big powerlines, at times popping out onto a street before beginning another segment. Get ready for some short, steep climbs.

The Chief Sealth Trail ends a bit northwest of Kubota Garden, which was created and maintained as a display garden by master landscaper Fujitaro Kubota, who blended Japanese landscaping concepts with Pacific Northwest plantings. The resulting cross between a Japanese garden and Northwest forest was acquired by the city in 1987 and is a horticultural gem worth many visits.

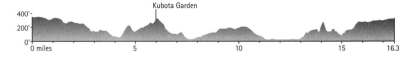

The Chief Sealth Trail offers excellent views of Mount Rainier beyond the powerlines.

Wind your way down to the Lake Washington shoreline next, and pick up the Lake Washington loop bike trail for a time. (To circle the entire lake, see Tour 16). Instead of dropping down to Seward Park, however, continue on through the Columbia City neighborhood, picking up Lake Washington Boulevard South, which sports public waterfront almost to the Interstate 90 floating bridge. An excellent ribbon of asphalt trail runs along the Olmsted-designed avenue by the water's edge.

Whether you're on the busy street or this path, however, expect slow going on a nice weekend day, as the area fills with families and people out for a scenic drive. Conversely, on selected weekend days throughout each summer, this 2.5-mile section of Lake Washington Boulevard is closed to car traffic from midmorning to late afternoon. During those days, the street becomes a great place for a slow ride through the family traffic and a chance to give young children a taste of riding on city streets. Check www.seattle.gov for dates and details.

You leave the lakeside by jogging west into Colman Park, which has a winding, little-used road that hauls you up to a wonderful viewpoint overlooking Interstate 90. From here, loop down under the view stop to ride on top of the freeway in the tunnel that takes you under the Mount Baker neighborhood and into Sam Smith Park. Note the curious art project beneath your tires. Large words set into the pavement invite a psychological game: gate/cave, home/away, dawn/twilight. I would add "park/ride."

This well-appointed bike trail takes you to the north edge of Beacon Hill, where along the way a sliver of park reminds you that you're

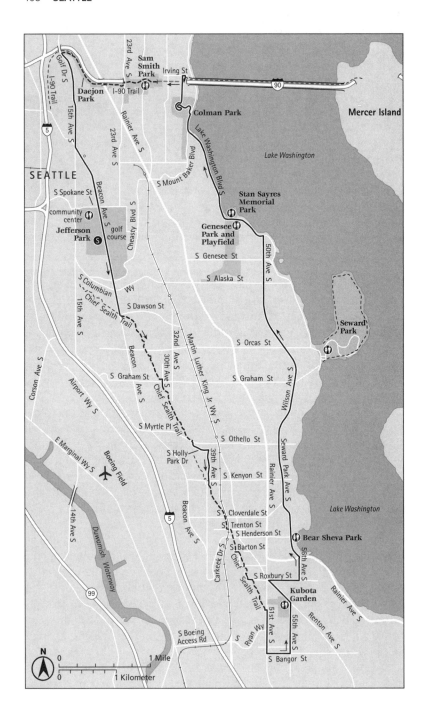

Mercer Island

SEATTLE

Lake Washington

Seward Park

Lake Washington

Parks and landmarks (labels on map):
23rd Ave S
Sam Smith Park
Irving St
I-90 Trail
Daejon Park
Golf Dr S
I-90 Trail
15th Ave S
Colman Park
Lake Washington Blvd
Rainier Ave S
23rd Ave S
S Mount Baker Blvd
Beacon Ave S
S Spokane St
community center
Jefferson Park
golf course
Cheasty Blvd
Stan Sayres Memorial Park
Genesee Park and Playfield
S Genesee St
50th Ave S
S Alaska St
15th Ave S
S Columbian Wy
Chief Sealth Trail
Wy
S Dawson St
32nd Ave S
Martin Luther King Jr Wy S
S Orcas St
Beacon
30th Ave S
Chief Sealth Trail
S Graham St
S Graham St
Corson Ave S
Ave S
50th Ave S
Wilson
Airport Wy S
S Myrtle Pl
Chief Sealth Trail
S Othello St
Boeing Field
39th Ave S
S Holly Park Dr
S Kenyon St
Seward Park Ave S
E Marginal Wy S
Rainier Ave S
14th Ave S
Duwamish Waterway
Beacon Ave S
S Cloverdale St
S Trenton St
S Henderson St
Bear Sheva Park
Carkeek Dr S
Chief Sealth Trail
S Barton St
56th Ave S
S Roxbury St
Kubota Garden
Rainier Ave S
99
S Boeing Access Rd
S Bean Wy
51st Ave S
55th Ave S
Renton Ave S
S Bangor St

N

0   1 Mile
0   1 Kilometer

on a small planet. Daejon Park, named for Seattle's sister city in the Republic of Korea, sports a beautiful, multicolored carved wood pavilion donated by that central Korean city.

At the end of the I-90 Trail, also called the Mountains to Sound Greenway, you are treated to great views of downtown Seattle, the stadia, and Elliott Bay. Drink in the panorama, then head south by cresting Beacon Hill to return to Jefferson Park.

Route Connections: Connect with the Lake Washington Loop (Tour 16) when crossing Rainier Avenue South or the Mountains to Sound Greenway ride (Tour 18) at Interstate 90. You could drop back down to the lake, traveling through Leschi and past Madrona Park and Denny Blaine Park, continuing north to join the Burke-Gilman Trail (Tour 1). You also could connect with the bike lane across Interstate 90 to Mercer Island (Tour 15).

MILEAGE LOG

0.0 Right out of parking at Jefferson Park Community Center (restrooms) onto Beacon Ave. S.

0.5 Cross S. Columbian Wy.

1.0 Left at S. Dawson St. onto Chief Sealth Trail.

1.5 Cross S. Orcas St. In 1 block, jog left onto S. Juneau St., then right in 100 yards to rejoin trail.

2.7 Cross S. Myrtle Pl. onto S. Holly Park Dr.; follow bike trail signs.

2.8 Right on 39th Ave. S.

3.3 Left to rejoin trail under powerlines.

3.5 Cross S. Thistle St., then immediate jog left to stay on trail.

3.7 Cross S. Cloverdale St. at stoplight.

3.8 Cross Martin Luther King Jr. Wy. S. at S. Trenton St. and cross light-rail tracks. In 1 block, cross S. Henderson St. to continue on trail.

4.1 Left onto S. Barton St.; steep climb. Road curves right, then immediately left back onto the trail.

4.4 Left on Marcus Ave. S., which becomes S. Roxbury St.

4.5 Right onto 48th Ave. S, then immediate left to rejoin trail.

4.7 Cross S. Bond St.

4.9 Right onto 51st Ave. S. as trail ends on Gazelle St.

5.3 Left on S. Bangor St.

5.5 Left on 55th Ave. S.

6.0 Arrive at Kubota Garden (restrooms). Depart left onto Renton Ave. S.

6.4 Right on S. Roxbury St.

6.7 Left onto 56th Ave. S.

6.9 Cross Rainier Ave. S. at light onto Seward Park Ave. S. Caution: two lanes of left-turning traffic.

7.3 Pass Atlantic City Boat Ramp and Beer Sheva Park (restrooms).

8.7 Straight onto Wilson Ave. S. as Seward Park Ave. S. turns right.

9.5 Cross S. Dawson St.; street becomes 50th Ave. S.

10.4 Left onto Lake Washington Blvd. S. Pass Stan Sayres Memorial Park (restrooms).

12.5 Left into Colman Park to stay on Lake Washington Blvd. S.

12.8 Right onto S. Irving St., and in ¼ block right onto I-90 Trail entrance. Loop right into tunnel and through Sam Smith Park (restrooms).

13.3 Cross Martin Luther King Jr. Wy. S.

13.6 Cross 23rd Ave. S., then left on sidewalk. Right in ½ block to continue on trail.

14.1 Pass Daejon Park.

14.4 Left at Y in trail, following sign that says "International District".

14.5 Left off trail onto Golf Dr. S.

14.6 Left at Y onto 15th Ave. S.

15.5 Left onto Beacon Ave. S.

16.3 Arrive at Jefferson Park Community Center parking to end tour.

14 South Seattle: Georgetown to Mount Baker

DIFFICULTY: moderate
TIME: allow 3 hours
DISTANCE: 20.3 miles
ELEVATION GAIN: 1254 feet

Getting There: Travel west on West Seattle Bridge, just south of downtown Seattle. Take Harbor Ave./Avalon Wy. exit. Turn right onto Harbor Ave. SW, travel 0.9 mile to a right turn into Jack Block Park, then another 0.2 mile to parking.

GPS Coordinates: N47 34 58 W122 22 19

Transit: King County Metro 37 (weekday commute hours only)

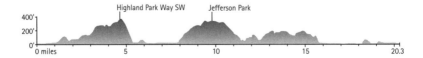

Georgetown's Oxbow Park contains a spiffed-up relic of Old Seattle: the Hat and Boots that used to be an iconic gas station along old Highway 99 that skirted this neighborhood.

Discovering a new neighborhood is one of the joys of urban bicycling, and this route guides you through some less-traveled areas of Seattle. A couple of the neighborhoods, like Georgetown and Sodo, may not have the bike traffic of some other neighborhoods because the biking "infrastructure" of bike lanes, dedicated trails, and signed routes has come more recently.

But finally it has arrived, so not only can you find some new urban haunts but you can spin through the city going east and west, making these new routes vital connections in our heretofore divided city. Alki to Lake Washington? No problem. Interstate 90 to Duwamish? This ride has it covered.

Begin by heading south from the northeastern edge of West Seattle (if you are directionally challenged, please use the modern-day equivalent of a compass, the GPS-enabled bike computer). Ride along the Alki Trail briefly, then head up along the eastern edge of West Seattle, on a

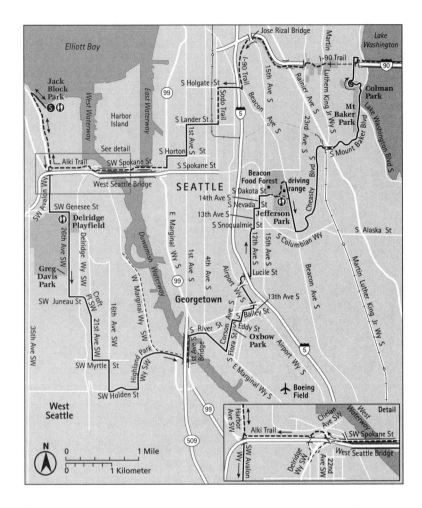

designated greenway bike route through the High Point and Delridge neighborhoods. You'll pass a golf course and numerous small parks.

From Delridge, drop down to the Duwamish Trail via the steep arterial of Highland Park Way SW. You'll be on this trail only briefly, too, before taking the protected bike-ped lane over the First Avenue South Bridge. Stop at the bridge to consider the industrial waterway below, with barges docked by rusting cranes and muscular working ships nosing into nooks next to windowless steel buildings. When you come down off the bridge on the Georgetown side, you'll get up close with some of it, weaving through a few streets lined by semitrucks. During the week, the big trucks are moving and this area is busy with industrial traffic, so this route is best ridden on the weekend.

The Georgetown neighborhood is modest, both in size and scale. It is bordered on the south by Boeing Field (officially the King County International Airport) and on the north by the warehouseland of Sodo, sandwiched between the Duwamish River and Interstate 5. But within its borders is a vibrant artist community that includes a small grid of tidy homes and a messy snag of angling roads containing an up-and-coming business district.

Loop around the south edge of South Seattle Community College's Georgetown Campus and arrive at your first stop, Oxbow Park, the home of the giant Hat and Boots buildings. Built in the 1950s as a gas station that sat along busy Highway 99 before Interstate 5 was built (the hat was the station, the boots were the restrooms), these historic buildings were moved to their current location and restored about a decade ago. They form a colorful centerpiece at this small park, which also includes a P-patch and a play area. If you want to stop and snack here, there's a small grocery on Carleton a block east of the park.

More entertaining sights lie ahead as you cycle into the neighborhood's small business district. Highlights are fine coffee shops, the bookstore of the fabulous local publisher Fantagraphics, which produces comics and graphic novels, and the Georgetown Trailer Park Mall, a parking lot ringed by travel trailers recycled into shops. Up a block on Airport Way South is the massive red-brick Old Rainier Brewery, which also has been converted to other uses . . . mostly. In 2013, sandwich boards for a microbrewery appeared on one of its corners. Cafés, bars, and shops, including a couple of excellent art galleries, round out the 'hood. Take some time to peruse, and make plans to return.

Next, climb onto south Beacon Hill, over railroad tracks and under Interstate 5, connecting to another neighborhood greenway route that leads north to Jefferson Park. On the park's sunny west edge, where there used to be fields of grass along busy 15th Avenue South, there's now the Beacon Food Forest, a combination of P-patch, orchards, and other edible landscape features that intends to bring much more local food to surrounding neighborhoods. A path leads through the park to the community center, on the north edge of the park's golf driving range. Bisect the range and the golf course and ride south briefly to another of the city's excellent verdant drives: Cheasty Boulevard South. Wend along this treed hillside down to the intersection of south Seattle's two big streets: Rainier Avenue South and Martin Luther King Jr. Way South. A bike-ped overpass lets you safely rise above the traffic.

Next you skirt stately Franklin High School and head down to Lake Washington through the Mount Baker neighborhood, along a tree-lined boulevard fronted by substantial old family homes, some of them quite elegant. At McClellan sits a coffee shop and pizzeria. You arrive at the lake at the Mount Baker Rowing Club and its adjacent swimming beach. On some summer weekend days, the city closes Lake Washington Boulevard to car traffic from here south to Seward Park, making it an excellent family bike outing. On this ride, turn left and, shortly, left again to ride through Colman Park. This takes you up above the Interstate 90 floating bridge. You will literally be on top of that freeway (although you'll never see it) as you cycle down into the I-90 Trail tunnel that cuts under the homes of Mount Baker.

Out of the tunnel, head west and skirt the edge of the freeway until reaching the northernmost point of Beacon Hill. Look down to your right and see the freeway cutting through a ravine between Beacon and Capitol hills. Spanning it is the Jose Rizal Bridge, and under the south edge of the bridge is one of the city's newer bike trails, an extension of the Mountains to Sound Greenway (Tour 18) that connects cyclists with Sodo via South Holgate Street. This short extension offers great views of the industrial neighborhood with the professional sports stadia and Elliott Bay in the distance.

Ride over Interstate 5 on Holgate and then down into traffic. Take care crossing to the Sodo Trail, a short connector laid next to the Link light-rail corridor. From South Lander Street, jog over to First Avenue South and ride a section of the Sodo area that is becoming a bit gentrified, with warehouses being turned into tony shops, local distilleries, and gathering places. From there it's a quick (but careful, as you're still in the land of big trucks) jaunt across Harbor Island and over the lower West Seattle Bridge to connect again to the Alki Trail and back to Jack Block Park.

Route Connections: From the starting point, connect with the West Seattle (Tour 11) and Duwamish Trail (Tour 12) rides. From the I-90 Trail, connect with the Chief Sealth Trail (Tour 13), Lake Washington Loop (Tour 16), and the Mountains to Sound Greenway (Tour 18).

MILEAGE LOG

0.0 Depart parking at Jack Block Park (restrooms).

0.2 Left onto trail. Cross onto street as you get close to bridge to head up SW Avalon Wy.

1.1 Straight under bridge onto SW Avalon Wy.

1.5 Left onto 30th Ave. SW.

1.7 Left onto SW Genesee St.; pass Delridge Playfield (restrooms).

1.9 Right onto 26th Ave. SW.

2.6 Pass Greg Davis Park.

2.9 Left onto SW Juneau St.

3.1 Right at T onto Croft Pl. SW.

3.3 Right onto 21st Ave. SW, which curves left and becomes SW Myrtle St.

4.1 Right onto 16th Ave. SW.

4.5 Left onto SW Holden St.

4.9 Left onto Highland Park Wy. SW.

5.4 Left at W. Marginal Wy. SW, then immediately right onto the trail on northwest corner of intersection.

5.7 After last street crossing approaching 1st Ave. S. Bridge, left at fork in trail, signed for 1st Ave. S. Bridge.

6.1 Right onto S. Michigan St. at bottom of bridge, at intersection with 1st Ave. S. In ½ block after going under bridge ramps, right onto Occidental Ave. S., and follow "To Georgetown" bike signs.

6.2 Left onto S. River St.

6.4 Right onto E. Marginal Wy. S. Caution: busy street.

6.7 Left onto Corson Ave. S. Caution: fast traffic; use pedestrian stoplight if necessary.

7.1 Pass Oxbow Park, with Hat and Boots historic buildings.

7.2 Right onto S. Eddy St.

7.3 Left onto S. Flora St.

7.4 Right onto S. Bailey St.

7.5 Left at 13th Ave. S, at intersection with Stanley. In 1 block, left onto Airport Wy. S.

7.8 Pass Georgetown Trailer Park Mall.

7.9 Right onto S. Lucile St. Climb over rail tracks and go under I-5.

8.1 Left on 12th Ave. S.

8.7 Right onto S. Snoqualmie St. In 1 block, left on 13th Ave. S.

8.9 Right onto S. Nevada St. In 1 block, left on 14th Ave. S.

9.1 Right onto S. Dakota St. In 1 block, cross 15th Ave. S. to Jefferson Park. Caution: busy street; use pedestrian light if necessary.

9.2 Left onto 16th Ave. S., then first right onto paved path next to Beacon Food Forest.

9.3 Continue uphill, curve right at top of playfields, then curve left to cycle around driving range.

9.6 Right at Jefferson Park Community Center building (restrooms), through parking to street.

9.7 Right onto Beacon Ave. S.

10.2 Left onto Cheasty Blvd. S. at S. Alaska St. at south end of golf course.

11.2 Cross S. Della St. and continue on Cheasty, which becomes S. Winthrop St.

11.4 Exit Winthrop at intersection of Rainier Ave. S. and Martin Luther King Jr. Wy. S. Right onto bike-ped overpass ramp that spans these two busy streets.

11.6 Right off overpass onto S. Washington St.

11.8 Left at Y at Franklin High School to cross 30th Ave. S. onto S. Mount Baker Blvd.

12.0 Continue on S. Mount Baker Blvd. at intersection with 36th Ave. S.

12.1 At intersection with S. McClellan St., continue on S. Mount Baker Blvd., which becomes Lake Park Dr. S.

12.5 Left onto Lake Washington Blvd. S.

12.6 Left into Colman Park to stay on Lake Washington Blvd. S.

13.3 Right on S. Irving St., then right in ½ block and stay right to enter I-90 Trail tunnel.

13.8 Cross Martin Luther King Jr. Wy. S.

14.0 Cross 23rd Ave. S., then left on far sidewalk and follow trail signs.

14.9 Take right fork to stay on lower trail at Y approaching link to Beacon Hill and International District.

15.6 Right onto S. Holgate St. at end of I-90 Trail/Mountains to Sound Greenway.

16.0 Cross 6th Ave. S., and left in ½ block onto Sodo Trail before railroad tracks. Caution: heavy traffic; use pedestrian light to cross if necessary.

16.5 Right onto S. Lander St.

16.8 Left onto 1st Ave. S. Caution: heavy traffic; use crosswalk at stoplight if necessary.

17.2 Right onto S. Horton St.

17.5 Left onto E. Marginal Wy. S. In 1 block, veer right onto sidewalk before bridge ramps and follow trail signs.

18.0 Follow trail signs for West Seattle Bridge Trail to cross Harbor Island truck lanes and S. Spokane St. to loop up onto lower bridge.

18.6 Take right fork off bridge, signed Alki Beach. In 1 block, cross 5-way intersection to continue on trail.

19.3 Right onto Harbor Ave. SW and Alki Trail.

20.1 Right into Jack Block Park.

20.3 Arrive at parking to end tour.

Opposite: *Jubilee Farm outside Carnation showcases local, small-scale agriculture and its supportive community.*

15 Mercer Island Loop

DIFFICULTY: easy
TIME: allow 1.5 hours
DISTANCE: 13.9 miles
ELEVATION GAIN: 712 feet

Getting There: From I-5, take I-90 east to Mercer Island and take exit 7A, 77th Ave. SE; turn left onto 77th Ave. SE. Turn right at stop sign onto N. Mercer Wy., go through light at 80th Ave. SE, then turn left onto 81st Ave. SE. Turn right on SE 24th St. and at T at 84th Ave. SE, turn left and drive to road end at entrance to Luther Burbank Park.

From I-405, take I-90 west to Mercer Island and take exit 7, Island Crest Wy. At top of ramp, turn right onto SE 26th St. At stop sign turn left onto 84th Ave. SE and drive straight past another stop sign at SE 24th St. into Luther Burbank Park.

   GPS Coordinates: N47 35 29 W122 13 36
   Transit: King County Metro 203, 213

Looking for a short, scenic ride on a sunny summer day? Consider East Seattle. That was the early name for the main community on Mercer Island, and though it's not officially part of the city now, it certainly feels like another Seattle neighborhood—albeit one accessible only by boat or floating bridge.

Mercer Island seems to be a workout route for cyclists who live in the area, judging by the number of people engaged in a businesslike trek on the quiet, wooded ring road during weekday evenings. But it also can be an enjoyable weekend ride combined with a visit to a lakeside beach.

Parking is easily accessible from the island exits off Interstate 90; simply head into Luther Burbank Park (or find the small lots along the landscaped Aubrey Davis Park, which was created when traffic designers put a landscaped "lid" on Interstate 90). Since this loop basically stays on one road for the entire route, it can be traveled in either direction, but I like taking it clockwise, because that side of the road offers better shoulders for more of the route.

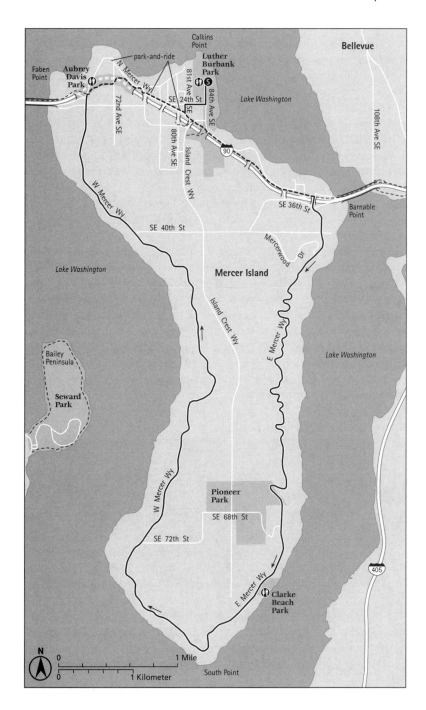

Calkins
Point

Bellevue

park-and-ride

Luther
Burbank
Park

Faben
Point

Aubrey
Davis
Park

81st Ave SE

N Mercer Wy

SE 24th St

84th Ave SE

Lake Washington

72nd Ave SE

SE

80th Ave SE

108th Ave SE

Island Crest Wy

90

SE 36th St

Barnable
Point

W Mercer Wy

SE 40th St

Mercerwood Dr

Lake Washington

Mercer Island

Bailey
Peninsula

Island Crest Wy

E Mercer Wy

Lake Washington

Seward
Park

W Mercer Wy

Pioneer
Park

SE 68th St

SE 72nd St

405

E Mercer Wy

Clarke
Beach
Park

N

0   1 Mile
0   1 Kilometer

South Point

Exiting the park via city streets, you pick up the I-90 Trail briefly. When entering or exiting this trail, be sure to check for commuting cyclists, who are commonly seen here, often moving fast. Head east on the trail, which uses sidewalks and crosses a couple of streets before reaching East Mercer Way, your gateway to the loop.

Shortly after beginning the loop ride around Mercer, you're treated to a series of linked curves hugging the hillsides. Thank the road designers for grading that is well calculated to provide a fun series of turns—unless you get behind a cautious Sunday driver. There is scant room to pass a car and no shoulder on parts of this section. However, local drivers are very used to bicyclists and know where the safe passing areas are. Be extracourteous to drivers here, as they put up with a lot of cyclists on their one road.

Development has come quite a long way since Seattle pioneer Thomas Mercer explored the island in the 1850s. Cyclists will see houses cleverly tucked into wooded hillsides and not-so-subtly looming over the waterfront. What you won't see while riding this loop is any commercial development. Services such as groceries and gas stations are confined to the island's north-central corridor. But if you brought a picnic or want a comfort stop, pull over at Clarke Beach Park at 6 miles. The well-kept beach and dock area have picnic tables, a grassy lawn, restrooms, and views of Mount Rainier rising behind Renton on Lake Washington's far southern shore.

Aubrey Davis Park on Mercer Island

At the southern tip of the island, East Mercer Way turns into West Mercer Way. As you ride along the island's western edge, you get peekaboo views through the trees of Seward Park across the lake and gables of the big houses fronting this side of the lake. After climbing through the last section of West Mercer Way, Seattle and the Interstate 90 floating bridge come into view.

At the island's northwest corner, cross the West Mercer Way off-ramp and pick up the I-90 Trail via the sidewalk to ride over the lid park past ballfields. Return to Luther Burbank Park and stretch your legs with a walk to the water or around the historic school building. The park is the site of a 100-acre self-sufficient farm that was operated in the early 1900s as part of a school for boys. A waterfront plaza, beach, and sculptures are worth a look.

For a postride beverage or some pub food, check out the Roanoke Inn, a historic spot on 72nd Avenue SE, a block north of Aubrey Davis Park on the Interstate 90 lid. The inn was a speakeasy in the days when travel to the island was by a ferry that docked at the island's nearby northern tip, and the place retains the flavor of a welcoming neighborhood tavern.

Route Connections: You can ride west on the I-90 Trail, then south along Lake Washington to connect to the South Seattle rides (Tours 13 and 14); travel east (a brief jaunt takes you to Bellevue for a visit to Mercer Slough) or west on the I-90 Trail to link to the Lake Washington Loop (Tour 16); or continue east or west on the Mountains to Sound Greenway (Tour 18).

MILEAGE LOG

0.0 Depart Luther Burbank Park north parking lot (restrooms) to begin tour.

0.2 Exit park access road/84th Ave. SE by turning right onto SE 24th St. at park entrance.

0.4 Left onto 81st Ave. SE. Road curves south behind park-and-ride.

0.5 Left onto I-90 Trail on near sidewalk at intersection with N. Mercer Wy. (east edge of park-and-ride).

1.7 Right onto E. Mercer Wy.

2.0 Straight through two intersections, then left after on-ramp to stay on E. Mercer Wy.

6.0 Right into Clarke Beach Park; descend to lakeshore.

6.1 Arrive at swimming area (water, restrooms).

6.2 Climb back to E. Mercer Wy., turning left to continue loop.

8.6 Continue forward through Brook Bay neighborhood.

11.1 Views of Seward Park beyond trees and homes to the right.

12.4 Straight at stop sign.
12.5 Merge right onto I-90 Trail at Aubrey Davis Park.
12.7 Arrive at Perogia Fields (restrooms).
13.4 Left off trail onto 81st Ave. SE at east edge of park-and-ride.
13.5 Right onto SE 24th St.
13.7 Left at 84th Ave. SE to access road into Luther Burbank Park.
13.9 Arrive at north parking lot to end tour.

16 Lake Washington Loop

DIFFICULTY: strenuous
TIME: allow 6 hours
DISTANCE: 48.9 miles
ELEVATION GAIN: 1919 feet

Getting There: From I-5 in Seattle, take exit 171, Lake City Wy./SR 522. Continue northeast on Lake City Wy. NE to Lake Forest Park, where road becomes Bothell Wy. NE. After entering Kenmore, turn right onto 61st Ave. NE, then immediately right onto NE 175th St. Tracy Owen Station at Log Boom Park is ahead 1 block; park here.
  GPS Coordinates: N47 45 28 W122 15 47
  Transit: King County Metro 306, 309, 312, 331, 342, 372, 522

Water is one of the Seattle area's most plentiful natural features, making local lakes and rivers some of our most enjoyable cycling destinations. Circumnavigating the queen of our blue heaven, Lake Washington, offers cyclists a route filled with great views, enticing stops, and insight into local history and development of our metropolitan area. A shorter half-loop option is possible, as are links to other Seattle tours.

Ride first through the desirable Eastside community of Juanita, leaving the lakeside almost immediately, skirting Saint Edward State Park and Big Finn Hill and O. O. Denny parks in a long, slow climb. Dropping down into Kirkland, regain lakeside views at Juanita Bay, where a large swimming beach at Juanita Beach Park beckons.

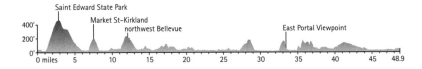

At the East Portal Viewpoint in Seattle, cyclists survey the traffic on the Interstate 90 floating bridge.

Just beyond the beach, a brief detour from the bike lane could take you through Juanita Bay Park, Kirkland's largest and most historic park, the terminus of two creeks and a calm haven for many types of birds. Enjoy the bustling downtown Kirkland scene, then head south along the lake, spotting numerous statues and sculptures in waterside parks faced by luxury apartment blocks.

Cross under State Route 520 and into Bellevue, climbing through north Bellevue's office parks and skirting the edge of its rising-ever-higher downtown. Cut over to side streets and trail sections along loud Interstate 405 and then intersect with the east-west I-90 Trail (see Tour 18).

At this point, a shorter loop is an option, if you go west across Mercer Island on the Interstate 90 bridge, then pick up this tour again at the East Portal Viewpoint. It's 4.8 miles from this junction to set your wheels on Seattle soil, and the shortcut removes a 19.5-mile south-end ride, making the shortened loop 34.2 miles total. A longer diversion is available, too, by turning left here and heading toward Issaquah, 7 miles east. That route runs on streets through the Factoria neighborhoods before becoming a freeway-side trail as you near Lake Sammamish.

To do the full loop, however, continue south on Lake Washington Boulevard. Again, trail segments merge with side roads as you parallel Interstate 405 to Renton.

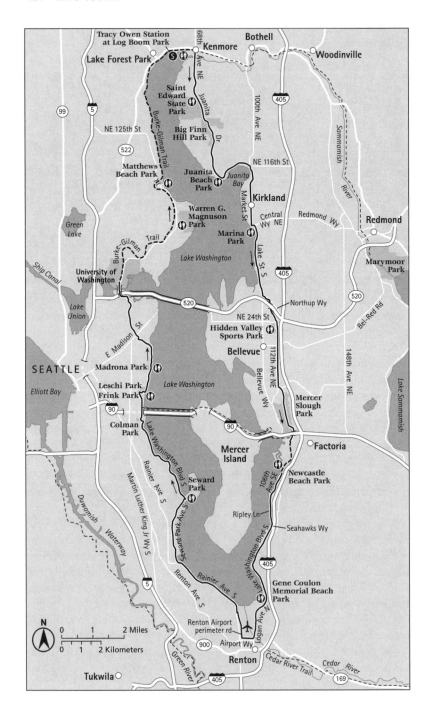

Next stop is Gene Coulon Memorial Park in Renton at the lake's southernmost point. Sited next to the Boeing Company's Renton plant, the park is a common cycling comfort stop. Plans call for a connection to the Cedar River Trail (Tour 25) just beyond Boeing's broad tarmacs, but until that happens, cyclists need to skirt the plant and the Renton Municipal Airport. A turn north onto Rainier Avenue South marks the tour's halfway point.

The western route hugs the lake for most of the ride, through the neighborhoods of southeast Seattle. Return to Lake Washington Boulevard at Seward Park, then leave the lakeside briefly for a view of the Interstate 90 bridge at the East Portal Viewpoint (here's where the shortened tour picks up the main route). Continue north along the lake through central Seattle (Tour 9), then cross the Montlake Bridge at Husky Stadium. Recent and ongoing construction work here related to a Link light-rail tunnel station and the replacement interchange for the State Route 520 bridge is likely to keep this connection in flux for years to come. But make your way to the Burke-Gilman Trail (Tour 1), which skirts the east edge of the University of Washington campus and heads north, providing a flat, pleasant end to the loop.

Route Connections: Head west through Seattle on the Burke-Gilman Trail (Tour 1); visit south Seattle (Tours 13 or 14); head east on the Cedar River Trail (Tour 25); head north to Snohomish (Tour 19); or make a wider loop via the Sammamish River Trail (Tour 17), combined with a ride from Redmond to Issaquah (Tour 20) and the Mountains to Sound Greenway (Tour 18). If you do the shorter loop, you could also circle Mercer Island (Tour 15).

MILEAGE LOG

0.0 Right from parking at Tracy Owen Station (restrooms) onto Burke-Gilman Trail and head north.

0.5 Right onto 65th Ave. NE, then immediate left onto NE 175th St.

0.7 Right onto 68th Ave. NE. Caution: busy intersection; use sidewalk over bridge.

1.1 Proceed straight (south) as 68th becomes Juanita Dr.

2.4 Pass entrance to Saint Edward State Park on the right (restrooms).

3.1 Pass entrance to Big Finn Hill Park on left.

4.1 Continue on Juanita Dr. at intersection with Holmes Pt. Dr.

6.0 Arrive at Juanita Beach Park (restrooms).

6.4 Right onto 98th Ave. NE. Pass Juanita Bay Park.

8.3 Left onto Central Wy. NE in downtown Kirkland. Caution: reduce speed. Pass Marina Park (restrooms) on the turn.

8.4 Right onto Lake St. S. (SR 908), which becomes Lake Washington Blvd.

9.1 Pass Marsh Park (restrooms).

10.6 Merge into left lane to turn onto Northup Wy. Caution: traffic.

11.0 Right onto 108th Ave. NE, then straight to cross under SR 520, then merge immediately into left lane and proceed up 112th Ave. NE. Caution: freeway on- and off-ramps.

12.2 Pass Hidden Valley Sports Park (restrooms).

13.2 Left onto NE 2nd St. at south edge of downtown Bellevue. In 1 block, road curves right.

14.4 Pass Mercer Slough Park. Continue in bike lane on road rather than taking hilly, narrow trail.

15.5 Pass intersection with I-90 Trail. Continue south on Lake Washington Blvd., crossing under I-90.

16.2 Merge right onto trail on southeast corner of intersection with Newport Wy.

16.8 Exit trail left onto Lake Washington Blvd. SE.

18.1 Forward through bollards to rejoin trail as road curves right.

18.8 Left onto 106th Ave. SE as trail ends, which becomes Ripley Ln., then Seahawks Wy.

19.2 Right onto Lake Washington Blvd. S.

21.1 Right into Gene Coulon Memorial Beach Park, then immediate left at stop sign.

21.2 Right into parking area by pavilion (restrooms, concessions). Right out of park to continue.

21.6 Right after crossing railroad tracks onto Lake Washington Blvd. S.

21.7 Right onto Logan Ave. N.

22.5 Merge right onto bike trail that parallels road.

22.9 Cross Cedar River on sidewalk, then immediate right and quick left onto Renton Airport perimeter road. Follow bike route signs on this road around airport.

24.2 Left to exit airport road, then in 50 yards right onto Rainier Ave. S. Caution: fast traffic.

26.9 Right onto Seward Park Ave. S.

28.7 Right to stay on Seward Park Ave. S.

29.1 Right onto S. Juneau St.

29.2 Straight at stop sign into Seward Park (restrooms).

29.3 Right onto Lake Washington Blvd. S.

32.5 Left to stay on Lake Washington Blvd. S. as lower road becomes Lakeside Ave. S. Continue uphill through Colman Park.

32.9 Cross S. Massachusetts St. to continue on Lake Washington Blvd. S.

33.1 Arrive at East Portal Viewpoint. Pass S. Irving St. on right (connection to I-90 Trail). Continue on Lake Washington Blvd. S. through Frink Park.

33.9 At intersection with S. Jackson St. and 34th Ave. S., take middle road to stay on Lake Washington Blvd. S.

34.2 Left at Leschi Park to stay on Lake Washington Blvd. S.

34.9 Straight at intersection with Madrona Dr. to stay on Lake Washington Blvd. S.

35.5 Curve left at Denny Blaine Park to stay on Lake Washington Blvd. S.

35.6 Cross 39th Ave E. to stay on Lake Washington Blvd. S.

35.8 Curve left at Y to stay on Lake Washington Blvd. S. at top of climb. In ½ block, straight onto E. Harrison St. as Lake Washington Blvd. curves right. Follow Lake Washington Loop signs.

36.3 Right onto Martin Luther King Jr. Wy. In 1 block, cross E. Madison St. at light, jogging briefly right, then left to cross Madison onto 28th Ave. E., which climbs, curves, and becomes 26th Ave. E.

37.0 Curve left at E. Galer St., then right in ½ block to return to 26th.

37.2 Cross E. Boyer St. Caution: traffic.

37.6 Left on E. Lynn St., then right in 1 block onto 25th Ave. E.

37.8 Straight through intersection with E. Roanoke St., then left into alley, and continue west through next alley.

37.9 Right onto 24th Ave. E. (follow bike route signs). In ½ block, cross over SR 520.

38.1 Forward through bollards as street turns right, then right onto Park Dr., which becomes E. Shelby St. and continues west to Montlake Blvd. NE.

38.3 Right onto sidewalk at Montlake Blvd. NE to cross Montlake Bridge.

38.5 Left at stoplight at Husky Stadium to cross Montlake Blvd. NE at intersection with NE Pacific St. Turn right onto sidewalk in front of UW entrance, circle right, and proceed forward to Burke-Gilman Trail. Caution: route might change due to ongoing construction.

38.6 Right onto trail.

39.8 Cross 25th Ave. NE to stay on trail at University Village shopping center.

42.1 Cross 65th Ave. NE. Side trip down cycletrack to right here takes you to Warren G. Magnuson Park (restrooms) in 0.25 mile.

43.9 Pass Matthews Beach Park (restrooms).

47.9 Pass Lake Forest Park shopping area.

48.9 Arrive at Tracy Owen Station at Log Boom Park to end tour.

17 Sammamish River Trail

DIFFICULTY: easy
TIME: allow 2.5 hours
DISTANCE: 28.4 miles
ELEVATION GAIN: 322 feet

Getting There: From I-5 in Seattle, take exit 171, Lake City Wy./SR 522. Continue northeast on Lake City Wy. to Lake Forest Park, where road becomes Bothell Wy NE. After entering Kenmore, turn right onto 61st Ave. NE, then immediately right onto NE 175th St. Tracy Owen Station at Log Boom Park is ahead 1 block.

GPS Coordinates: N47 45 28 W122 15 47
Transit: King County Metro 306, 309, 312, 331, 342, 372, 522

Suburban recreating doesn't get much smoother than a ride on the Sammamish River Trail, the flat, buffered green ribbon that hugs that river's east bank from Bothell to Redmond. It's well used but mostly free of traffic noise or interruptions, and it offers comfort stops at evenly spaced intervals.

Begin at either end, at Marymoor Park in Redmond or at parks bordering the trail in Bothell or Woodinville. I suggest starting from Tracy Owen Station in Kenmore, which borders Lake Washington's north shore, because from there you get the flavor of how the Sammamish links with the granddaddy of local bike routes, the Burke-Gilman Trail (Tour 1).

Heading northeast through Kenmore, you immediately begin to parallel the Sammamish River, which connects Lake Sammamish with Lake Washington. You're also paralleling Bothell Way NE here, but the dense greenery along the trail, which is significantly below street level, makes you soon forget you're surrounded by traffic and commerce. Cycle past the Wayne Golf Course, the Park at Bothell Landing—which has services accessible via a quaint, arched wooden bridge—and Brackett's Landing Park before crossing under the massive girders of the Interstate 405 and State Route 522 interchange.

As the trail stretches out into the warehouse area of Woodinville, ride by Jerry Wilmot Gateway Park, an excellent amenity stop. Restrooms, water fountains, and attractive stone planters effusive with trees and

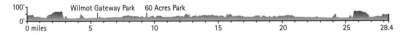

100'	Wilmot Gateway Park	60 Acres Park				
0'						
0 miles	5	10	15	20	25	28.4

flowers and linked with an arcing overhead trellis create a shady, comfortable place to dismount and watch the wheels go by. Just beyond the parking lot is the busy intersection of State Route 202 and NE 175th Street, which would take you into downtown Woodinville if a side trip interests you, or connect you with the Woodinville to Snohomish ride (Tour 19), which starts here.

Continue south on the Sammamish River Trail to view some youthful competition at the Northshore Athletic Fields (at 7.4 miles) and 60 Acres Park (at 9.8 miles), both trailside as you head south toward Redmond. Opposite 60 Acres, at NE 116th Street, is the northern border of Willow's Run Golf Course, just west of the trail across the river. A side trail called the Puget Power Trail, accessible at 11.1 miles via an attractive red bridge, runs under the lines out to Willows Road in the midvalley.

At 12.7 miles you reach tiny Luke McRedmond Landing, and in another 0.2 mile the trail splits, with the upper route leading to the surface streets of Redmond and the Town Center a few blocks away and the riverside branch continuing south to Marymoor Park.

Marymoor is an Eastside gem, offering open space, a constant stream of events, and numerous attractions for its many regional users. State Route 520 dead-ends at its northeast corner, giving it major access for festivals and concerts. Vast grassy fields and generous frontage along Lake Sammamish provide hours of exploration. For cyclists, the Velodrome is the logical terminus, where, if you haven't had enough

Wilmot Gateway Park is a popular meeting point. It connects the Burke-Gilman and Sammamish River trails.

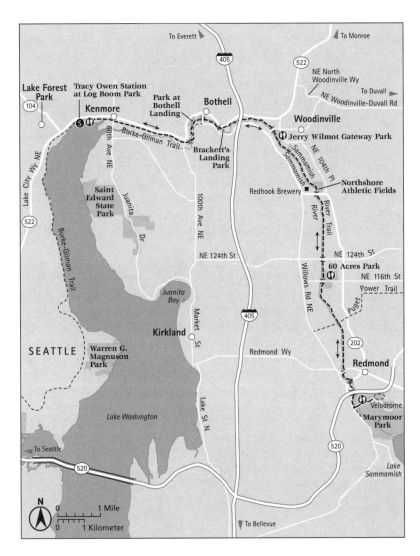

riding, you can circle round and round, trying your skill at banking, passing, and group dynamics. Classes and events are often held at the Velodrome, but it is also a significant training site for racers and has a bank of bleachers from which to watch the action.

After some Marymoor-style repose, hop back on the velo and head north again to finish off the refreshing ride by retracing your route. As an additional treat, when you reach the Northshore Athletic Fields on the return trip, head west briefly on NE 145th Street for a stop at

Redhook Brewery's Forecaster's Public House, almost immediately on your right. Here you'll find one of the most extensive areas of bike racks outside of a public school, and with good reason: there's often scant room to fit your two-wheeler in with the crowd. If wine is more your style, pedal a bit farther on the same road to find the facing Chateau Ste. Michelle and Columbia wineries.

The Velodrome isn't Redmond's only cycling claim to fame. It also hosts the nation's oldest bicycle race, the Derby Criterium, a multilap race on a downtown course. Begun in 1939 as the Redmond Bike Derby, it was a fundraiser to help the town pull out of the Great Depression (according to Historylink.org). Today the race is the centerpiece of Redmond's biggest weekend festival.

Route Connections: If you're interested in a longer ride, continue south from Tracy Owen Station on the Burke-Gilman Trail (Tour 1) or, if you're truly energetic, continue around Lake Washington (Tour 16) or south from Marymoor Park around Lake Sammamish to Issaquah (Tour 20). You could also head north to Snohomish from Woodinville (Tour 19).

MILEAGE LOG

0.0 Right from parking at Tracy Owen Station (restrooms) onto Burke-Gilman Trail and head north.

2.5 Pass Wayne Golf Course clubhouse, then follow signs to right to cross river.

3.4 Pass the Park at Bothell Landing.

4.2 Pass Brackett's Landing Park. Trail continues on marked street for 0.2 mile.

5.7 Arrive at Jerry Wilmot Gateway Park (restrooms) in Woodinville.

7.4 Pass Northshore Athletic Fields. (Exit trail and turn right onto NE 145th St. here to go to wineries and brewery.)

9.8 Pass playfields at 60 Acres Park (restrooms).

11.1 Pass bridge on the right that connects to Puget Power Trail leading out to Willows Rd.

12.7 Trail splits; follow main route over Sammamish River south to Marymoor Park. (Side branch leads to Redmond Town Center via Redmond Wy.).

13.4 Cross back over river and pass Marymoor's ball fields.

14.2 Arrive at Velodrome (restrooms). Reverse route to return.

28.4 Return to parking at Tracy Owen Station to end tour.

18 Mountains to Sound Greenway

DIFFICULTY: challenging
TIME: allow 5.5 hours
DISTANCE: 37.3 miles
ELEVATION GAIN: 2246 feet

Getting There: Take I-5 to exit 163, Columbian Wy.; merge to Columbian Wy., then left at first light onto S. Spokane St. In 0.3 mile, right onto Beacon Ave. S. Jefferson Park Community Center is on right in 0.1 mile.

GPS Coordinates: N47 34 11 W122 18 28
Transit: King County Metro 36, 50, 60

Want to go from urban to suburban to small town, or from a saltwater bay to mountain foothills? Just think like the people at Mountains to Sound Greenway, whose motto is "the Greenway connects it all."

This ride, which begins in sight of Elliott Bay in the center of Seattle, ushers you through those environments and more. The route utilizes a recently expanded trail that ties together communities along the Interstate 90 corridor. It takes you through or along numerous parks, across a floating bridge, and through a marsh.

Begin at the north end of Beacon Hill, departing from the Jefferson Park Community Center next to the city-owned golf course. Then, with Seattle's sports stadiums and shipping cranes as a backdrop, cycle east on a green ribbon that runs next to Interstate 90 and through the Mount Baker tunnel to the protected bikeway along the floating bridge. Across the big Homer M. Hadley Memorial Bridge, then Mercer Island, then the East Channel Bridge, and you're soon in the Mercer Slough, a gloriously messy swamp under the tangle of ramps and pillars necessary for a freeway interchange. Birdsong may be drowned out by the buzzing traffic, but focus on the waterways and lush greenery as you pedal the raised bikeway through it all.

Exit the slough into Factoria and Eastgate, neighborhoods of south Bellevue, where you must ride bike lanes for a time. Cross under Interstate 90 and pick up the trail again, which runs next to the

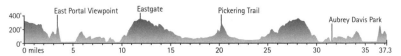

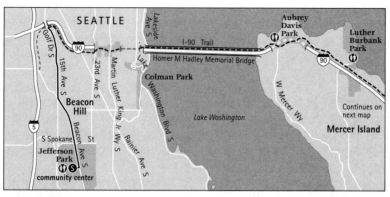

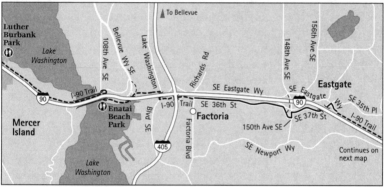

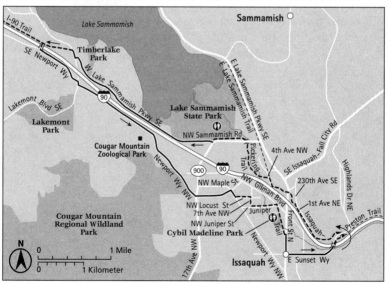

freeway and then crosses it again on a bike-ped overpass between Lake Sammamish and Cougar Mountain. Newport Way NW sweeps you past the Cougar Mountain Zoological Park into Issaquah, where a series of short trails takes you to its historic downtown.

At the halfway point, this is a good place for a break. Sample the coffee shops and cafés or, if the season is right, witness the running of the salmon through the creek at the Issaquah Salmon Hatchery, a couple of blocks from Front Street at Sunset Way. A short interpretive walk with bridges over Issaquah Creek and viewing of the hatchery ponds is a good way to straighten your legs for a bit.

New trails on the north side of Issaquah and up toward Sammamish Plateau get you out of town again, and you turn west to head back upstream, as it were. As you return on the Greenway, a couple interesting sights await. On the wooded edge of Issaquah, stop at the Pickering Barn, which hosts a bustling farmers market on summer Saturdays. Bike along the playfields and large Lake Sammamish State Park, where trails, beaches, and watersports beckon.

Farther west on the Greenway trail, a series of mossy switchbacks through a wooded ravine takes you back to the freeway-side trail that leads back to Bellevue and Seattle. Although there's much more to the Mountains to Sound Greenway than is sampled on this tour—after all, the entire Greenway stretches across the Cascade Mountains to Ellensburg—you will agree upon completion of the ride that this Greenway really does "connect it all."

Route Connections: From Issaquah, a side trip north to Marymoor Park in Redmond would add about 10 miles, following the directions to loop Lake Sammamish (Tour 20); or instead of returning on the

A family cycles along the safe—if a bit loud—I-90 Trail next to the freeway at Beacon Hill. Bikes are separated from cars by a three-foot cement wall.

Greenway, you could simply keep going and continue north from Redmond to return to Seattle on the Sammamish River Trail (Tour 17) and the Burke-Gilman Trail (Tour 1), which links with the Central Seattle ride (Tour 9) to return to your starting point. Other opportunities for side trips as you cross the lake trail at Enatai Beach Park include looping Mercer Island (Tour 15) or looping the south or north portions of Lake Washington (Tour 16). Or once you've returned to Beacon Hill, keep going south to sample the Chief Sealth Trail (Tour 13), which heads deep into southeast Seattle.

MILEAGE LOG

0.0 Left out of Jefferson Park Community Center (restrooms) parking onto Beacon Ave. S.

1.0 Right onto 15th Ave. S., which becomes Golf Dr. S.

2.0 Right onto the I-90 Trail on NE corner of intersection with 12th Ave. S. and S. Charles St.

2.9 Exit trail left onto sidewalk on 23rd Ave. S. In ½ block, cross 23rd at the light.

3.1 Cross Martin Luther King Jr. Wy. S. at the light, continuing forward into tunnel.

3.3 Exit tunnel, then immediate right down to I-90 Trail across the floating bridge.

5.6 Pass Aubrey Davis Park (restrooms).

6.2 Pass Mercer Island park-and-ride.

8.2 Exit I-90 Trail ramp, then follow trail left at Enatai Beach trailhead (to Enatai Beach Park; restrooms) and downhill to loop under bridge.

8.8 Stay right at Y after passing under I-405. Climb trail bridge and continue through the marsh.

9.1 Right as trail comes to a T. Ride under freeway, then in 50 yards left at crosswalk and left onto trail. Follow trail signs to Factoria.

9.8 Exit trail at corner of Richards Rd., which goes north, and Factoria Blvd., which goes south; continue forward in bike lane on SE 36th St., which becomes SE 38th St.

11.2 Left onto 150th Ave. SE. In 1 block, right onto SE 37th St. In ½ block, bear left at Y and stay on 37th to go under freeway in short tunnel.

11.8 Right onto SE Eastgate Wy., following bike route sign. In ½ block, right onto trail.

12.7 Left onto bike-ped bridge over freeway. Steep climb.

12.9 Exit bridge onto short unpaved trail, then left onto SE Newport Wy.

13.7 Cross Lakemont Blvd. SE.

14.9 Pass entrance to Cougar Mountain Zoological Park.

16.0 Cross 17th Ave. SW/SR 900.

16.5 Cross intersection at NW Maple St., then right onto sidewalk trail on far side. In ½ block, left onto Juniper Trail behind shopping center.

16.7 Right onto sidewalk trail at 7th Ave. NW.

16.8 Left onto NW Juniper St.

17.2 Right onto Rainier Blvd. Trail on far sidewalk, or use street.

17.4 Pass Cybil Madeline Park on right (restrooms).

17.6 At NW Dogwood St., soft right onto Front St. N.

18.1 Left onto E. Sunset Wy.

18.8 Cross onto sidewalk trail on NE corner of I-90 on-ramp.

19.2 Left as trail splits; go under Highlands Dr. NE, then left again onto Issaquah–Preston Trail.

20.2 Cross Front St. N. at crosswalk to continue on trail.

20.4 Right as trail comes to a T at 4th Ave. NW.

20.5 Left at crosswalk and light at medical center on SE 64th Pl. to join Pickering Trail.

20.8 Right after bridge to stay on Pickering Trail. In 0.4 mile, cross side trail to Pickering Barn.

20.9 Cross under NW Sammamish Rd. Trail curves left.

21.1 At Lake Sammamish State Park soccer fields, merge onto bike lane on NW Sammamish Rd.

21.8 Pass entrance to Lake Sammamish State Park (restrooms). Road becomes W. Lake Sammamish Pkwy. NE.

23.4 Pass entrance to Timberlake Park.

24.0 Right at roundabout to stay on W. Lake Sammamish Pkwy NE. In ½ block, follow bike signs to left onto I-90 Trail.

24.4 Climb switchbacks.

24.7 Arrive at I-90 overpass and continue straight westbound.

25.4 Left off trail onto SE Eastgate Wy. In 1 block, left onto SE 37th St., through tunnel under I-90.

25.9 Left onto 150th Ave. SE. In 1 block, right onto SE 38th St., which becomes SE 36th St.

27.2 Cross Factoria Blvd. in left-turning lane and merge onto trail on SW corner of intersection. Caution: congested intersection.

27.9 Right onto Lake Washington Blvd. SE. In ½ block, left onto trail after going under freeway.

28.4 Left at T in trail after bridge, then continue on trail under freeway.

28.9 Curve under freeway and stay right on trail. Pass Enatai Beach Park (restrooms).

29.0 Right onto I-90 Trail at Enatai Beach trailhead.

31.7 Pass Aubrey Davis Park (restrooms).

32.0 Cross W. Mercer Wy. to continue on trail.

33.8 Exit I-90 bridge. At Y, stay left to enter tunnel.

34.4 Cross Martin Luther King Jr. Wy. S.

34.6 Cross 23rd Ave. S., then left on sidewalk. Right in ½ block to continue on trail.

35.4 Left at Y in trail, following sign that says International District.

35.5 Left off trail onto Golf Dr. S.

35.6 Left at Y onto 15th Ave. S.

36.5 Left onto Beacon Ave. S.

37.3 Arrive at Jefferson Park Community Center parking to end ride.

19 Woodinville to Snohomish

DIFFICULTY: moderate
TIME: allow 4.5 hours
DISTANCE: 36.6 miles
ELEVATION GAIN: 1870 feet

Getting There: Take I-405 to exit 23, SR 522, and take SR 522 east toward Woodinville and Wenatchee. Exit onto SR 202 E./131st Ave. NE toward Woodinville and Redmond. Proceed south on 131st for 0.3 mile to Wilmot Gateway Park. Park on left by playfields.

GPS Coordinates: N47 45 10 W122 09 56
Transit: King County Metro 236, 237, 311, 372, 522

The suburbs and small towns of Puget Sound counties are bursting at the seams as new residents move to our desirable region, which sometimes means it's tough for municipalities to keep up with the growth. Those challenges also offer great opportunities for enlightened city planners to include bike trails to ease the congested roads and move more people faster. Such is the way with northeast King and southeast Snohomish counties, which are grappling with sprawl and trying to

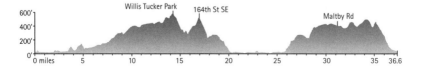

Cyclists enjoy a rest break in downtown Snohomish after time-trials out on Riverview Road.

maintain the quaint old town centers, open space, wildlife corridors, and quality of life for all. This route explores some such terrain.

Start on the west edge of well-established Woodinville, and ride west on the big rail-trail next to the Sammamish River into Bothell to a fork that heads north under Interstate 405 and by the adjoining campuses of Cascadia Community College and the University of Washington's Bothell campus, themselves also chafing at their confinements. Then pick your way north through the technology corridors of Bothell and Canyon Park, where great new techie gadgets and software apps are being created behind the reflective office park windows facing the intermittent North Creek Trail segments. You'll find yourself out on a road, then back on the trail, over and over, which illustrates the challenge of such growth.

Take the bike lane and shoulder of the expanding Bothell–Everett Highway, State Route 527, to Mill Creek. You'll find bike lanes, paved shoulders, and sidewalks where a new development has been put in, but these disappear unceremoniously when the development ends. It's a bittersweet situation: where these amenities are absent, an open field of view toward the mountains might appear. Cut east through the Seattle Hill area, passing Willis Tucker Park, an expanding suburban playground that hosts a farmers market and summer movie nights. Carefully cross busy, fast State Route 9 to Cathcart, where you turn north along the well-biked but undersized (oh, for a consistent shoulder!) Broadway Avenue toward Snohomish.

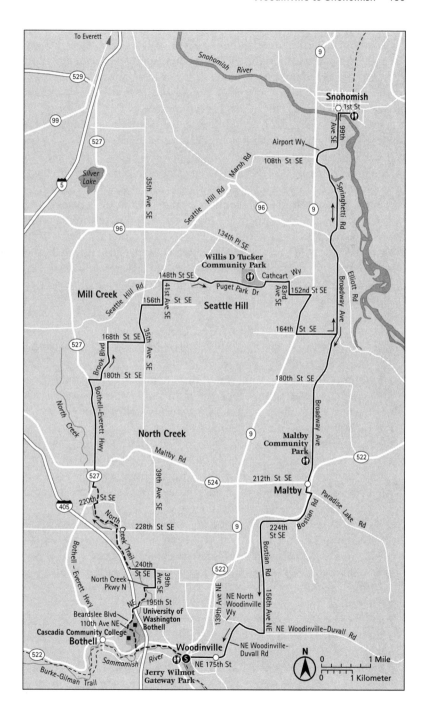

Heading toward the Snohomish River valley, take care to spy Springhetti Road on the right, which springs up quickly on a downhill glide and is easy to miss. Drop down into the lush farmland, then pass by the town's airport and into old Snohomish, where the coffee and ice cream cones abound. This is the turnaround point. Head back up Broadway, but continue south past Cathcart to Maltby, where you cross State Route 522 and take side roads back into Woodinville. Be alert on the last screaming downhill, as you need to merge to the turning lane for a left halfway down the hill to spin back through Woodinville's business district to return to the starting point.

Route Connections: This route is a great connector between long rail-trails. You can ride up from Seattle on the Burke-Gilman Trail (Tour 1) or from Eastside communities on the Sammamish River Trail (Tour 17). When you reach Snohomish, you can continue north on the Centennial Trail (Tour 51). Linked routes could serve as a multiday excursion to north Snohomish County, Skagit County, Bellingham, or even Vancouver, British Columbia.

MILEAGE LOG

0.0 Depart Wilmot Gateway Park (restrooms) heading west on Sammamish River Trail toward Seattle.

1.2 Right off main trail after small bridge, following "regional trail" sign onto side spur that goes under SR 522; spur trail winds north next to UW Bothell/Cascadia Community College campuses.

1.8 Right to stay on trail as it comes to 110th Ave. NE.

1.9 Curve right to stay on trail at Beardslee Blvd.

2.0 As trail ends at freeway on-ramp, forward onto Beardslee Blvd., cross over I-405, then left at on-ramp to return to trail.

2.4 Cross onto "Technology Corridor" trail on left side of street. Cross trail bridge, then left to continue on trail.

2.5 Right onto North Creek Pkwy. N. as trail continues unpaved.

2.7 Left onto 120th Ave. NE., which becomes 39th Ave. SE here.

3.5 Left onto near-side sidewalk trail on 240th St. SE at T.

4.6 Slight right as trail continues on sidewalk along Fitzgerald Rd., which becomes 27th Ave. SE.

4.9 Cross 228th St. SE to continue on the trail.

5.0 Left on trail to continue on paved portion.

5.2 Forward at trail crossing to continue on paved portion.

5.6 Right at Y after small bridge.

5.8 Right onto sidewalk on 220th St. SE.

5.9 Left on near-side (west) sidewalk at 20th Ave. SE to pick up trail.

6.3 Left onto 214th St. SE as trail ends.

6.4 Right into bike lane on Bothell–Everett Highway/SR 527. Caution: high-traffic road; bike lanes disappear at intersection with Maltby Rd./SR 524.

8.5 Right onto 180th St. SE.

8.9 Left onto Brook Blvd. Caution: fast traffic.

9.8 Right onto 168th St. SE.

10.5 Left onto 35th Ave. SE.

11.3 Right onto 156th St. SE.

11.7 Left onto 41st Ave. SE.

12.3 Right onto 148th St. SE.

13.1 Right onto Puget Park Dr.

14.0 Pass Willis D. Tucker Community Park (restrooms).

14.6 Right onto Cathcart Wy.

15.1 Right onto 83rd Ave. SE.

15.3 Left on 152nd St. SE.

15.8 Right onto SR 9. Caution: fast traffic.

16.6 Left onto 164th St. SE. Caution: fast traffic. Use crosswalks if necessary.

17.4 Left onto Broadway Ave.

19.3 Slight right onto Springhetti Rd. Caution: easy to miss on fast downhill.

21.2 At stop sign, continue forward on Airport Wy, which becomes 99th Ave. SE.

22.3 Cross bridge into downtown Snohomish. Bridge sidewalk OK in heavy traffic. Road becomes Ave. D.

22.4 Right onto 1st St.

22.5 Arrive at turnaround point: corner of Ave. B (public restrooms). Depart west on 1st St.

22.6 Left on Ave. D; cross bridge.

23.8 Straight at stop sign to continue on Springhetti Rd.

25.7 Left onto Broadway Ave.

28.7 Cross 180th St. SE.

30.1 Pass Maltby Community Park (restrooms, water on right by playfields).

30.5 Left at Y onto Yew Wy. Caution: railroad tracks.

30.8 Left at curve as Yew meets 212th St. SE. Caution: fast-moving traffic.

30.9 Left at corner onto Paradise Lake Rd. to cross SR 522.

31.0 Right onto Bostian Rd., which becomes 75th Ave. SE, then 156th Ave. NE when entering Woodinville.

34.6 Right onto NE Woodinville–Duvall Rd. Caution: traffic.

35.1 Left at stoplight to stay on NE Woodinville–Duvall Rd., which becomes NE 175th St. Caution: fast traffic on steep downhill.

35.9 Cross 140th Ave. NE at stoplight. Continue forward.

36.5 Left onto 131st Ave. NE. Caution: heavy traffic.

36.6 Arrive at Wilmot Gateway Park to end ride.

20 Redmond to Issaquah and Preston

DIFFICULTY: challenging
TIME: allow 6 hours
DISTANCE: 49.4 miles
ELEVATION GAIN: 2061 feet

Getting There: Take SR 520 east to W. Lake Sammamish Pkwy. NE exit. Travel south 0.6 mile on W. Lake Sammamish Pkwy. NE, then turn left into Marymoor Park. Inexpensive paid parking in 0.3 mile on the left.

GPS Coordinates: N47 39 42 W122 07 32

Transit: King County Metro 232, 542, 545

Redmond's Marymoor Park is a location from which you can go nearly any direction on a bike: north to Woodinville, west into Bellevue, or east to the Snoqualmie Valley over winding Union Hill or Novelty Hill roads. That leaves only one compass point left, and that's the direction for this tour: head south toward Issaquah around Lake Sammamish.

This route south will be much enhanced for road cyclists in coming years as the East Lake Sammamish Trail is paved. Until then, loop the lake by heading south along its west side, then returning up its east side. Both roads have good bike lanes, although the west side is bike-able only southbound, and there is a brief section with no shoulder. If that is a concern, go up and back on the east side of the lake on the wide, well-paved road surface.

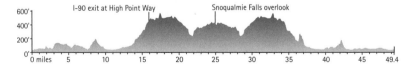

Banking turns on the Velodrome in Marymoor Park

The lake ride is mostly a means to an end, though. Other than intermittent views and two lakefront parks (passed early in the ride), it's not an exciting destination on its own. But heading down the lake links you to more great riding, either west toward Seattle on the I-90 Trail (Tour 18) or east toward Issaquah and beyond. The latter is the goal of this tour.

The fast-growing town of Issaquah is a place to check out. The attractions are plentiful, from the quaint shops of Front Street and homey but professional Village Theater to the in-town salmon hatchery and nearby hiking and mountain biking trails of Tiger, Cougar, and Squak mountains—the Issaquah Alps. A microbrewery and candy factory offer gastronomical temptations.

Stop in Issaquah for a rest and provisions before hopping onto the freeway—that's right, Interstate 90—which takes you to the Preston–Snoqualmie Trail. Cycling on the interstate is allowed east of Front Street, but the tour picks it up at the Sunset Way on-ramp. You ride just 2 loud miles on a very wide shoulder to the High Point Way exit. High Point connects to the trail at Preston, where there are restrooms and provisions at the Preston General Store. If you want to skip the big highway and your tires can handle a packed gravel trail, veer onto the Issaquah–Preston Trail at the Interstate 90 on-ramp, then continue east on the Issaquah Creek Trail, which comes out onto the road at High Point Way.

Beyond Preston, the paved trail becomes quiet and wooded. Moss envelopes the trunks of tall evergreens and bigleaf maples. Sturdy bridges cross an occasional deep ravine or riverbed. It's necessary to

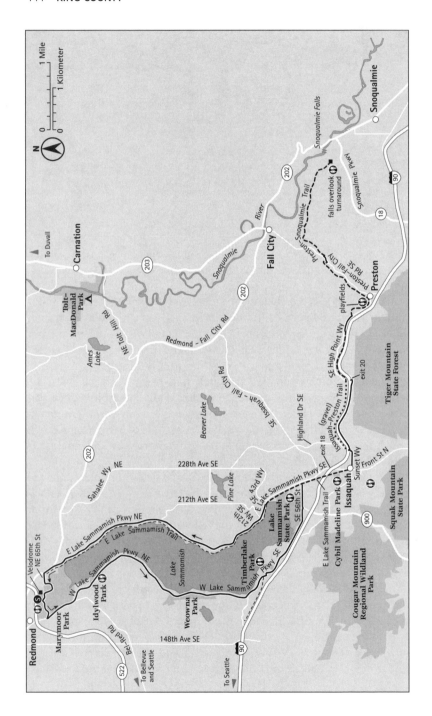

traverse two roads to continue up to the trail end, high in the forest, where there's a stunning overlook of Snoqualmie Falls and the Salish Lodge. This is the true heart of the ride, so plan enough time to enjoy it at a leisurely pace. Return to Issaquah by reversing the route to the Interstate 90 off-ramp, pick up a short trail into Issaquah, then ride back to Redmond on the east side of Lake Sammamish.

Note: This tour can be ridden in two sections. Simply loop Lake Sammamish and drop into downtown Issaquah for a 28-mile trip, or ride the Preston–Snoqualmie Trail from a start in Issaquah for a 24-mile trip. To skip the freeway ride and take an even shorter 20-mile ride through Preston and on the trail, begin at the High Point Way exit off Interstate 90.

Route Connections: Head north to Woodinville on the Sammamish River Trail (Tour 17); connect at Issaquah to the Mountains to Sound Greenway (Tour 18); or ride east to the Snoqualmie Valley roads (Tour 21).

MILEAGE LOG

0.0 Right out of Marymoor Park Velodrome parking to W. Lake Sammamish Pkwy. NE.

0.3 Left onto W. Lake Sammamish Pkwy. NE.

1.2 Left to stay on W. Lake Sammamish Pkwy. NE.

2.1 Pass Idylwood Park (lakefront access, restrooms) on the left.

5.1 Continue straight at intersection with Northup Wy.

5.6 Pass Weowna Park.

7.5 Pass Timberlake Park.

8.4 Travel three-fourths of the way around the roundabout at I-90 entrance, and turn left to continue on W. Lake Sammamish Pkwy. SE, which becomes NW Sammamish Rd., then SE 56th St.

10.1 Pass Lake Sammamish State Park (restrooms).

11.5 Right onto E. Lake Sammamish Trail at intersection with E. Lake Sammamish Pkwy. SE. Caution: heavy traffic; use crosswalk.

12.4 Right onto sidewalk at NE Gilman Blvd. In ½ block, cross Gilman at crosswalk, then left into bike lane.

12.7 Right onto Rainier Blvd. N.

13.0 Pass Cybil Madeline Park (restrooms).

13.1 Jog left onto Front St. N.

13.4 Left onto Sunset Wy.

14.1 Right onto I-90 via on-ramp, or cross intersection and join Issaquah Creek Trail and then Issaquah–Preston Trail (partially packed gravel).

16.3 Right off I-90 at exit 20, SE High Point Wy.

16.4 Left onto 270th Ave. SE and go under freeway. Continue on High Point Wy.

18.6 Left onto trail at Opus I-90 business center at SE 78th St.

19.1 Pass playfields (restrooms).

19.3 Cross SE 87th Pl. and continue on trail beyond trailhead parking.

21.4 Cross Preston–Fall City Rd. SE and turn right to continue on trail behind concrete barrier on east side of road. Caution: fast traffic.

21.5 Left onto SE 68th St. and cross the Raging River.

21.8 Rejoin trail at end of this short street. Trail climbs, then again runs behind roadside barriers.

22.1 Pavement ends at gravel path leading to short series of switchbacks. Walk bike up to rejoin trail.

22.2 Continue on trail at top of switchbacks.

25.2 Arrive at Snoqualmie Falls overlook (restrooms) at end of trail. Retrace route to return.

28.3 Arrive back at switchbacks; walk bike down to continue.

28.4 Rejoin trail at bottom of switchbacks.

28.8 At Preston–Fall City Rd. SE, turn right onto near-side sidewalk.

28.9 Cross busy road and continue on trail.

30.6 Exit trail at parking, cross SE 87th Pl., and rejoin trail eastbound.

31.7 Rejoin High Point Wy. as trail ends.

33.9 Right onto I-90 at on-ramp.

36.0 Exit I-90 at exit 18, Sunset Wy.

36.2 Right onto sidewalk trail at off-ramp stoplight.

36.6 Left as trail splits and go under Highlands Dr. NE, then left again onto Issaquah–Preston Trail.

37.7 Cross Front St. N. at crosswalk and continue on trail.

37.9 Right as trail comes to T at 4th Ave. NW.

39.6 Exit trail at Lake Sammamish State Park boat ramp (restrooms); continue north in bike lane.

40.0 Continue on E. Lake Sammamish Pkwy. SE at roundabout with SE 43rd Wy.

40.5 Cross 212th Wy. SE.

41.5 Cross SE 24th Wy.

44.0 Cross Thompson Hill Rd.

48.0 Left onto NE 65th St. at light and sign for Marymoor Park. Proceed through industrial park to Marymoor entrance.

48.3 Left onto Marymoor Wy., then forward onto trail within park to return to parking.

49.4 Arrive at Velodrome parking to end tour.

21 Redmond to Carnation and Duvall

DIFFICULTY: challenging
TIME: allow 5 hours
DISTANCE: 40.9 miles
ELEVATION GAIN: 1967 feet

Getting There: Take SR 520 east to its end. Make first right, onto NE Union Hill Rd., cross 178th Pl. NE, then turn right into Bear Creek Park-and-Ride.

GPS Coordinates: N47 40 29 W122 06 01
Transit: King County Metro 216, 248, 268, 269, 545

Climbing and descending the hills of Redmond to explore the farm country around Duvall and Carnation makes for a pleasant afternoon and a good bit of exercise. On a balmy summer day, you'll find plenty of two-wheeled company taking variations of this route.

Begin the tour at the end of State Route 520, where you will find the convenient Bear Creek Park-and-Ride, a bit northeast of Marymoor Park. Escape the shopping-area scene very quickly by heading east out of Redmond on NE Union Hill Road, then cutting through preserved marshlands and a nearby park to pick up Novelty Hill Road.

Booming development has significantly increased traffic in this area, but an adequate bike lane makes the long climb relatively safe. The traffic thins as you reach the Redmond Ridge development, and the wooded roadside opens into northern vistas. Take care as you plunge down the steep, three-quarter-mile run to the Snoqualmie Valley. A winding two-lane road with scant shoulders means that cyclists should command a lane and ride with traffic on this stretch. Drivers seem to be used to it.

Pastoral views abound as you skirt the valley's west edge. The Snoqualmie River meanders through plowed fields and pastures, and picturesque farm buildings appear at intervals along the road.

The tour dips briefly into Duvall, and riders are encouraged to explore the town with a detour down Main Street and a stop riverside at McCormick Park just south of the bridge at the west end of

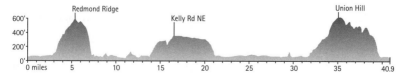

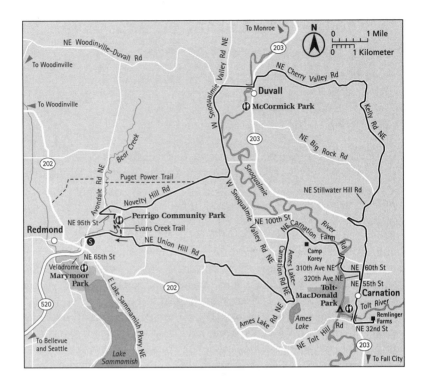

South Stevens Street. Mountain bikers are often seen on the unpaved Snoqualmie Valley Trail, which runs along the river as it skirts the town.

Continue the route on NE Cherry Valley Road north of Duvall. After climbing its first few steep blocks, you are rewarded with views north across the river valley to Mount Baker and east to the closer Cascade peaks. Make a stop at the historic cemetery and farmstead, or pull over at the Cherry Valley Dairy's farm stand a bit farther along.

Enjoy the views while making a steady climb away from the valley, because the scenery turns green and woodsy as the road turns south. The next vista comes when you again rejoin the Snoqualmie Valley after a grand slalom curve downhill to meet State Route 203, the Carnation–Duvall Road. Take care entering and riding along this stretch into Carnation, as State Route 203 is the busiest road in the valley. Still, a wide shoulder offers safety for careful riders.

When visiting Carnation, I look forward to two things: a stop at Remlinger Farms and a visit to Tolt-MacDonald Park. Remlinger's represents perhaps the pinnacle of on-farm marketing. It holds a harvest festival, celebrates Halloween with massive pumpkin patches, and

Old Carnation Road

operates a farm store, café, and bakery that must be seen to be believed. It's just a mile south of Carnation, well worth the detour.

Pick up some snacks or drinks at Remlinger's and take them to Tolt-MacDonald Park. Named for a civic leader who marshaled the efforts of Boy Scouts to build the public amenities, the park holds a sweet spot on the Snoqualmie River where you can doff your shoes and cool pedal-weary feet. The park has overnight camping and plenty of day-use sites and picnic tables, as well as acres of open space. Its entrance at NE 40th Street is well signed off Tolt Avenue, the main road through town.

Depart Carnation by heading north, then cut west across the valley on Carnation Farm Road. This route takes you over a scenic bridge that's next to the county's Chinook Bend Natural Area, which offers great bird-watching. A bit farther along is the historic Carnation Farm, homestead of the well-known dairy. The dairy is now called Camp Korey, and its cluster of neat, red-roofed white buildings host a getaway camp for children with life-altering medical conditions. On the west side of the road, overlooking the valley, the dairy's heritage is recalled by a statue of the "World Champion Milk Cow."

Leaving the valley behind, the last leg of the tour takes cyclists up a thigh-burning climb of NE Union Hill Road, which flattens out in the last few miles and then drops you back to civilization.

Route Connections: Continue south at Carnation to the Snoqualmie Valley Farm Tour (Tour 22), north from Redmond to the Sammamish River Trail (Tour 17), or south from Redmond to Issaquah and Preston (Tour 20).

MILEAGE LOG

0.0   Right out of Bear Creek Park-and-Ride lot onto NE Union Hill Rd.

1.0   Left onto Evans Creek Trail through Perrigo Community Park.

1.7   Pass side trail to restrooms, water.

2.0   Left off trail onto NE 95th St.

2.4   Right onto Avondale Rd. NE.

2.5   Right onto Novelty Hill Rd. after 1 short block.

5.2   Pass Redmond Ridge shopping area (restrooms, gas station).

7.2   Left onto W. Snoqualmie Valley Rd. NE at bottom of hill.

10.1   Right onto NE Woodinville–Duvall Rd.

11.2   Left onto SR 203 in Duvall. (Go right to visit town of Duvall, then retrace your route to here to resume the tour.)

11.4   Right onto NE Cherry Valley Rd. (first right, sharply uphill, after turning onto SR 203), which becomes Kelly Rd NE, then NE Stillwater Hill Rd.

21.1   Left at end of NE Stillwater Hill Rd. onto SR 203, which becomes Tolt Ave. through Carnation.

24.2   Pass entrance to Tolt-MacDonald Park (restrooms) at NE 40th St. in downtown Carnation.

24.7   Cross bridge over Tolt River.

24.8   Left onto NE 32nd St. for visit to Remlinger Farms.

25.3   Arrive at Remlinger Farms (restrooms, café). Retrace route to SR 203.

25.9   Right onto SR 203 and recross bridge, retracing route through Carnation.

27.2   Left onto NE 55th St. Caution: fast traffic. In 1 block, right onto 320th Ave. NE.

27.4   Left onto NE 60th St., which curves and becomes 310th Ave. NE.

28.5   Left onto NE Carnation Farm Rd.; cross bridge.

30.2   Pass Camp Korey.

30.7   At intersection with W. Snoqualmie Valley Rd. NE, continue forward onto Ames Lake–Carnation Rd. NE.

33.4   Right onto NE Union Hill Rd.

36.7   Right at T with 238th Ave. NE to stay on NE Union Hill Rd.

36.9   Bear left at stop sign at 3-way intersection to stay on NE Union Hill Rd.

40.9   Left into Bear Creek Park-and-Ride lot to end tour.

22 Snoqualmie Valley Farm Tour

DIFFICULTY: easy
TIME: allow 3 hours
DISTANCE: 35.6 miles
ELEVATION GAIN: 587 feet

Getting There: From SR 520, take Redmond Wy. exit and turn right onto SR 202 east (Redmond–Fall City Rd.). Turn left on NE Tolt Hill Rd., then left onto SR 203 (Fall City–Carnation Rd.). Cross bridge into Carnation and drive 0.5 mile to a left at NE 40th St. Tolt-MacDonald Park is at road's end.

From I-90, take exit 22, Preston/Fall City, and follow Preston–Fall City Rd. SE, which becomes SR 203 (Fall City–Carnation Rd.) at intersection with SR 202 (Redmond–Fall City Rd.). Continue straight on SR 203 across bridge into Carnation and drive 0.5 mile to a left at NE 40th St. to Tolt-MacDonald Park at road's end.

GPS Coordinates: N47 38 39 W121 54 56
Transit: Route Snoqualmie Valley Transit (SVT) to Duvall

Spend a lazy afternoon in the lush farm country of the Snoqualmie River valley with this flat tour between two of the area's main towns. Beginning at Tolt-MacDonald Park in Carnation, the tour loops through the farm country north of Carnation, then circles back through town and makes a southern swing to Fall City.

From the free parking lot, where a row of big poplars shields your car from the afternoon sun, bike out to Tolt Avenue, Carnation's main street, turn left, and ride north through town. The road turns into State Route 203, the valley's busy highway, which is best avoided by cyclists. That main road has higher speed limits and more traffic, and cyclists have the opportunity to use other, mellower roads.

As you exit town, take the side roads that link up with the Old Carnation Farm Road at a bridge across the Snoqualmie River. Turn west and climb to the edge of the valley, which offers great views of the lush marshlands on the river's edge, flanked by broad fields. As you reach the peak of this climb, a whopping 100 feet above sea level, you can enjoy the picturesque scene of the original Carnation Farm,

200'
0'
0 miles   5   10   15   20   25   30   35.6

The statue of Elsie, here decked out for Halloween, stands at the site of the original dairy farm of the Carnation company. The farm is now a retreat center for kids with serious illnesses.

for which the town is named. This was the dairy that made it big in the milk business. Remember their catchy slogan, "from contented cows," and Bessie, their friendly mascot cow? A giant statue of her stands proudly on the far side of the farm buildings. Today, the cluster of neat, red-roofed white buildings host a getaway camp for children with life-altering medical conditions.

Cycle past the farm and continue along the edge of the valley. Along West Snoqualmie Valley Road NE you'll cycle by a working dairy (mind the farm equipment), and your senses will discover the true smells and sounds of the milk-production world. A right turn into the valley takes you along the river and spinning by plots of land cultivated by small, market farmers, some of it owned and leased by the Puget Consumers Co-op Farmland Trust, a nonprofit organization started by the Seattle-based natural-food grocery chain that buys land to keep it as farmland in perpetuity. Swing past a horse farm and over a tributary's bridge and rejoin the route back toward Carnation, offering the opportunity of waving to Bessie once more.

The second leg of this tour heads south from Carnation, past the park where your car sits (in case you forgot something). At the south edge of Carnation, cross the bridge out of town and, if you want a brief side trip to see another type of farming operation, make an immediate

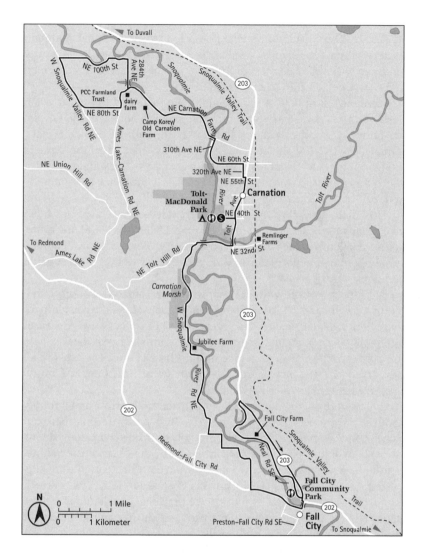

left to cycle a half mile to the huge farm store at Remlinger Farms (see Tour 21). To continue on this tour's route, turn right out of Carnation onto NE Tolt Hill Road and ride a half mile until you cross the river again. Just beyond that bridge, turn left and head south on West Snoqualmie River Road NE. The curvy, shady lane is lightly used, due to the straighter and wider Fall City–Carnation Road (State Route 203) on the east side of the valley. It's not unusual to see cars stopped by the roadside, buying cut flowers or vegetables from a farm stand or admiring the bucolic scenery.

Pass by the Carnation Marsh, stewarded by the National Audubon Society, with its osprey nests and leafless dead tree "snags" in the boggy landscape, then pedal by an alternative use of the land: the trimmed and flower-bedecked Carnation Golf Course.

Productive farmland is nestled along the road, and in August you'll be treated to rows of riotous color in fields where cutting flowers are grown. Next you arrive at Jubilee Farm, with its big white barn hunched by the side of the road, gaping door open when the farmers are working, which is almost every summer day. The well-loved farm also offers processed foods and hosts regular events, such as farm tours and festivals.

This main road through the western side of the valley has been given many names, as reflected in the mileage log, but it's all one route, taking you south to the small town of Fall City. Along the way, you may come upon lush fields of corn lining the road, as well as modest cattle and horse ranches.

Fall City sports a tiny main street with a well-stocked market, a couple of taverns, and a take-out burger joint, as well as a riverside park that offers a good place to picnic. A curious sight is the Native American totem pole welcoming you to town, which seems to have a bear clutching a blue space-alien child. A plaque at the base of the piece explains all the carved symbols. Across from the totem is the King County Library, in case a restroom stop is needed.

Continue through Fall City to a bridge across the river and a roundabout that connects to State Route 203. Turn north on this road, but only briefly, then left at Fall City Community Park to ride along sleepy Neal Road SE and past Fall City Farm, one of the older of the valley's market farms and a pioneer in small-farm trends like community supported agriculture. Neal Road connects to State Route 203 via a street-end barrier easily skirted by bikes. Take the adequate shoulder of State Route 203 for a couple miles to get back to Fall City and retrace your steps to Carnation via the back roads.

End the tour by sticking your feet in the cool water of the Snoqualmie at the park in Carnation, or ride up the town's main street to the upscale tavern for a snack and a cold drink before heading home.

Route Connections: If you feel like a challenge after making the short trip from Carnation to Fall City, take the 3-mile climb to view the famous Snoqualmie Falls; you can also connect with the rest of the Snoqualmie Falls ride (Tour 23), which takes you through the towns of Snoqualmie and North Bend. Or use the farm tour as a continuation of the Duvall–Carnation loop from Redmond (Tour 21).

MILEAGE LOG

0.0 Exit Tolt-MacDonald Park (restrooms) parking lot toward Carnation on access road.

0.3 Left onto Tolt Ave.

1.1 Left onto NE 55th St. Caution: fast traffic. In 1 block, right onto 320th Ave. NE.

1.3 Left onto NE 60th St., which curves and becomes 310th Ave. NE.

2.3 Left onto NE Carnation Farm Rd.; cross bridge.

4.0 Pass Camp Korey, site of the old Carnation Farm.

4.4 Continue onto Ames Lake–Carnation Rd NE past a working dairy farm.

4.8 Right onto NE 80th St.; PCC Farmland Trust land is on the right.

5.5 Right at Y to stay on 80th.

5.6 Right onto W. Snoqualmie Valley Rd NE.

6.6 Right onto NE 100th St.

8.0 Right onto 284th Ave. NE.

8.5 Left to rejoin NE Carnation Farm Rd.

10.7 Right, after crossing bridge, onto 310th Ave. NE.

11.7 Right onto 320th Ave. NE, then left on NE 55th St.

12.3 Right onto Tolt Ave.

12.9 Pass entrance to Tolt-MacDonald Park.

13.1 Right, after crossing bridge, onto NE Tolt Hill Rd.

13.9 Left onto W. Snoqualmie River Rd. NE, past Carnation Marsh.

16.4 Pass Jubilee Farm.

17.9 Left onto SE 24th St., which becomes 316th Ave. SE, then SE 28th St., then 321st Ave. SE, then SE 31st St., and finally 324th Ave. SE.

19.7 Left onto Redmond–Fall City Rd. (SR 202).

20.4 Arrive at Fall City.

20.7 Left onto Preston–Fall City Rd. SE and over Snoqualmie River bridge.

21.1 Left onto Fall City–Carnation Rd. SE (SR 203). Pass Fall City Community Park.

21.2 Left onto Neal Rd. SE.

22.5 Pass Fall City Farm.

23.9 Right through street-end barrier onto Carnation–Fall City Rd. (SR 203).

26.2 Right onto Preston–Fall City Rd. SE (SR 202). Cross bridge over river.

26.3 Right onto River St., which becomes Redmond–Fall City Rd. (SR 202).

27.4 Right onto 324th Ave. SE, which eventually becomes W. Snoqualmie River Rd. NE.

34.1 Right onto NE Tolt Hill Rd.

34.9 Left onto Tolt Ave. (SR 203).

35.0 Left into parking by river immediately after bridge. Caution: traffic. Proceed forward on trail at end of parking.

35.6 Return to Tolt-MacDonald Park's parking lot to end tour.

23 Snoqualmie Falls

DIFFICULTY: moderate
TIME: allow 3 hours
DISTANCE: 21.1 miles
ELEVATION GAIN: 854 feet

Getting There: Take I-90 east to exit 22, Preston/Fall City. Turn left off exit and go over I-90 on SE 82nd St. Turn right onto Fall City–Preston Rd. SE at stop sign. Go north 4.7 miles. At intersection with SR 202, turn right to follow signs that say "202 East, North Bend/Snoqualmie Falls." At Fall City, cross bridge and turn immediately left onto SR 203, Fall City–Carnation Rd. SE. At Fall City Community Park immediately on the left, park in the unpaved lot.

GPS Coordinates: N47 34 13 W121 53 15

Transit: King County Metro 209

Take this short tour to visit Snoqualmie Falls, enjoy some rolling hills, get a great view of rocky Mount Si, and take a spin through the Cascades foothill towns of Snoqualmie and North Bend.

Depart from the eastern edge of Fall City and avoid most of the climb up busy State Route 202 by turning south onto Fish Hatchery Road. This populated side road parallels the loud highway but also runs along the peaceful Snoqualmie River for a time.

It's 3 miles of riding up into the foothills, as the overhead line of mountain peaks that were visible from the valley floor give way to a thick march of evergreens growing up to the ditches on both sides and

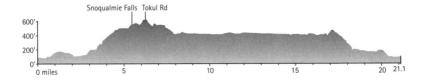

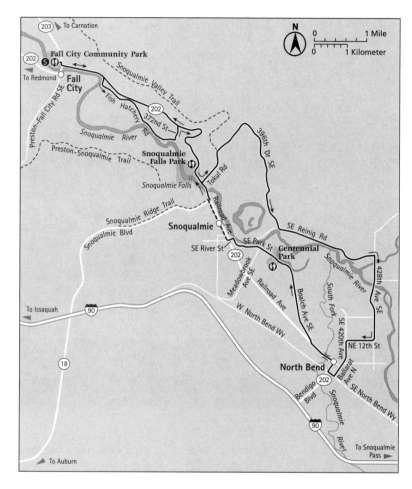

receding into the hills beyond the road ahead. The climb is steady but not overly difficult, and a wide shoulder makes the traffic bearable.

A short climb takes you back onto State Route 202 for the last mile of climbing before reaching the impressive Snoqualmie Falls, which is always worth a look. Stop at the parking area for the falls, take the short walk 100 yards to the overlook near the luxurious Salish Lodge, or make a hike out of it and take the steep half-mile trip down to the river emerging from the base of the falls. Restrooms and refreshments are available here.

Cross the busy highway at the slow corridor around the lodge and continue toward North Bend on back roads, skirting the town of Snoqualmie on the outbound. The route takes you into the "Reinig Road Sycamore Corridor," where a bit of history from when the area

Mount Si

was run by a logging mill can still be seen. A large stand of sycamores was planted by immigrants who lived in the Snoqualmie Falls company town and worked in the mill. The trees, with their mottled gray bark and heavy canopies, are now quite large and shade the edge of the valley.

Break out into a farming area and aim straight at Mount Si, which provides an impressive backdrop to the rural valley you traverse to get to North Bend. A leisurely cycling speed is perfect for examining its craggy walls. In the foreground, enjoy a King County natural area at 9.8 miles that offers trails down to a bend in the river. A neighboring ranch with its nicely maintained barns, paddocks, and pastures completes the postcard-perfect scene.

The small town of North Bend offers a number of attractions as well. Although the route calls for turning right onto SE North Bend Way, the town's main street, detour left a block to visit Scott's Dairy Freeze for an ice cream treat. To the right along your downtown route, pass Twede's

Café, which was made famous as the Mar-T Diner in the quirky 1980s television series *Twin Peaks*. You can still get Agent Cooper's favorite cherry pie at the diner, which plays up its screen notoriety. Turn right at the diner's corner to exit North Bend and continue the tour, or make another detour and head left down Bendigo Boulevard to the factory discount stores, grouped in a shopping center a mile south next to Interstate 90.

Plentiful local traffic is found on the road between Snoqualmie and North Bend, although a generous shoulder makes for a safe ride. The only exceptions are the old bridges, which have no shoulder or pedestrian-bikeway and must be traversed with caution. A rear-view mirror to gauge the traffic behind you comes in handy at such unavoidable spots.

The route takes you back to the edge of the Snoqualmie River, with more views of Mount Si beyond the town's golf course and some quiet country scenes. Turn onto Snoqualmie's main street and soon pass an old rail station and train display—and one of the most massive cross sections of a tree trunk you'll ever see. Across the street are a candy factory, a café, and a small grouping of shops. Exiting Snoqualmie, you approach another narrow bridge, but this one has a separated pedestrian-bikeway on the right. Take care at the narrow ramp to the protected lane.

For the final leg of this short ride, pass by the lodge and the falls, then enjoy a thrilling, curving downhill ride back to the edge of the Snoqualmie Valley.

Route Connections: You can continue north from Fall City to visit Snoqualmie Valley farms (Tour 22); for a really long ride, you could head west to Redmond (Tour 21) from Carnation, then up through Duvall and return to Fall City via Tour 22.

MILEAGE LOG

0.0 Right out of Fall City Community Park's parking area onto Fall City–Carnation Rd. SE (SR 203).

0.1 Left at stop sign onto Fall City–Snoqualmie Rd. SE (SR 202).

0.9 Right onto Fish Hatchery Rd.

2.8 Left onto 372nd St.

3.0 Right onto Fall City–Snoqualmie Rd. SE (SR 202).

4.5 Arrive at Snoqualmie Falls Park (restrooms, water, overlook to falls).

4.6 Left on Tokul Rd. just beyond Salish Lodge.

6.0 Bear right to stay on unmarked main road as Tokul curves sharply uphill. Main road becomes 396th Dr. SE.

8.0 Left onto SE Reinig Rd.

9.8 Right onto 428th Ave. SE.

11.3 Road curves right and becomes NE 12th St.

11.8 Road then curves left and becomes SE 420th Ave.

12.0 Continue forward as 420th becomes Ballarat Ave. N. in downtown North Bend.

12.4 Right onto SE North Bend Wy.

12.6 Right onto Bendigo Blvd. (SR 202), which curves left (west) and departs town.

13.3 Left onto Boalch Ave. SE, which becomes SE Park St.

15.0 Pass Centennial Park (restrooms).

15.8 Road curves left and becomes SE River St.

15.9 Right onto Railroad Ave.

16.1 Arrive at downtown Snoqualmie; historic rail station, tree cross section in park on the right.

17.1 Arrive back at Snoqualmie Falls; return to Fall City via SR 202.

21.0 Right onto SR 203.

21.1 Left into Fall City Community Park's parking area to end tour.

24 Green River and Interurban Trails

DIFFICULTY: moderate
TIME: allow 4 hours
DISTANCE: 39.3 miles
ELEVATION GAIN: 398 feet

Getting There: From I-5 southbound, take exit 156, Tukwila Interurban Avenue, turn right onto Interurban Ave. S., travel 0.5 mile, then turn right on 42nd Ave. S., cross Green River, and turn right into Tukwila Community Center parking lot.

From I-5 northbound, take exit 156, Tukwila Interurban Avenue, turn left onto Interurban Ave. S., travel 0.3 mile, then turn right on 42nd Ave. S., cross Green River, and turn right into Tukwila Community Center parking lot.

GPS Coordinates: N47 29 28 W122 16 47
Transit: King County Metro 124, 154, 193

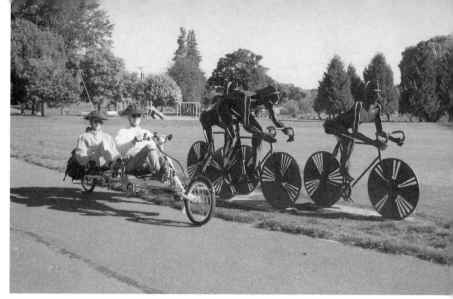

Cycling past the Slip Stream *sculpture in Van Doren's Landing Park*

The Green River has a bad reputation, through no fault of its own. It has faced the common challenges of many American rivers that flow through urban areas: pollution, industrial uses, neglect. But in true American fashion, let's ignore all those problems and instead recognize this river as a historic waterway, important in Native American and early pioneer settlement. A ride along the river presents a bit of the area's history as well as a view of the suburban development that's happening south of Seattle. It also provides a great link to other south King County rides.

Begin the ride at the Tukwila Community Center and ride south along the river to Fort Dent Park. The area, a former Duwamish tribe settlement, was once the confluence of the Green River and the long-gone Black River, an outflow from Lake Washington and nearby White Lake. The Washington National Guard built a small fort here after the 1855 Battle of Seattle against the tribes and named it after the battalion's leader, Frederick Dent, who was also the brother-in-law of President Ulysses S. Grant.

Skirt the edge of Fort Dent Park, then continue on the Green River Trail where it intersects with the northern terminus of the Interurban Trail. As you head south under the many lanes of Interstate 405 and into Tukwila's light industrial warehouse area, it's hard to imagine the open land that the Green River once wound through in its path from Mount Rainier to Puget Sound. But you do still feel the flow of nature as you bike along the flat, winding path that tracks the river's route.

The trail leads behind warehouses that skirt Southcenter Mall. What was once fertile farmland has been replaced largely by suburban sprawl, although there are occasional runs along plowed fields and rows of produce. You'll even see a lot of birds and some other small wildlife, like rabbits, among the trailside greenery.

The snaking trail veers slightly westward but continues to roughly parallel Interstate 5 as it skirts the eastern edge of Des Moines and enters Kent. At South 212th Street, you leave the trail briefly and ride along Russell Road, past Van Doren's Landing Park and the Green River Natural Resources Area. This former sewage lagoon now hosts a wildlife refuge and wetland. On the south edge of the GRNRA, the Puget Power Trail intersects with the Green River Trail, heading east-west. Continue south, however, and soon reenter the off-road Green River Trail at Russell Woods Park.

Apartment complexes and townhomes are plentiful along this stretch, making the trail more populated with children and family pets. The trail runs by the historic Neely Soames Homestead, the oldest standing residence in the Kent area. Due to its location at an easy river landing for steamboats headed for Seattle, it served as the area's first post office and general store.

From the frontier homestead, travel back even further in time for some prehistoric barbecue at Cave Man Kitchens, an area fixture since 1970. The original owners kept chickens on the site, and if you could catch one, you'd get a free chicken dinner. Today you catch your chicken, beef, or pork sandwich smothered in sweet, tangy sauce at the counter across from the smokehouse and enjoy it at one of the brick-red picnic tables beneath a dinosaur mural. To get there, head south on the trail from the Neely Soames Homestead to where the trail again joins Russell Road. Make a left off the trail onto South 240th Street, also known as West James Street, and travel a half dozen blocks on a street bike lane to the West Valley Highway (State Route 181, also known here as Washington Street). Make a left, staying on the near sidewalk to avoid riding on this busy street, and the Cave Man is on your left in a scant two blocks.

Back on the route, pass between the two halves of the Riverbend Golf Course, with a bridge linking the links. Just south, the City of Kent's Old Fishing Hole provides a stocked pond for young fishers. Anglers under 14 years old can catch up to six fish. The park has a totem pole and benches.

The Green River Trail ends at Foster Park in south Kent, linking up with the rail-straight Interurban Trail. If you wish to turn around at this point, turn left onto the Interurban back to Fort Dent. The Interurban is as linear as the Green River is curvaceous, and you're slowed only

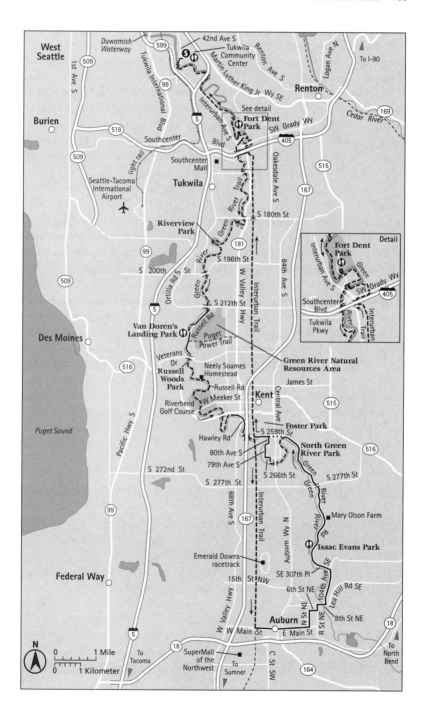

by other trail users and road crossings. Heed the roads: much of the Interurban Trail runs between highways and warehouses, so truck traffic is plentiful, but well-signed crossings make the route safe.

To continue on this tour's route and see more of the Green River, turn south on the Interurban Trail. This takes you past the Emerald Downs horse-racing track and to the town of Auburn. This trail currently continues south past the SuperMall of the Northwest to the tiny town of Pacific, just north of the Pierce County line, and hopefully someday will connect to a good route into Tacoma.

As you turn east onto Auburn's Main Street, ride through its modest downtown and a couple of neighborhoods before heading north again out of town along the east side of the Green River. This moderately busy highway has good river views, plenty of trees, and a nice restroom stop at a park along the river. The road takes you back to the intersection with the Interurban Trail at Foster Park, and from there you follow the trail north back to Tukwila.

Route Connections: Continue north to West Seattle via the Duwamish Trail (Tour 12) or east at Auburn to Black Diamond and Flaming Geyser State Park (Tour 27).

MILEAGE LOG

0.0 Left out of Tukwila Community Center (restrooms) parking onto near-side sidewalk. Cross bridge.

0.1 Left off bridge down short embankment, then right onto trail. Exit trail immediately into office park parking lot and continue along river's edge.

0.4 Reenter trail as parking lot ends.

1.1 Trail travels under I-5, then next to on-ramp.

1.4 Curve left to stay on trail at intersection with I-5 and Interurban Ave. S.

2.1 Cross 141st St., then left and follow bike trail signs.

2.6 Cross bridge into Fort Dent Park (restrooms), with playfields on the left.

3.3 Pass under vehicle bridge, then curve left to follow "River Trail" signs and cross over river on bridge's pedestrian-bike lane. Caution: ride slowly on this narrow bridge to safely share with oncoming traffic.

3.9 Right to stay on Green River Trail at intersection with Interurban Trail.

6.3 Left onto arched pedestrian bridge to cross river. Right off bridge to continue.

7.2 Pass Riverview Park.

8.4 Pass Three Friends Fishing Hole.

9.2 Pass under S. 212th St., then soft right onto Russell Rd. Pass Green River Natural Resources Area.

9.8 Right onto trail through Van Doren's Landing Park (restrooms).

10.0 Exit trail back onto Russell Rd.

10.6 Right onto trail at bridge into Russell Woods Park.

11.6 Pass Neely Soames Homestead.

11.7 Rejoin Russell Rd. briefly, then right onto trail through Riverbend Golf Course.

12.6 Trail passes under W. Meeker St. and continues through golf course.

14.4 Exit trail onto cul-de-sac, then continue forward to pick up trail again in 0.1 mile.

14.5 Exit trail right onto Hawley Rd.

14.6 Rejoin trail at street end.

14.9 Trail curves left, goes under SR 167, the Valley Freeway. Stay right at Y to enter Foster Park.

15.2 Right onto Interurban Trail. (Note: To shorten route, left on Interurban Trail and return to parking in 9.9 miles.)

15.5 Take care when crossing railroad tracks, on which are operated remote-controlled locomotives.

18.0 Pass Emerald Downs racetrack.

19.5 Left onto W. Main St. in Auburn.

20.8 Left onto N St. NE.

21.1 Right onto 6th St. NE.

21.3 Left onto R St. NE.

21.4 Right onto 8th St. NE over bridge to cross Green River. Get in left turn lane immediately. Caution: heavy traffic.

21.7 Left onto 104th Ave. SE at stoplight. Caution: busy intersection.

22.5 Left onto SE 307th Pl., also known as Green River Rd.

23.2 Pass Issac Evans Park (restrooms, water) on left.

24.0 Pass Mary Olson Farm.

24.9 Pass North Green River Park.

25.2 Bear left at Y with 94th Pl. S. to stay on Green River Rd., which becomes S. 259th St.

25.9 Left at large boulders and bollards to rejoin trail (or stay straight on 259th to skip this short trail section).

27.2 Trail ends under a railroad bridge. Right onto Ives Ave.

27.4 Left onto S. 266th St., which becomes 79th Ave. S., then S. 261st St., then 80th Ave. S.

28.0 Left onto S. 259th St.

28.4 Right onto Interurban Trail.

29.0 Cross at light at W. Willis St. Curve left briefly to stay on trail, then right through trail opening in chain-link fence, then bear right to stay on trail.

29.8 Continue on trail under SR 167, the Valley Freeway.

35.0 Continue on trail under I-405, then under SW Grady Wy.

35.5 Right at intersection with Green River Trail.

36.1 Right onto bike lane on narrow bridge bike-walkway into Fort Dent Park (restrooms). When exiting bridge, curve right and follow "River Trail" signs.

37.2 Right on trail parallel to Interurban Ave. S. at S. 141st St.

37.9 Trail curves right at I-5 on-ramp.

38.7 Exit trail into parking behind office park. Continue along river.

39.2 Exit parking lot onto trail briefly, then exit to ramp and right onto bridge to community center.

39.3 Arrive at Tukwila Community Center parking to end tour.

25 Cedar River Trail and May Valley

DIFFICULTY: moderate
TIME: allow 3 hours
DISTANCE: 28.2 miles
ELEVATION GAIN: 1031 feet

Getting There: From I-5, take exit 154 to I-405 northbound. From I-405, take exit 4A and turn right onto Maple Valley Hwy./SR 169. Take first right into Renton Community Center, proceed left, and pass aquatic center to parking by community center.

GPS Coordinates: N47 28 52 W122 11 55

Transit: King County Metro 101, 102, 106, 107, 110, 140, 143, 167, 169

Do you ever, on a flat and open stretch of trail, just tune out your surroundings and listen to your body working with your bike? Legs

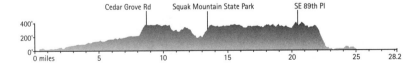

operate like pistons, heart churns like an engine. Try this on the Cedar River Trail's flat, open route, and you might get a feel for the trail's first use: as a railroad. The trail, paved from Renton to Maple Valley and then continuing to Landsburg as gravel, began life as a part of the Milwaukee Railroad. Reappropriated by the government through the "railbanking" mechanism, it's a great jumping-off point for exploring the cusp of rural lands in south King County. The straight trail ride is at times loud and busy, but the exploration of the charms still existing in May Valley make it a worthy ramble through the civilization happening southeast of Seattle. And once you see the maze of suburban roads emanating from the trail, you'll find other rambles to explore.

Begin the tour by crossing the bridge behind the Renton Community Center. Head south along the river, enjoying a couple miles of peaceful, green landscape. Emerge like a locomotive out onto the fringes of State Route 169, the Maple Valley Highway, past a golf course and multiple housing developments.

The ride to Maple Valley is just over 20 miles round-trip, and the paved trail stops just short of the actual town, ending at a bridge over the river where the gravel portion begins. If you went this way, you'd exit the paved trail at the Testy Chef, a small diner that locals say lives up to its name. Across the busy highway sit the Cedar Grange and the Maple Valley Grocery, but you'd need to ride about 2 miles farther south on that fast-moving street to find any other conveniences. You

A broad, paved boardwalk runs along the Cedar River from downtown Renton toward Lake Washington.

might plan this trip on a Sunday when the Cedar Grange is offering its pancake breakfast.

If it's not the right day, however, there is a better way to see more of the area, and that's the goal of this route. Instead of riding into Maple Valley, continue south on the loud trail only until it meets Cedar Grove Road. Follow the road up the hill, past the Cedar Grove Composting facility, with its steady stream of trucks, and on to a left at the Issaquah-Hobart Road, then onto SE May Valley Road for a long and winding route, mostly rural and enjoyable, back to Renton.

May Valley still reveals its farming heritage at spots, but those are outnumbered by signs of suburbanization. For instance, a development called Sunset Valley Farms shows a number of homes with suburban-size yards filling a small side valley that one could picture having been a pastoral family farm.

At Squak Mountain State Park, you'll find restrooms and picnic tables off the parking area. The park, replete with hiking and riding

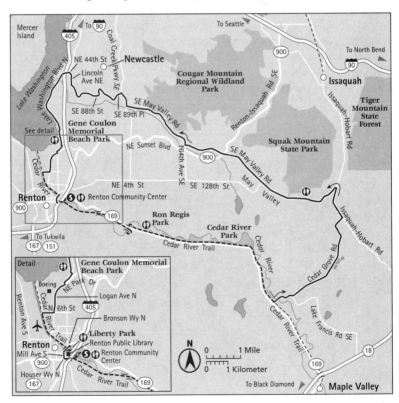

trails, stretches some distance north. Cross State Route 900, Renton–Issaquah Road SE, and then the landscape becomes more pastoral for a time. SE May Valley Road has minimal to nonexistent shoulders, but it is signed for 30 miles per hour, with regular reminders that it is a "recreation trail" for pedestrians and cyclists.

A brief stint onto wide and busy Coal Creek Parkway SE is followed by a series of narrow suburban streets with moderate hills and many twists and turns: SE 89th Place begets SE 88th Place begets Lincoln Avenue NE begets NE 44th Street, and you're in Newcastle, then back in Renton. As the streets narrow, so do the side yards, until townhomes and shopping centers give way again to Interstate 405.

Cross over Interstate 405 and head south on Lake Washington Boulevard N to Gene Coulon Memorial Beach Park on the lake's south edge. Soon you're in downtown Renton, jogging down once again to the river, then emerging at the library and Liberty Park to return to the tour's start.

Route Connections: Connect with the Lake Washington Loop (Tour 16) or continue south on the gravel section of the Cedar River Trail to Landsburg for the Green River Gorge ride (Tour 26).

MILEAGE LOG

0.0 Begin on trail behind Renton Community Center (restrooms) parking area. Left onto trail under I-405 on a bridge crossing Cedar River.

0.1 Left on trail on west side of river.

3.2 Pass Ron Regis Park (restrooms).

4.1 Pass Cedar River Park.

6.1 Pass Cedar Grove Natural Area.

8.0 Left onto Cedar Grove Rd.

11.6 Left onto Issaquah-Hobart Rd.

12.6 Left onto SE May Valley Rd. Caution: traffic when merging to left-turn lane.

14.1 Squak Mountain State Park (restrooms) on right.

15.1 Stay right at intersection with SE 128th Wy.

16.5 Cross SR 900/Renton–Issaquah Rd.

17.7 At stop sign at 164th Ave. SE, stay on SE May Valley Rd.

19.9 Right onto Coal Creek Pkwy. SE.

20.4 Left onto SE 89th Pl. Caution: road curves; fast-moving traffic. Road becomes SE 88th Pl., then SE 88th St., then 114th Ave. SE, then Lincoln Ave. NE, then NE 44th St.

22.9 At ramps for I-405, go straight over I-405.

23.0 Left onto Lake Washington Blvd. N.

24.9 Right into Gene Coulon Memorial Beach Park, then immediate left at stop sign.

25.0 Right into parking area by pavilion (restrooms, concessions).

25.5 Right onto park road, which ends at intersection of Houser Wy. N. and Lake Washington Blvd.

25.6 Right onto NE Park Dr., which becomes Logan Ave. N.

26.3 Right onto N. 6th St.

26.6 Left onto Cedar River Trail at street end.

27.5 As trail enters Liberty Park, hard left onto sidewalk at top of ramp. In 100 yards, left onto Bronson Wy. N. In ½ block, left onto Mills Ave. S.

27.7 Cross Houser Wy. N. at light. In ½ block, left onto N. 3rd St. (lower road).

27.8 Left onto trail. Proceed under I-405 and in 50   ds, left to Renton Community Center.

28.2 Arrive at parking to end tour.

26 Green River Gorge and Black Diamond

DIFFICULTY: moderate
TIME: allow 3 hours
DISTANCE: 26.5 miles
ELEVATION GAIN: 1383 feet

Getting There: Take I-5 to I-90 eastbound. At Issaquah, take Front St. exit. Turn right on Front St., which becomes Issaquah-Hobart Rd., which becomes 276th Ave. SE. Travel approximately 11 miles. Trailhead parking is on north bank of Cedar River, just south of SE 247th St.

  GPS Coordinates: N47 22 32 W121 58 15

  Transit: King County Metro 168, 907 (3 miles to Landsburg Park)

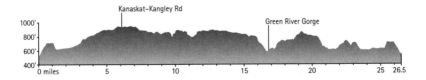

Southeast King County, somewhat less encumbered by the rumble of development or the bustle of farm activity, is home to some of the best back-road riding still available in the area. A ride through the Green River Gorge east of Black Diamond offers quieter roads, mostly gentle terrain, and beautiful wooded scenes. This tour provides merely an introduction to the multiple routes cyclists can create around the Green River, and it may be combined easily with other adjacent tours for many enjoyable outings of varied length and difficulty.

Begin this loop at Landsburg, a wide spot in the road adjacent to the Cedar River Watershed, one of the sources of Seattle's water supply. From here, water is screened, chlorinated, and fluoridated to slake the thirst of more than a million people. However, fill up your water bottle at home, because you'll find no facilities at the parking site.

Many cyclists get a treat at the Black Diamond Bakery when exploring south King County.

What you will see is a whitewater kayak training course under the bridge that spans the Cedar River. "Gates" elevated above the river are raised and lowered depending on the flow to provide a course for river rats to hone their skills. A foot trail from the parking area leads to the Big Bend open space along the river.

Ride south and east on 276th Avenue SE, which becomes Landsburg Road SE, a somewhat strenuous hill with which to begin. At the intersection of Landsburg Road SE and Kent–Kangley Road, the ride's first turn, sits the Ravensdale Market, a good stop for snacks if you plan to picnic on this ride. Restrooms are just south in Ravensdale Park. Turn left onto Kent–Kangley, the busiest road on the tour but one that sports a wide shoulder for easy riding. Cycle east past wooded hillsides and

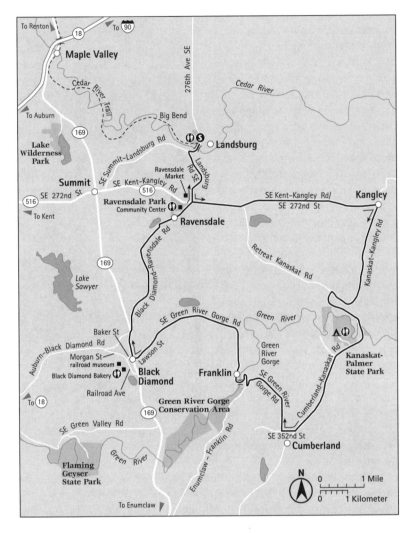

the occasional open valley sporting small ranches to a comfort stop at Kanaskat-Palmer State Park.

The 320-acre park has campgrounds and day-use areas, with restrooms, water, and picnic sites. Its main attraction is the Green River access, also a favorite of paddlers. The curving riverfront through the park goes from class II to IV, providing challenges for kayakers and rafters of many skill levels. A recreation area begins at the park and follows the river downstream almost continuously through Hanging Gardens State Park to Flaming Geyser State Park; a coalition of enthusiastic users is seeking to preserve the area and develop the recreational opportunities of this verdant ribbon that supporters call "the best of the last wild places in King County."

South of Kanaskat-Palmer State Park, turn right toward the SE Green River Gorge Road just before the tiny burg of Cumberland. This segment provides the visual high point in the ride: a winding, secluded road that leads to a sturdy one-lane bridge spanning the gorge. A stoplight warns approaching motorists of oncoming traffic, but cyclists can use the wide sidewalks to traverse the bridge. Stop midspan to enjoy its breathtaking views down into the gorge. A former inn sits boarded up at the bridge's eastern approach, implying the grandness of this attraction to previous generations. Perhaps conservation of the area will make it a destination yet again.

The road climbs and winds, alternating past woods and clear-cuts, into Black Diamond, where a visit to the Black Diamond Bakery is virtually required for anyone pedaling into town. Depart Black Diamond heading north, then shortly angle northeast toward Ravensdale, beyond which lies the Landsburg parking site.

Route Connections: Connect to Auburn via Flaming Geyser State Park and Green Valley Road (Tour 27) or ride north on the gravel section of the Cedar River Trail to link to Renton and May Valley (Tour 25).

MILEAGE LOG

0.0 Depart parking area north of Landsburg bridge by turning south and crossing bridge.

0.2 Bear left at Y at SE Summit–Landsburg Rd, staying on Landsburg Rd. SE.

1.5 Left onto SE Kent–Kangley Rd./SR 516.

2.6 Stay left at intersection with Retreat Kanaskat Rd. to stay on Kent–Kangley (also signed here as SE 272nd St.).

5.8 Right onto Kanaskat–Kangley Rd.

8.6 Left onto Cumberland–Kanaskat Rd.

10.4 Right into Kanaskat-Palmer State Park.

11.2 Arrive at day-use area (restrooms, water, picnic tables). Retrace route to exit park.

11.9 Right onto Cumberland–Kanaskat Rd. when exiting park.

14.2 Right onto SE 352nd St.

14.5 Right onto 309th Ave. SE, which becomes SE Green River Gorge Rd.

16.3 Right at intersection with Enumclaw–Franklin Rd. to continue on SE Green River Gorge Rd.

16.7 Cross one-lane Green River Gorge Bridge.

20.4 Road becomes Lawson St. as it enters Black Diamond.

20.8 Right onto 3rd Ave., also known as SR 169/Enumclaw–Black Diamond Rd. (For side trip to Black Diamond Bakery, turn left onto Baker St., then left onto Railroad Ave.)

21.4 Turn right onto Black Diamond–Ravensdale Rd., which becomes SE Ravensdale Wy.

25.0 Cross Kent–Kangley Rd. at Ravensdale Market. Proceed north on Landsburg Rd. SE.

26.3 Right onto SE Summit–Landsburg Rd.

26.5 Arrive back at Landsburg bridge and parking to end tour.

27 Auburn to Flaming Geyser State Park

DIFFICULTY: moderate
TIME: allow 3.5 hours
DISTANCE: 31.5 miles
ELEVATION GAIN: 1009 feet

Getting There: Take I-5 or SR 167 to SR 18 eastbound. Take first exit in Auburn, C St. SW. Left off ramp, in 0.2 mile left onto W. Main St., then left into parking by Interurban Trail in another 0.4 mile.

GPS Coordinates N47 18 28 W122 14 22

Transit King County Metro 152, 180, 181, 186, 910, 919

South King County is home to some excellent road biking, along rural roads and through lush farming communities. This route, heading east from Auburn, skirts new development, visits the small town of Black Diamond with a great bakery, and returns through lush, green farmland.

Start the tour by parking next to the Interurban Trail adjacent to Auburn's quiet West Main Street. Access is easy and quick from Interstate 5 or State Route 167. Ride east through town and briefly alongside busy State Route 18 as you head northeast on the shady, winding SE Auburn–Black Diamond Road. (An alternate route along

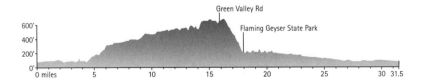

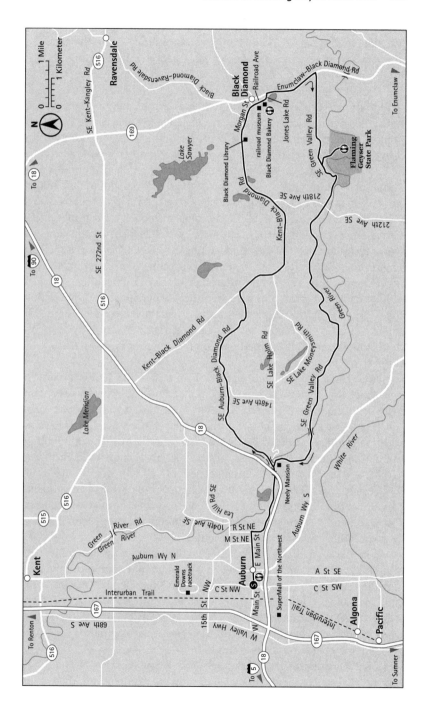

SE Lake Holm Road, found just after you cross the Green River, can be taken if the group wants a more strenuous activity and a quieter road, but the curvy, steep section to start, which offers no shoulder for biking, might be unpleasant for less experienced riders.)

By either route, your first destination is Black Diamond and its two main tourist attractions: the railway museum and the Black Diamond Bakery. They are situated just a matter of yards from one another, in a small shopping area that also houses a bookstore and general store.

The railroad station has a well-preserved engine sitting on a short stretch of track and displays of goods shipped from the area, such as coal and logs. Other relics of the town's past are lined up, too, such as a one-room jail dating from 1910. The museum, open on summer afternoons, is worth a quick tour. The bakery is a favorite of the region's cyclists, and not just for the comfort-stop essentials of water and clean restrooms. A café offers a full menu, but there is a generous seating area for those just having an espresso drink or bakery item.

Ride back to Auburn along the country jewel that is SE Green Valley Road. Here in designated farming areas, housing developments are still nonexistent, although massive new homes of hobby farmers are sprinkled along the road. It is mostly an area of working farms, with picturesque barns and horse pastures.

Before reaching the main valley, drop down into Flaming Geyser State Park, adjacent to the road. Part of a patchwork of preserved green spaces that begins on the Green River at Kanaskat-Palmer State Park and continues through the stunning Green River Gorge, this park is home to a unique sight: a flame that continually burns in a bubbling stream due to release of natural gases. It's only a short walk from the parking area to view the "flaming geyser."

The park also features mossy, woodland trails and Christy Creek, home to chinook, chum, and coho salmon. At the entrance to the park is an open area used by model-airplane aficionados, often seen buzzing their remote-control planes over the flat, grassy field.

While the road out to Black Diamond is shady with rolling hills, this route back is light, airy, and flat. There are even a couple of opportunities to pick up country farm products. End the loop by turning back onto the Auburn–Black Diamond Road west into Auburn under State Route 18. At the turn, the venerable Neely Mansion sits on the left, a homestead of one of the first families of the area. Its grounds are open to visitors during summer weekends.

Route Connections: Head north from Auburn on the Green River and Interurban Trails ride (Tour 24) or loop north and east to the Green River Gorge (Tour 26).

Bucolic SE Green Valley Road

MILEAGE LOG

0.0 From parking adjacent to Interurban Trail, right onto E. Main St.

1.5 Right onto R St. NE.

1.7 Road becomes SE Auburn–Black Diamond Rd. Caution: railroad tracks—cross at an angle; intersection with truck traffic.

3.4 Cross SE Green Valley Rd.

3.5 Cross bridge and continue straight on SE Auburn–Black Diamond Rd. at intersection with SE Lake Holm Rd.

8.1 Merge right at intersection with Kent–Black Diamond Rd.

12.2 Arrive at Black Diamond; road becomes Roberts Rd.

12.8 Right onto Morgan St., which becomes Railroad Ave.; pass railroad museum and bakery (restrooms).

13.8 Right onto 3rd Ave., which becomes Enumclaw–Black Diamond Rd.

15.1 Right onto SE Green Valley Rd.

17.9 Left into Flaming Geyser State Park.

18.2 Right into park off access road.

19.1 Arrive at parking (restrooms, picnic area). Retrace route to continue.

20.3 Left onto SE Green Valley Rd. when exiting park to continue tour.

26.7 Cross bridge over Green River.

28.3 Left onto SE Auburn–Black Diamond Rd.

30.0 Left onto E. Main St.

31.5 Arrive at Interurban Trail parking to end tour.

28 Vashon and Maury Islands

DIFFICULTY: strenuous
TIME: allow 5 hours
DISTANCE: 37.4 miles
ELEVATION GAIN: 2822 feet

Getting There: From I-5, take exit 163, West Seattle Bridge, and follow it west. Continue into West Seattle on Fauntleroy Wy. SW as bridge ends. Follow Fauntleroy as it curves left, then right, to Lincoln Park for parking near the ferry. Use north lot farthest from ferry, except on Sunday, when closer lot may be used. After parking, cycle 0.2 mile south on Fauntleroy to ferry dock.

   GPS Coordinates: N47 31 45 W122 23 34
   Transit: King County Metro C line

Ferry across to Vashon Island for a rural 40-mile workout that is one of the most scenic to be found in our region. Off the well-traveled main road, cyclists enjoy tree-lined back roads low on traffic and high on pastoral and water views.

   The inevitable hill climb to start the ride is one of the most challenging of any from a ferry dock. It's a steady 2-mile grade, after which you veer onto the island's west side for a long spin that takes you south down most of the island. Views across Colvos Passage to the Kitsap Peninsula and the Olympics are interspersed with valleys where deer or grazing livestock can be seen. Mostly, though, the view is a predictable tunnel of Northwest evergreens that line the roads. The way south takes you past the Wax Orchards berry operation and picturesque Misty Isle Farms and its naturally raised beef. Vashon is a bounteous agricultural island, and many small farms, a few with roadside stands offering fresh veggies, can be found along its roads.

   As the route turns back onto the Vashon Highway, you're just 2 miles from the Tahlequah ferry to Tacoma. A wonderful side trip to Point Defiance Park is only a few minutes beyond that ferry dock. However, this tour turns north and loops around the tiny Burton peninsula before continuing onto Maury Island.

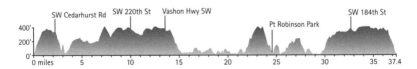

Riding past the self-serve produce stand at Plum Forest Farm

A note on picnicking: On this route, retail establishments are scarce, so it's best to plan ahead and bring your provisions. However, a small store sits roadside at the entrance to the Burton area. A great midpoint to stop, rest your legs, enjoy the views, and fuel up is Burton Acres Park. The park includes beach access, restrooms, and picnic tables.

From Burton, curve northeast around quiet Quartermaster Harbor. You could skip Maury Island and shorten the tour by 8 miles by turning left at Dockton Road, but continue to Maury and you'll be delighted by the quaint lighthouse and pebbly beach at Point Robinson Park. This is a great place for an extended rest.

The small Point Robinson Lighthouse, with well-informed guides who take you up the spiral stairs to view the working Fresnel lens, is a gem for visitors. From the catwalk you can view Seattle across the narrow channel and perhaps see "hardhat" divers going into the 300-foot-deep water right off the point to harvest geoduck clams. Looming next to the lighthouse is the Coast Guard's electronic beacon, making this a rare facility where both old and new warning systems for sailors are in effect.

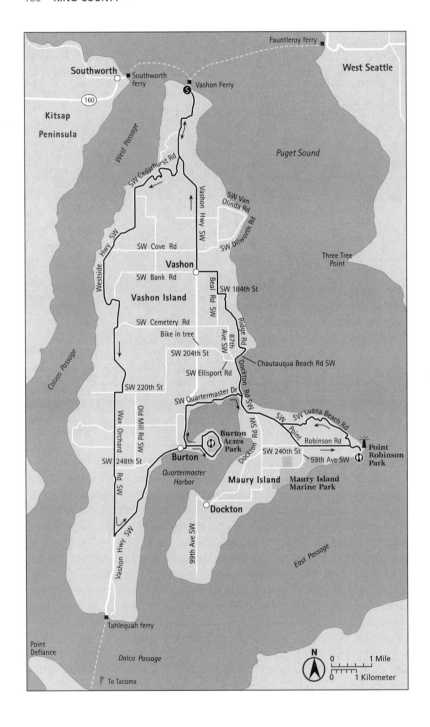

Walk the curved, sandy beach and view a case of excellent mariners' antiques in the gift shop before climbing back out of the park and onto the road leading back to Vashon. The ride hugs the islands' eastern coasts until climbing toward the commercial center of Vashon, offering many views of the city to the northeast.

If visiting Vashon on a Sunday, be forewarned that many of its shops are closed and there is no bus service on the island. However, downtown Vashon does host a number of great cafés and gift shops, as well as a bustling farmers market. A cycling curiosity can be found on a side trip 2 miles south of town; just off the northeast corner of SW 204th Street and Vashon Highway SW, discover a short trail into the woods that leads to a bike encased in the trunk of a large tree. You'd have to backtrack on the highway to find this, but it's worth a side trip. From town, it's a quick and easy 5 miles to return to the ferry for the 15-minute crossing back to Fauntleroy.

Route Connections: Loop West Seattle (Tour 11), continue on the ferry to Southworth for the Port Orchard ride (Tour 29), or continue south on Vashon Highway SW to the Tahlequah ferry to Tacoma for the Point Defiance ride (Tour 55).

MILEAGE LOG

  0.0 Depart ferry dock uphill.
  2.0 Right onto SW Cedarhurst Rd.
  3.8 Road curves left and becomes Westside Hwy. SW.
  7.9 Road curves right and becomes SW Cemetery Rd. briefly.
  8.1 Continue forward as road again becomes Westside Hwy. SW.
  9.6 Right onto SW 220th St.
  9.8 Left onto Wax Orchard Rd. SW.
 13.2 Left onto Vashon Hwy. SW.
 16.2 Right onto SW Burton Dr. for a short peninsula loop.
 16.5 Right onto 97th Ave. W., which becomes SW Bay View Dr.
 17.3 Pass Burton Acres Park (restrooms) on left.
 18.2 Right back onto SW Burton Dr. to return to main road.
 18.6 Right onto Vashon Hwy SW.
 19.6 Right onto SW Quartermaster Dr.
 21.0 Right onto Dockton Rd SW to ride Maury Island (left to shortcut omitting Maury Island).
 21.6 Left at Y onto SW Point Robinson Rd. as main road goes right.
 23.1 Stay left at intersection with 59th Ave. SW to continue on SW Point Robinson Rd.
 24.2 Right to stay on SW Point Robinson Rd. into park.

24.6 Arrive at Point Robinson Park (restrooms). Retrace route to depart park.

25.0 At intersection with SW Point Robinson Rd., stay right to turn onto SW Luana Beach Rd.

27.4 Right to return to SW Point Robinson Rd.

28.0 At intersection with Dockton Rd. SW, stay right to continue back to Vashon on Dockton.

28.8 At intersection with SW Quartermaster Dr., stay right to continue on Dockton.

29.5 Right onto Chautauqua Beach Rd. SW at intersection with SW Ellisport Rd.

29.9 Left onto SW 204th St., which becomes Ridge Rd. at mile 30.2.

31.5 Road curves left and becomes SW 184th St.

31.7 At T where 184th ends, turn right on Beal Rd. SW.

32.2 Left onto SW Bank Rd.

32.7 Right onto Vashon Hwy. SW. (Left here would take you to the bike in a tree in 1.7 miles.)

37.4 Arrive at ferry dock to end tour.

Opposite: S'Klallam totem pole and longhouse in Little Boston

KITSAP COUNTY

29 Port Orchard

DIFFICULTY: easy
TIME: allow 3 hours
DISTANCE: 30.9 miles
ELEVATION GAIN: 987 feet

Getting There: From I-5, take exit 163, West Seattle Bridge, and follow it west. Continue into West Seattle on Fauntleroy Wy. SW as bridge ends. Follow Fauntleroy as it curves left, then right, to Lincoln Park for parking near the ferry. Use north lot farthest from ferry, except on Sunday, when closer lot may be used. After parking, cycle 0.2 mile south on Fauntleroy to ferry dock.

GPS Coordinates: N47 31 45 W122 23 34
Transit: King County Metro C line

The creaking of ferry pilings as the big boat snuggles up to the dock is a familiar sound to cyclists who head across Puget Sound for relaxing rides on the Kitsap Peninsula. Bicyclists are first on and first off the ferry—unless you arrive at the last minute—and get a front-row view of docking procedures. Disembarking at Southworth, on the far side of the Vashon Island run from West Seattle, riders are treated to one of the few ferry landings that does not require a steep uphill charge right off the dock. It's a mellow beginning for a ride that is equally relaxing throughout. Hills are not a challenge on this 30-mile spin along the shore toward Bremerton.

Accessibility and a moderate climate make this waterfront property desirable, so the ride passes a great variety of homes, from a surprising number of modest bungalows to the occasional luxury vacation home. At 2 miles, slip through a hidden passage to continue along the water at Harper Pier. Stop here to watch people fishing or scuba diving off the pier. Left of the pier, find a foot trail around overgrown bushes that leads to a one-lane road serving the homes along the beach. The road dead-ends at the pier but connects on the other end to allow for continuous riding.

Another quaint side road exists on the outbound leg of this tour. After riding Colchester Drive SE for about a mile, veer right onto

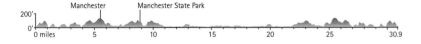

A cyclist's inspiration rises above flat, scenic Sinclair Inlet.

Miracle Mile Drive East for a brief jaunt (0.3 mile—perhaps that's the miracle) along a scenic side road.

Manchester provides the next diversion, where you can turn off the route toward the water and find a grocery store, pleasure-boat docks, a small park, and great views of downtown Seattle and the shipping traffic heading to Bremerton.

Just beyond the town and the fenced US Navy fuel supply depot is Manchester State Park, worth a short trip down its side road. The park, alongside Clam Bay's small cove, housed a defensive military installation, the remnants of which still exist. At the picnic area you'll see a mining casement and former torpedo warehouse (now a picnic shelter), and if you continue down the old road east, you'll find a cement battery nestled among the trees. From that point, looking north across Rich Passage to Bainbridge Island, you'll realize the strategic placement of these defenses when you see the location of matching batteries among the trees at Fort Ward Park.

Manchester State Park is also part of the Cascadia Marine Trail, so

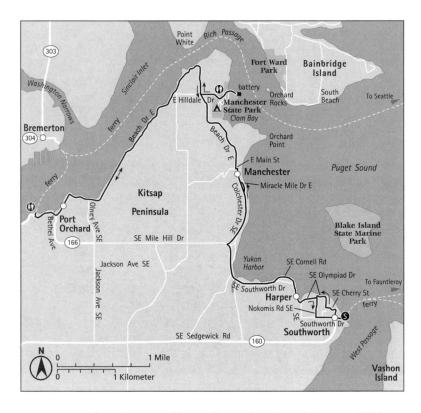

you may spot kayakers traveling and camping along this route. Offshore is Blake Island, also part of the Cascadia Marine Trail.

Next stop: Port Orchard, after a lovely 5-mile ride along Sinclair Inlet, with views north and west over small bays and inlets. The town of Port Orchard has a relaxing marina at which to have a picnic or just kick back and watch the boat traffic in and out of Bremerton harbor. The Puget Sound Naval Shipyard is visible just across the bay. Enjoy the laid-back feel of Port Orchard, try the bakery, or check out the antique shops, then head back along the water to retrace your steps to Southworth. This ride gets a nomination as the one most likely to put the tang of rotting seaweed into your nose as it delivers some of the best coastal riding around Puget Sound.

Route Connections: A passenger ferry connects Port Orchard to Bremerton, so you could visit that navy town or extend the tour if desired: for a longer return to your car, ride this ferry to Bremerton, then get on the one-hour Bremerton-Seattle ferry and bicycle back to West Seattle from downtown Seattle's Colman Dock (an additional 13 miles), or from Bremerton you could ride out to Seabeck (Tour 30) or ride the

Winslow to Bremerton ferry-to-ferry route (Tour 33) in reverse direction to Bainbridge Island, then take the Bainbridge ferry back to Seattle.

MILEAGE LOG

0.0 Exit ferry dock onto SE Southworth Dr.

0.3 Just beyond grocery store and post office, right onto SE Cherry St.

0.7 Right onto SE Olympiad Dr.

1.1 After road curves, right to stay on Olympiad Dr.

1.5 As Olympiad ends, right onto SE Southworth Dr.

2.0 Exit road at Harper Pier. Use foot trail to left of pier, walk bike around street-end barrier, and continue on SE Cornell Rd.

2.6 Right onto SE Southworth Dr.

3.5 Right onto Yukon Harbor Dr. SE.

4.4 Right onto Colchester Dr. SE.

5.3 Right onto Miracle Mile Dr. E.

5.6 Right onto Colchester Dr. SE.

5.8 Left onto E. Main St. in Manchester. (On right at intersection are grocery and town park.)

5.9 Right onto Beach Dr. E.

7.9 Right onto E. Hilldale Rd. toward Manchester State Park.

8.2 Enter park.

8.8 Arrive at park picnic area (restrooms). Ride an additional 0.2 mile to park battery. Retrace route to Beach Dr. E.

10.1 Right onto Beach Dr. E.

15.7 Arrive at Westbay Center in Port Orchard. Turn right onto Bay St. at stoplight.

16.3 Arrive at Port Orchard marina (restrooms) and bay. Retrace route onto Bay St. to return.

16.9 Left onto Beach Dr. E.

18.9 Pass E. Hilldale Rd., which would take you to Manchester State Park in 0.3 mile.

24.6 Left onto E. Main St. in Manchester.

24.8 Right onto Colchester Dr. E.

26.5 Left on Yukon Harbor Dr. SE.

27.4 Left onto SE Southworth Dr.

28.4 Left onto SE Cornell Rd.

29.0 Exit Cornell by walking bike around street-end barrier at Harper Pier. Continue forward on SE Southworth Dr.

29.5 Left onto SE Olympiad Dr.

29.9 Right onto Nokomis Rd SE.

30.3 Left onto SE Southworth Dr.

30.9 Arrive at ferry dock to end tour.

30 Bremerton to Seabeck and Scenic Beach

DIFFICULTY: strenuous
TIME: allow 4.5 hours
DISTANCE: 37.1 miles
ELEVATION GAIN: 2788 feet

Getting There: From I-5 southbound, take exit 164 (northbound, exit 164B) and follow signs to Washington State Ferries' Colman Dock at Pier 52. No parking at ferry terminal; park in paid lots or at on-street meters.
GPS Coordinates: N47 36 10 W122 20 20
Transit: Multiple bus lines

Kitsap County is a great place for getting away, and this tour takes riders along a road less traveled than some of the northern county routes. Explore the naval town of Bremerton, loop around Dyes Inlet, and ride out to the western side of the county to the tiny village of Seabeck and a secluded beach park. There are a few good hill climbs on this tour and some roads with no shoulders, but the traffic is relatively low and the scenic value is high.

Bremerton, as home of the Puget Sound Naval Shipyard, seems to be awash in navy-gray paint. On the ferry ride into port, view the USS *Turner Joy*, a destroyer berthed at a waterfront pier and open for touring. Downtown Bremerton has experienced a bit of a rejuvenation, and it merits a visit too. A naval museum, historical museum, and downtown park and boardwalk are worth a look, and you'll find a number of small shops near the ferry.

Depart Kitsap County's largest city by skirting the south edge of Dyes Inlet and the north edge of Kitsap Lake as you head inland along Seabeck Highway NW. The rolling hills and seemingly endless forest give way to the tiny town of Seabeck, on the east shore of Hood Canal. A cluster of shops alongside quiet Seabeck Bay, including a café, pizza place, well-stocked general store, and espresso stand, provide ample

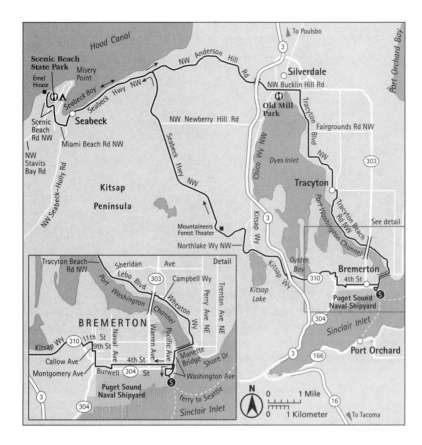

provisions for a lunch at the nearby town park, or have lunch in the village and enjoy the comings and goings of locals.

The town began as an early logging settlement, known as Kah-mogk ("Quiet Waters") by Native Americans. A sawmill was begun in 1866 and operated until 1882, at which time mill operations were moved to Port Hadlock farther north on the canal.

Just 2 miles beyond town is Scenic Beach State Park, which was the homestead of Joe Emel Sr., before becoming a state park. Now Emel House, home of the Seabeck Community Club, sits between a grassy lawn and a bluff overlooking a pebbly beach. Colorful gardens and lush forest surround it. Across the canal, close enough to chart a climbing path, the stunning Olympic peaks loom. It's a quiet place for viewing wildlife and sea life or simply contemplating two of Washington's finest natural wonders: salt water and craggy mountains.

Scenic Beach is a peaceful place for a stroll.

Reluctantly depart Scenic Beach by returning through Seabeck. The return route tackles imposing NW Anderson Hill Road, so get ready for repeated climbs in the first few miles beyond Seabeck, which moderate as you get closer to Silverdale. (To avoid the impressive hills that must be climbed, you could retrace the outbound route instead.)

At Silverdale, a comfort stop can be taken at Old Mill Park, a roadside county park marking the north edge of the inlet. The tour's last leg takes you south on a mostly flat ride along Puget Sound on the east side of Dyes Inlet through the Tracyton community, along a road signed as a Blue Star Memorial Highway route. These highways, designated throughout the country since World War II, are dedicated to men and women who served in our armed forces. The blue star refers to the star on the flag of the armed services. Often the roads have been chosen for their scenic nature, and this one lives up to the designation.

End the tour by crossing the Manette Bridge into downtown Bremerton.

Route Connections: Take the foot ferry from Bremerton to Port Orchard for that ride (Tour 29) or head north along the coast to the Bainbridge ferry (Tour 33, ridden in reverse).

MILEAGE LOG

0.0 Exit ferry dock onto Washington Ave.

0.3 Left onto 4th St.

1.4 Left onto Naval Ave., then right in 2 blocks onto Burwell St.

1.7 Right onto Montgomery Ave.

2.0 Left onto 9th St., then in 1 block right onto Callow Ave.

2.2 Left onto 11th St.

2.3 Right onto Kitsap Wy./SR 310.

3.6 Cross under SR 3; continue forward.

5.3 Left onto Northlake Wy. NW. Caution: busy intersection; use left turn lane.

6.5 Left at Y onto Seabeck Hwy. NW. Caution: railroad tracks with bad angle just ahead.

7.5 Pass Mountaineers Forest Theater on right.

11.7 Cross intersection with NW Newberry Hill Rd.; service station on right.

12.5 Pass intersection with NW Anderson Hill Rd.

16.6 Arrive at Seabeck.

17.2 Right onto Miami Beach Rd. NW.

17.5 Stay right at Y with Seaview Dr.

18.1 Left onto Scenic Beach Rd. NW.

18.2 Stay right at Y with NW Stavits Bay Rd.

18.6 Arrive at Scenic Beach State Park (restrooms). Take first left to Emel House.

18.8 Arrive at Emel House parking. Retrace route to return.

20.5 Left to rejoin Seabeck Hwy. NW.

24.0 Left onto NW Anderson Hill Rd.

28.3 At roundabout just beyond SR 3 underpass, continue on NW Anderson Hill Rd. toward Silverdale.

28.6 Left onto NW Bucklin Hill Rd.

29.1 Arrive at Kitsap County's Old Mill Park (restrooms).

29.8 Right onto Tracyton Blvd. NW.

33.7 Right to stay on Tracyton Blvd., which becomes Tracyton Beach Rd. NW, then Lebo Blvd., then Campbell Wy.

35.6 Right onto Wheaton Wy.

36.6 Right onto Manette Bridge to downtown Bremerton.

36.8 Left onto Washington Ave.

36.9 Right onto Burwell St. In 1 block, left on Pacific Ave.

37.1 Arrive at ferry dock to end tour.

31 Bainbridge Island Loop

DIFFICULTY: challenging
TIME: allow 4 hours
DISTANCE: 33.9 miles
ELEVATION GAIN: 2230 feet

Getting There: From I-5 southbound, take exit 164 (northbound, exit 164B) and follow signs to Washington State Ferries' Colman Dock at Pier 52. No parking at ferry terminal; park in paid lots or at on-street meters.

GPS Coordinates: N47 36 10 W122 20 20
Transit: Multiple bus lines

You know Bainbridge is bike-friendly as you pedal from the ferry to begin the tour. Kitsap Transit's Bainbridge Island Bike Barn, adjacent to the ferry terminal, offers a number of covered, secure storage units for commuter bicycles as well as some personal-size lockers. Green bike-route signs placed regularly along the island roads are another clue. Along the tree-covered lanes and beach drives of Bainbridge Island, you'll see a purely Northwest amalgam: a family-centered lifestyle embracing the natural world, in a setting that doesn't get much more ideal.

This tour, which mostly paces the route used for the annual February cycling event known as the "Chilly Hilly," traces the eastern curves of the island and heads north, but you'll get only occasional glimpses of the water as you pedal toward Fay Bainbridge State Park, a great place for the first break. The park lies at the northeasternmost point of the island. Welcoming you is the Port Madison Bell, brought from San Francisco in 1883 to be used as a "town crier" for the area, which was then a booming sawmill and shipbuilding area. There are restrooms, picnic tables, and many bleached-white driftwood logs on which to contemplate the waves and the view of Seattle. You'll see the green swaths of Discovery Park, Golden Gardens Park, and Carkeek Park, with a low point in between where lie the Ballard locks and Shilshole Bay.

Cut across the northern end of the island, past Madison Bay toward Agate Pass. As you turn west, the corner of Phelps Road NE and Madison

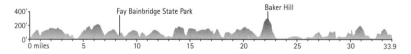

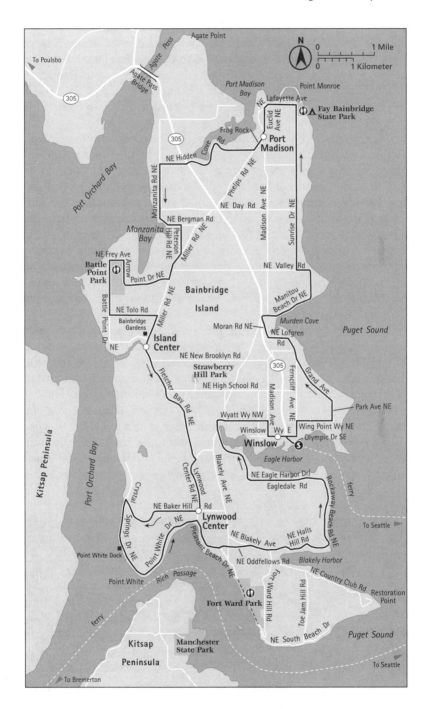

To Poulsbo

Agate Point

305

Agate Pass

Agate Pass Bridge

Port Madison Bay

Point Monroe

Lafayette Ave

NE Lafayette Ave

Fay Bainbridge State Park

Euclid Ave NE

Frog Rock

305

Cove Rd

NE Hidden

Port Madison

Phelps Rd NE

Manzanita Rd NE

NE Day Rd

Madison Ave NE

Sunrise Dr NE

NE Bergman Rd

Manzanita Bay

Peterson Hill Rd NE

Miller Rd NE

NE Valley Rd

NE Frey Ave

Battle Point Park

Arrow Point Dr NE

Bainbridge Island

Manitou Beach Dr NE

Murden Cove

Puget Sound

NE Tolo Rd

Miller Rd NE

Moran Rd NE

NE Lofgren Rd

Battle Point Dr NE

Bainbridge Gardens

Island Center

NE

NE New Brooklyn Rd

305

Ferncliff Ave NE

Grand Ave

Park Ave NE

Strawberry Hill Park

NE High School Rd

Fletcher Bay Rd NE

Wyatt Wy NW

Madison Ave NE

Wing Point Wy NE

Kitsap Peninsula

Winslow

Wy E

Olympic Dr SE

Winslow

Port Orchard Bay

Eagle Harbor

NE Eagle Harbor Dr

Blakely Ave NE

Eagledale Rd

Lynwood Center Rd NE

Rockaway Beach Rd NE

ferry

To Seattle

Crystal Springs Dr NE

NE Baker Hill Rd

Lynwood Center

Point White Dr NE

Pleasant Beach Dr NE

NE Blakely Ave

NE Halls Hill Rd

Point White Dock

NE Oddfellows Rd

Blakely Harbor

NE Country Club Rd

Restoration Point

Point White

Rich Passage

Fort Ward Hill Rd

Toe Jam Hill Rd

ferry

Fort Ward Park

NE South Beach Dr

Puget Sound

Kitsap Peninsula

Manchester State Park

To Bremerton

To Seattle

N

0   1 Mile
0   1 Kilometer

Avenue NE offers a locally famous landmark. Nestled at the base of the trees is "Frog Rock," which looks like two stacked boulders with a crease across the middle. Locals keep the rock covered in frog-green paint, sporting big eyes and a bright red mouth formed by the crease. A smaller rock, painted like a ladybug, is its companion. Cyclists use it as a regrouping point.

Carefully cross busy State Route 305, which connects Winslow with the Agate Pass Bridge and the Kitsap Peninsula, then turn south and you're riding roughly along the island's western edge. Skirt Manzanita Bay and conquer the roller-coaster hills leading to Battle Point Park, another welcome rest stop with sheltered picnic areas and playfields.

Back on Miller Road NE, watch for Bainbridge Gardens on the right as you head downhill toward Lynwood Center Road. There's a cute espresso shop with light café fare nestled among the big trees, along with plants for sale. A few steps away is a pair of pear trees pruned into a heart shape as a symbol of the Japanese-American owner's feeling toward the island residents, who welcomed them back after internment during World War II.

From here, you could turn inland past Island Center for a quick return to Winslow if you want to cut the ride shorter. To do this, turn left onto NE New Brooklyn Road, then make a right on Madison Avenue NE, which leads to Winslow Way. But this tour continues to the south part of the island, offering a few alluring sights and one more hilly challenge.

Lynwood Center Road NE leads to NE Baker Hill Road, which is one of the most difficult big climbs of Bainbridge, worth the effort because of the wonderful western waterfront riding along Point White beyond. If you've had enough of big hills, skip the climb and still get the beach ride by continuing south to the Lynwood Center shopping area and,

Frog Rock is a popular place for cyclists to regroup.

just before the business strip, make a right onto Point White Drive NE, ride out to the Point White Dock, and return. In either case, cross back east across the island at Lynwood Center, skipping the very southernmost points of the island. Skirt the south edge of IslandWood, an incredible nonprofit environmental learning center, then ride through a hilly neighborhood on the island's east edge before reentering Winslow via Eagle Harbor.

Route Connections: Head west over the Agate Pass Bridge to ride south to the Bremerton ferry (Tour 33) or north off the bridge to the Kingston ferry (Tour 34) or Port Gamble and Poulsbo (Tour 36). You can also join this tour with the ride south to Fort Ward (Tour 32).

MILEAGE LOG

0.0 Exit ferry dock onto Olympic Dr. SE.

0.2 Right onto Winslow Wy. E.

0.4 Left onto Ferncliff Ave. NE.

0.6 Right onto Wing Point Wy. NE.

1.3 Left onto Park Ave. NE, which becomes Grand Ave.

2.6 Right onto Ferncliff Ave. NE, which becomes NE Lofgren Rd.

3.3 Curve right to join Moran Rd. NE.

3.8 Right onto Manitou Beach Dr. NE when parallel to SR 305.

3.9 Take right fork in road to stay on Manitou Beach Dr. NE.

4.5 Left onto Falk Rd. NE.

5.1 Left onto NE Valley Rd.

5.3 Right onto Sunrise Dr. NE.

8.1 Right into Fay Bainbridge State Park.

8.5 Arrive at parking area and beach (restrooms, water). Retrace route to road.

8.9 Exit park by turning right onto Sunrise Dr. NE, which curves left to become NE Lafayette Ave.

9.4 Left onto Euclid Ave. NE.

9.9 Left onto Phelps Rd. NE.

10.1 Pass by "Frog Rock," at intersection of Phelps and Madison Ave. NE.

10.4 Right onto NE Hidden Cove Rd.

11.6 Cross SR 305. Caution: traffic at highway speeds.

12.0 Left onto Manzanita Rd. NE, which becomes Doris Ave. NE, then NE Bergman Rd.

13.3 Right onto Peterson Hill Rd. NE.

13.7 Right onto Miller Rd. NE.

14.3 Right onto Arrow Point Dr. NE, which curves north.

15.3 Arrive at Battle Point Park (restrooms, water).

15.4 Exit park by turning left onto Arrow Point Dr. NE.

15.8 Left onto NE Frey Ave.

16.1 Left onto Battle Point Dr. NE.

17.0 Left onto NE Tolo Rd.

17.8 Right onto Miller Rd. NE, which becomes Fletcher Bay Rd. NE.

20.5 Right onto Lynwood Center Rd. NE.

21.4 Right onto NE Baker Hill Rd.

23.0 Left onto Crystal Springs Dr. NE. Caution: stop sign at end of descent.

23.7 Arrive at Point White Dock. Past southern tip of Point White, road becomes Point White Dr. NE.

25.9 Right onto Pleasant Beach Dr. NE.

26.6 Left onto NE Oddfellows Rd.

27.2 Merge right onto NE Blakely Ave.

27.9 At 5-way intersection, go straight across and uphill onto NE Halls Hill Rd., which becomes Rockaway Beach Rd. NE, then NE Eagle Harbor Dr./Eagledale Rd.

32.3 Road curves right and becomes Wyatt Wy. NW.

32.9 Right onto Grow Ave. NW.

33.1 Left onto Winslow Wy. E.

33.7 Right onto Olympic Dr. SE toward ferry dock.

33.9 Arrive at ferry dock to end tour.

32 Winslow to Fort Ward

DIFFICULTY: moderate
TIME: allow 2.5 hours
DISTANCE: 19.7 miles
ELEVATION GAIN: 1193 feet

Getting There: From I-5 southbound, take exit 164 (northbound, exit 164B) and follow signs to Washington State Ferries' Colman Dock at Pier 52. No parking at ferry terminal; park in paid lots or at on-street meters.
   GPS Coordinates: N47 36 10 W122 20 20
   Transit: Multiple bus lines

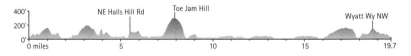

*It's worth a stop to see bikes from many eras in the bicycle museum at
Classic Cycle in downtown Winslow.*

Tackling the entire length and breadth of Bainbridge Island is a full-day
affair suitable for strong legs and lungs, but a jaunt around the island's
south end can be handled with much less time and effort. However, its
challenges are still best met by a cyclist with at least moderate experience
and the ability to take on a half-dozen decent climbs. This tour explores
the island's southern waterfront areas and offers views of Rich Passage,
Bremerton, and the verdant hills of the Kitsap Peninsula beyond. It's a
great summer morning's ride to be followed by lunch in Winslow and a
visit to view the many historic bicycles on display at the local bike shop.

Cycle in and out of Winslow via Wyatt Way NW. The outbound route
reverses the full island tour (see Tour 31) by heading south along NE
Eagle Harbor Drive/Eagledale Road and the island's eastern edge. Here,
stylish houses crowd the bluffs above the bay, offering only glimpses
of their million-dollar views of Seattle. Prepare for an abrupt and steep
hill climb, which comes quickly as Rockaway Beach Road NE turns
west and becomes NE Halls Hill Road.

Although you don't see it, you're cycling around the inlet of Blakely
Harbor before heading toward South Beach, first by climbing Country
Club Road, then by screaming down Toe Jam Hill Road. Prepare for

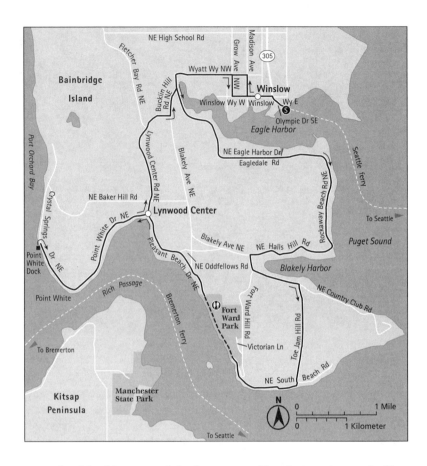

some hard braking toward the bottom, and be glad you're not huffing up this curving, wooded grade.

At the bottom of the hill lies South Beach, and you're rewarded with a waterfront spin at the island's southernmost point. First you're waterside, and the modest homes that brave this briny face are to your right. Then the road jogs up half a block, and the houses sit between you and the water. Soon you arrive at the ramparts of Fort Ward, accessed via a short gravel connector.

Fort Ward displays the remains of Battery Vinton, one of the four gun batteries installed at the fort at the end of the 1800s. The plan was to protect the Bremerton Naval Shipyard from enemy ships with forts that began farther north, at Port Townsend and Whidbey Island. Fort Ward was a second line of defense. The water of Rich Passage beyond, which contained an underwater minefield, was the third protection.

From the boat dock and picnic area in Fort Ward State Park, pause to look across the demined Rich Passage to the greenery of Manchester State Park, the site of the fourth gun battery. Just south of it, the US Navy's fuel depot at Orchard Point is visible. Picturing the Bremerton ferry that navigates this narrow passage as an enemy frigate, it's easy to see how such a ship would be a sitting duck from gun batteries on each side and mines lurking below.

The guns were never used against an enemy, however, and were removed from Fort Ward and sent to France, expected to be needed in World War I. Along with Forts Casey, Flagler, and Worden, and some ruins at Manchester, Fort Ward sits as a reminder that preparation is the best defense.

A short road, closed to car traffic, cuts through the west edge of Fort Ward, near the shoreline, then exits onto Pleasant Beach Drive NE as you head north toward Lynwood Center. Another look at waterfront living is afforded with an out-and-back ride to Point White Dock, a public fishing area on the island's southwest edge. The flat road hugs the coastline, providing great views across to Bremerton; stately homes face the road and water. The tour concludes by climbing Bucklin Hill Road, dropping back to Eagle Harbor, and then rising again into Winslow.

Route Connections: Loop the entire island (Tour 31) or head north from Winslow to the Agate Pass Bridge to ride south to the Bremerton ferry (Tour 33) or north to the Kingston Ferry (Tour 34) or Port Gamble and Poulsbo (Tour 36).

MILEAGE LOG

0.0 Exit ferry dock onto Olympic Dr. SE.

0.2 Left onto Winslow Wy. W.

0.5 Right onto Madison Ave.

0.8 Left onto Wyatt Wy. NW, which becomes NE Eagle Harbor Dr. as it curves left.

1.9 Merge into left lane; turn left at Y to stay on NE Eagle Harbor Dr./Eagledale Rd. Caution: congested area, busy road with fast downhill traffic.

4.3 NE Eagle Harbor Dr. becomes Rockaway Beach Rd. NE, which becomes NE Halls Hill Rd.

6.5 Left onto NE Country Club Rd.

7.3 Right onto Toe Jam Hill Rd. Caution: steep downhill; use moderate speed.

8.5 Curve right onto NE South Beach Dr.

9.4 At intersection with Fort Ward Hill Rd., go straight into waterfront housing development.

9.5 At street end, go straight onto brief gravel road into park, then left onto paved park road.

9.8 Arrive at Fort Ward Park picnic area (restrooms).

10.4 Exit park onto Pleasant Beach Dr. NE.

10.8 Stay left at Y with Blakely Ave. NE to continue on Pleasant Beach Dr. NE.

11.0 Left to stay on Pleasant Beach Dr. NE at intersection with NE Oddfellows Rd.

11.7 Left onto Point White Dr. NE.

13.9 Arrive at Point White Dock. Reverse route to return to Lynwood Center.

16.1 Left onto Lynwood Center Rd. NE.

17.4 Merge right onto Bucklin Hill Rd. NE at stop sign.

17.5 Left at stop sign to continue on Bucklin Hill Rd. NE.

17.9 Merge left onto NE Eagle Harbor Dr. Caution: busy intersection.

18.1 Curve right, then road becomes Wyatt Wy. NW.

18.7 Right onto Grow Ave. NW.

19.0 Left onto Winslow Wy. W.

19.5 Right onto Olympic Dr. SE to ferry.

19.7 Arrive at ferry dock to end tour.

33 Bainbridge Ferry to Bremerton Ferry

DIFFICULTY: challenging
TIME: allow 4 hours
DISTANCE: 32 miles
ELEVATION GAIN: 2234 feet

Getting There: From I-5 southbound, take exit 164 (northbound, exit 164B) and follow signs to Washington State Ferries' Colman Dock at Pier 52. No parking at ferry terminal; park in paid lots or at on-street meters.
  GPS Coordinates: N47 36 10 W122 20 20
  Transit: Multiple bus lines

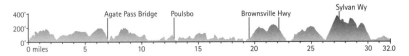

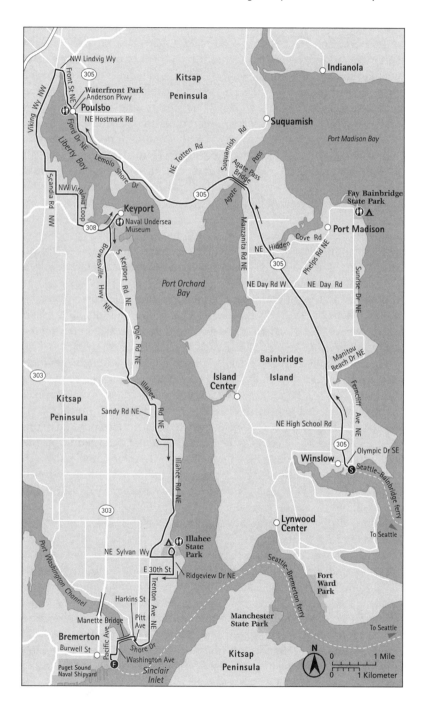

As you sail across the calm waters of Elliott Bay on the ferry to Bainbridge Island, consider the maritime activity and heritage of our region. On Puget Sound, many thousands of people move around for work and recreation every day, as they have done since the first Native American tribes plied the waters with canoes, fishing and trading, later to be joined by immigrants who brought their own maritime traditions. In today's interconnected society, the shipping lanes of the Salish Sea provide a strategic link to Pacific Rim countries. Along with all this activity, Northwest waterways and ports have been monitored and protected by the US Armed Forces for generations. This ride skirts the three major US Navy installations in the region and offers much history to explore.

Begin this ride by heading up-island to the Agate Pass Bridge via the main drag, State Route 305. I often recommend getting off the main roads, and there's a great route that skirts the island's edges and connects with State Route 305 near the bridge (see Tour 31). But sometimes a straight route is advisable, and in this case, it's easy, because State Route 305 is safe, with a generous shoulder, and much less hilly than the alternatives. Save the climbing and meandering for later in the route.

Once on the Kitsap Peninsula, climb a bit along the highway, then head west on side roads into Poulsbo. You might think you're docking your wheels at a fjord in Scandinavia, considering the snowcapped Olympic peaks that appear so close across Liberty Bay from the quiet, scenic harbor. That concept is reinforced by the painted ships and nautical village themes visible along the town's main drag. The Nordic people who settled here obviously found an affinity with their homeland.

Turn south on Viking Way NW and head to Keyport, the first of two stops where you can steep yourself in navy history. You might not realize it, but along the way you will be skirting the edge of the most imposing of the area's three naval stations: Naval Base Kitsap Bangor. Nuclear-powered submarines ply the waters at Bangor.

If that piques your interest, you're in luck, because the next stop is the Naval Undersea Museum at the Undersea Warfare Center in Keyport. Head toward Keyport on quiet Scandia Road, through a small, farm-focused river valley. After a challenging climb out of the valley, coast into Keyport to the modern, free museum. Exhibits include submarine and weapons technology, as well as a diving and salvage focus. A local bike group meets up Sundays in the museum's expansive parking lot, which is flanked by two imposing white deep-sea vehicles and the sail of the nuclear submarine USS *Sturgeon.*

The sail of a nuclear submarine guards the entrance to the Naval Undersea Museum at Keyport.

Take a brief side trip to check out the tiny marina at Keyport, and then head south along the western edge of Port Orchard Bay toward Bremerton. The tour continues down Brownsville Highway NE and Illahee Road NE, but if you want a bit more climbing and views east, turn onto South Keyport Road and continue on Ogle Road NE. A small grocery fronts the serene bay where Brownsville meets Illahee, but otherwise there are no services on this stretch. Settle in for a long, steady climb as Illahee becomes Trenton Avenue.

One last stop before Bremerton is Illahee State Park, situated at the base of the hills facing Bainbridge Island. Two big guns from the USS *West Virginia* angled toward the forest mark the park's entrance, along with a plaque honoring Earl Henry Harkins, a shipyard worker and Bremerton booster who was the park's first caretaker and also an appointed commissioner on the state parks and recreation board.

Finally, arrive at Bremerton, Kitsap County's largest city and home to Naval Base Kitsap Bremerton. Cycle down to the water across from the city center and follow a narrow one-way road to the recently built Manette Bridge. Cross the concrete structure on its bike lane or ample pedestrian walkway, then turn left into downtown. This city bleeds navy gray, and you will see it writ large on the left as you enter the city. The Vietnam-era destroyer USS *Turner Joy* is docked here as a museum ship, open for tours and even for overnight stays.

As your last stop, learn all about the navy's great influence on the area at the Puget Sound Navy Museum, situated in a stately building between the ferry dock and a delightful water-focused park. Announcing the museum is the sail of the USS *Parche,* which museum information calls "the most decorated ship in the history of the US Navy." Painted symbols and letters cover the large black tower of the ship, which conducted secret "special operations" between 1976 and 2004. Inside the free museum, you'll learn (in general) about the navy's special operations submarines, why they are silent, secret, and important. An interactive exhibit shows life aboard an aircraft carrier, and a shipyard exhibit explains that hundreds of navy ships were built here, beginning in the 1890s and continuing to the 1960s.

A diorama shows the layout of the shipyard, which stretches west along Sinclair Inlet from the ferry landing. In 1939 there were 6000 workers in the shipyard, but during World War II that number swelled to more than 32,000, who worked outfitting and modernizing more than 400 ships. Modernizing aircraft carriers was the shipyard's most important postwar job, and that work continued until 1960.

It's only fitting, after all this navy lore, to get back on a ship for the ride home. As you glide onto the ferry, give a "tip of the helmet" to our seafaring soldiers.

Route Connections: From Bremerton, take the foot ferry to Port Orchard (Tour 29) or ride out to Seabeck (Tour 30), or, before leaving Bainbridge, loop the island (Tour 31) or ride south to Fort Ward (Tour 32).

MILEAGE LOG

0.0 Exit Bainbridge ferry dock onto Olympic Dr. SE.

0.2 At stoplight, continue straight on SR 305.

1.0 Cross NE High School Rd., which heads west.

2.3 Cross Manitou Beach Dr. NE, which heads east.

5.3 Cross NE Hidden Cove Rd., which heads east to Fay Bainbridge State Park.

6.8 Cross Agate Pass Bridge. Caution: travel in car lane.

7.2 Cross Suquamish Rd., which heads north toward Kingston (Tour 34).

8.8 Left onto Lemolo Shore Dr. Caution: fast traffic.

11.2 Lemolo Shore Dr. becomes Fjord Dr. NE as you enter town.

11.9 Left onto NE Hostmark Rd., which curves right and becomes Front St. NE.

12.1 Left onto Anderson Pkwy. in downtown Poulsbo.

12.2 Arrive at Waterfront Park (restrooms). Return to Front St. NE to continue.

12.3 Left on Front St. NE.

13.1 Left onto NW Lindvig Wy.

13.4 Left onto Viking Wy. NW. Caution: double-turn lane.

15.6 Left onto Scandia Rd. NW.

16.4 Left onto NW Virginia Loop Rd.

17.6 Left onto SR 308.

18.5 Arrive at Naval Undersea Museum (restrooms) at Keyport.

18.6 Left onto Washington Ave.

18.7 Arrive at Keyport waterfront (grocery-deli). Retrace route to leave town.

19.2 Left onto Brownsville Hwy. NE.

19.9 Cross S. Keyport Rd. NE.

22.8 Left onto Illahee Rd. NE.

23.5 Curve left at intersection with Sandy Rd. NE to stay on Illahee. In 1 block, Illahee curves right.

24.8 Pass Breakwater Point.

27.3 Illahee becomes Trenton Ave. NE.

27.4 Left onto NE Sylvan Wy.

27.9 Left into Illahee State Park (restrooms).

28.0 Exit park straight onto Ridgeview Dr. NE.

28.4 Ridgeview curves right and becomes E. 30th St. Gear down for short, steep climb.

28.9 Left onto Trenton Ave. NE. Caution: cross-traffic does not stop.

30.5 Right onto Shore Dr. at Bachman Park as Trenton ends. As road splits, take center, one-way lane.

31.0 Right onto E. 10th St. In 1 block, left onto Pitt Ave.

31.2 Left onto Harkins St. In 1 block, right around the roundabout and forward onto Manette Bridge.

31.5 Left onto Washington Ave.

31.8 Right onto Burwell St.

31.9 Left onto Pacific Ave.

32.0 Arrive at Bremerton ferry dock to end tour.

34 Bainbridge Ferry to Kingston Ferry

DIFFICULTY: moderate
TIME: allow 2.5 hours
DISTANCE: 21 miles
ELEVATION GAIN: 1380 feet

Getting There: From I-5 southbound, take exit 164 (northbound, exit 164B) and follow signs to Washington State Ferries' Colman Dock at Pier 52. No parking at ferry terminal; park in paid lots or at on-street meters.
 GPS Coordinates: N47 36 10 W122 20 20
Transit: Multiple bus lines

The big ferry to Bainbridge Island is the jumping-off point for a great many adventures on the Kitsap and Olympic peninsulas, such as hiking or camping at destinations like Hurricane Ridge or the Hoh Rain Forest. But delights lie much closer, too: multiple choices await the cyclists who queue up at Colman Dock in Seattle. From this central point in Kitsap County, three out of the four cardinal compass points aim you toward fun.

This tour connects you to the next ferry north—the Kingston-to-Edmonds run—and a couple of other great rides on the north Kitsap Peninsula. And with another ferry dock as your destination, you can cross back over and loop back to the city on the second leg of your ride.

Start with a modified diversion up the northeast side of the island, taking rural roads to Fay Bainbridge State Park (worth a stop if you're not in a hurry—and you shouldn't be). Cut west after the park and connect with State Route 305 in 3 miles. In another 2 miles you're taking over a lane on the Agate Pass Bridge, then you're off the island and onto the Kitsap Peninsula.

Take your first right, toward Suquamish, where you again should take a break and visit the renovated gravesite of Chief Noah Sealth, for whom Washington's largest city was named (albeit with an Anglicized spelling). The Suquamish tribe, with support from the City of Seattle, has created a colorful interpretive plaza around the grave. Just downhill from the cemetery, the tribe has erected connected totem poles in

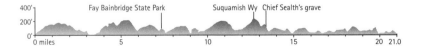

Exit Bainbridge Island via the Agate Pass Bridge on your way to Kingston.

a dignified plaza with flags and plaques honoring the Suquamish people who served in the armed forces.

A climb and some rolling hills along Miller Bay take you into Kingston, where this route guides you back to the ferry dock. But to continue exploring, see the Route Connections that follow.

Route Connections: Continue straight on Miller Bay Rd. to State Route 104 at Kingston Crossing, where you could continue north to Point No Point (Tour 35). Or you could turn left onto State Route 104 and head to Port Gamble, the Hood Canal Bridge, and Port Townsend beyond (Tour 37) or to Poulsbo (Tour 36). If you're ready for another ferry ride, head back across Puget Sound to Edmonds, and then connect with the Interurban Trail north to Mukilteo (Tour 50) or south to Green Lake in Seattle (Tour 5).

MILEAGE LOG

0.0 Exit Bainbridge ferry dock onto Olympic Dr. SE.

0.2 Right onto Winslow Wy. E.

0.4 Left onto Ferncliff Ave. NE, which becomes NE Lofgren Rd.

2.4 Curve right to join Moran Rd. NE.

2.9 Right onto Manitou Beach Dr. NE when parallel to SR 305.

3.5 Left onto Falk Rd. NE.

To Port Gamble 104

104

NE West Kingston Rd

Kingston

To Edmonds

F

Central Ave

South Kingston Rd NE

Edmonds–Kingston ferry

307

To Poulsbo

Kitsap

Peninsula

Miller Bay Rd NE

Miller Bay

Indianola

Augusta Ave NE

Chief Sealth's grave

Division Ave NE

Suquamish

NE South St

Suquamish Wy NE

To Poulsbo

NE Totten Rd

Agate Pass

Agate Pass Bridge

Port Madison Bay

305

Agate

305

NE Lafayette Ave

Fay Bainbridge
State Park

Euclid Ave NE

NE Hidden
Cove Rd

Phelps Rd NE

Sunrise Dr NE

Port Orchard
Bay

Puget Sound

NE Valley Rd

Bainbridge

Island

Manitou Beach Dr NE

Moran Rd NE

NE Lofgren
Rd

Ferncliff Ave NE

305

Winslow

Winslow Wy E

S

Seattle–Bainbridge ferry

To Seattle

N

0   1 Mile

0   1 Kilometer

4.1 Left onto NE Valley Rd.
4.4 Right onto Sunrise Dr. NE.
7.1 Pass Fay Bainbridge State Park (restrooms) on right.
7.2 Left onto NE Lafayette Ave.
7.8 Left onto Euclid Ave. NE.
8.2 Left onto Phelps Rd. NE.
8.5 Right onto NE Hidden Cove Rd.
10.0 Right onto SR 305 northbound.
11.6 Cross Agate Pass Bridge. Caution: no bike lane, ride with vehicles.
12.0 Right onto Suquamish Wy. NE.
13.3 Left onto Division Ave. NE.
13.4 Right onto NE South St.
13.5 Pass cemetery with Chief Sealth's grave.
13.6 Left onto Suquamish Wy. NE.
13.7 Stay on Suquamish as it curves left and becomes Augusta Ave.
       NE, which becomes Miller Bay Rd. NE.
18.7 Right onto NE West Kingston Rd.
20.3 Left at Y to continue on NE West Kingston Rd. into town.
20.9 Right onto Central Ave.
21.0 Left at parking by Kingston ferry dock to end tour.

35 Point No Point and Little Boston

DIFFICULTY: moderate
TIME: allow 3 hours
DISTANCE: 27.9 miles
ELEVATION GAIN: 1529 feet

Getting There: From I-5, take exit 177, Edmonds, and proceed west on SR 104. Continue on SR 104, which becomes Edmonds Wy. Follow signs to parking at Washington State Ferries dock, or choose day parking at fringes of downtown Edmonds and cycle to ferry.
   GPS Coordinates: N47 48 46 W122 23 00
   Transit: Community Transit 110, 116, 130, 196, 416

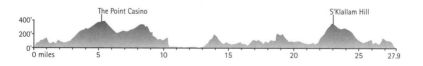

The lighthouse at Point No Point

This spin out to Point No Point Lighthouse from Kingston provides some moderate challenges and interesting sights in a fairly short ride. It's a good option if your group gets a late start at the ferry or if you want to combine a Kitsap Peninsula ride with a city ride, such as Green Lake to Edmonds (Tour 5).

Begin and end in friendly, accessible Kingston, which offers a variety of shops, cafés, and pubs, as well as a lively Saturday morning farmers market in the park adjacent to the ferry dock. If you're aiming for a picnic lunch at the beach by the lighthouse, you can carry it from Kingston, stop at the grocery at Kingston Crossing as you turn north toward Hansville, or pick up deli sandwiches at the small grocery in Hansville.

The Hansville Road offers rolling hills and pleasant scenery of farms, forests, and a couple small lakes, but the country idyll is marred by lack of shoulder on its northern half and a fairly steady stream of vehicles, including the occasional gravel truck or semi. You pass the Point Casino, operated by the S'Klallam tribe, whose community center you'll ride through on the return leg. Other roadside attractions include Buck Lake County Park and the young vines of the Hansville Hill Vineyard.

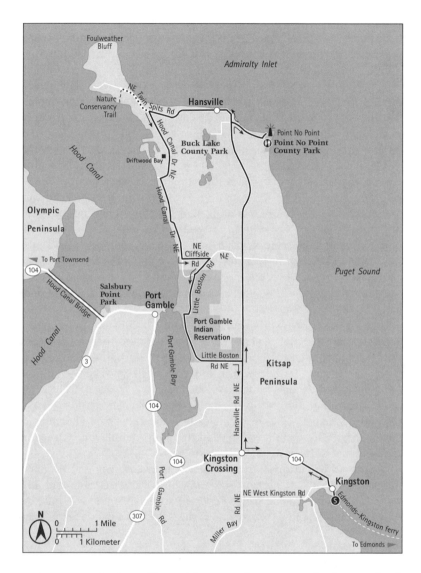

As you reach Hansville, a right turn takes you a mile down a dead-end road to the lighthouse and beach at Point No Point County Park. Continue a few hundred yards past the turn to shop at the modest Hansville grocery.

The small, well-maintained Point No Point Lighthouse, white with red trim and roofs, looks over a curving point on Puget Sound that is a popular fishing destination, both for casting from the beach and from boats moored offshore. Trails take you through the scrubby beach vegetation to explore the county park. Whidbey Island is visible across Admiralty Inlet.

Continuing around this northern tip of the Kitsap Peninsula, churn through the roller-coaster hills west of Hansville. A short detour up NE Twin Spits Road takes you to the Nature Conservancy property near Foulweather Bluff, where a half-mile trail hike on the left in a quarter mile leads to a stunning beach. Then ride south, through the "covenanted" community of Driftwood Bay and the houses overlooking Hood Canal Bridge at Cliffside before coming to Little Boston.

Plan some time for a visit with the S'Klallams, who have an extensive community center complex here at Port Gamble Indian Reservation. A grand longhouse boasts four carved totem poles depicting traditional tribal activities, as well as massive 12-foot-tall doors carved with tribal history that slide to open the cavernous space for gatherings and events. A popular time to ride this tour is the weekend in mid-September when the tribe hosts S'Klallam Days, which has traditional dancing, crafts, and food.

Does it seem strange that the center of a Washington Indian reservation is named Little Boston? Early settlers found that the adjacent waterway reminded them so much of Boston Harbor, they named it such, and it stuck. Here, however, you're more likely to be served wild rice than baked beans with your smoked salmon.

This short but interesting loop holds one challenge on the return to Kingston: S'Klallam Hill. A long, steady grade keeps you churning as you head back toward Hansville Road. Topping the hill, you retrace the remaining route to downtown Kingston.

Route Connections: From Kingston Crossing, go west on State Route 104 to Port Gamble, Poulsbo and Chief Sealth's Grave (Tour 36), or cross the Hood Canal Bridge beyond Port Gamble and continue on to Port Townsend (Tour 37). Or ride to the Bainbridge Island ferry (Tour 34, in reverse).

MILEAGE LOG

0.0 Depart ferry dock onto Kingston Rd.
0.5 Stay right to continue out of Kingston west on SR 104.
2.7 Right onto Hansville Rd. NE at Kingston Crossing.
4.7 Pass intersection with Little Boston Rd NE.
5.0 Pass the Point Casino.
9.1 Pass Hansville Hill Vineyard.
9.7 Arrive at Hansville.

10.5 Right onto NE Point No Point Rd.
11.5 Arrive at Point No Point County Park (restrooms) and lighthouse. Retrace route to main road.
12.7 Right to continue north on Hansville Rd. NE, which curves west and becomes NE Twin Spits Rd.
15.0 Left onto Hood Canal Dr. NE. (Continue straight ahead for side trip to Foulweather Bluff.)
15.7 Arrive at Driftwood Bay.
16.8 Left at stop sign to stay on Hood Canal Dr. NE.
17.8 Caution: road drops and curves, then heads sharply uphill.
18.9 Left onto NE Cliffside Rd. Caution: steep climb.
19.5 Right onto Little Boston Rd. NE.
21.0 Arrive at S'Klallam Tribe's community center and longhouse.
22.3 Road curves and begins long climb east.
23.2 Right onto Hansville Rd. NE.
25.4 Left onto SR 104 at Kingston Crossing.
27.9 Arrive at ferry dock to end tour.

36 Port Gamble, Poulsbo, and Chief Sealth's Grave

DIFFICULTY: moderate
TIME: allow 3.5 hours
DISTANCE: 33.4 miles
ELEVATION GAIN: 1789 feet

Getting There: From I-5, take exit 177, Edmonds, and proceed west on SR 104. Continue on SR 104, which becomes Edmonds Wy. Follow signs to parking at Washington State Ferries dock, or choose day parking at fringes of downtown Edmonds and cycle to ferry.
   GPS Coordinates: N47 48 46 W122 23 00
   Transit: Community Transit 110, 116, 130, 196, 416

Gain a great historic perspective on early settlement of the area in this 33-mile ride that loops west and south from Kingston, a short ferry

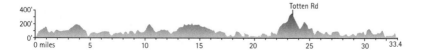

The grave of Chief Sealth stands proudly in the small cemetery at Suquamish.

ride across Puget Sound from Edmonds. Travel through rolling hills to small but significant port towns, including an early logging town, a Scandinavian invasion, and the last resting place of a great Native American chief.

Begin the tour on the adequate shoulder of State Route 104 heading west toward the Hood Canal Bridge. First stop is Port Gamble, just before the bridge. Cycle past well-kept Victorian homes as you enter town, and continue straight into its small town center as the road curves left. Nearly all the shops are visible from the turn, as the town extends less than two blocks to the hills overlooking the bay. Within those few blocks, however, sits a miniature history of area settlement.

Port Gamble is and always has been a mill town. Like many small towns along Hood Canal, it served the lumber barons who fed an insatiable appetite for wood by settlers flocking to western cities. Pioneer lumbermen Andrew Pope and William Talbot came up from San Francisco looking for logging opportunities and created a company

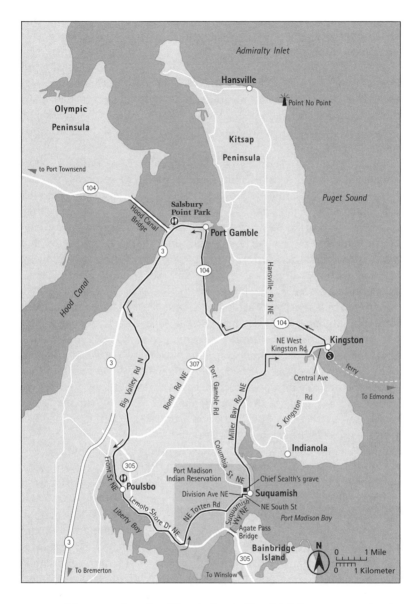

town at this strategic point. The timber mill, which began operating in the mid-1800s, was shut down in 1995.

What remains today is a town still wholly owned by Pope and Talbot, housing perhaps 100 residents. Economic efforts have turned to tourism, and the well-preserved town now has a row of antique shops to accompany its unique general store and an excellent historical museum. The Port Gamble General Store, dating from 1916, sells snacks, ice cream, and espresso, as well as a wide array of locally produced items. A recently expanded café beckons. Upstairs in the store is the free Of Sea and Shore Museum, which displays crabs, fish, shark teeth, and what claims to be the world's largest collection of seashells. The lower level of the store houses the historical museum, well worth its modest fee.

Adjacent to Port Gamble is Salsbury Point Park, which offers a great view of the essential Hood Canal Bridge. You can cross it to the Olympic Peninsula and Port Townsend (Tour 37), but to complete this ride, stay on the Kitsap side.

Head south to Poulsbo via State Route 3 and then Big Valley Road North, a quiet country highway with small horse farms, a few hay and cattle operations, and much less traffic than the main highway. Located at about halfway through the tour, Poulsbo is a great place for lunch and an extended break.

Poulsbo bills itself as "Washington's little Norway," a statement reinforced by a glance down its main street. The Poulsbohemian Coffee Shop reflects the droll wordplay for which Norwegians are famous. It shares the street with an imposing Sons of Norway lodge. Scandinavian flags vie with hanging baskets overflowing with flowers, and the storefronts are topped with wooden ships' peaks or the floral painted designs known as rosemaling. A Scandinavian bakery, grocery, gift shops, and cafés front a still and scenic harbor on Liberty Bay. This is the Poulsbo never viewed by travelers heading to Olympic National Park or other points west, because State Route 305 skirts the edge of town.

From Poulsbo, drop down along Liberty Bay before heading east, crossing busy State Route 305 just west of the Agate Pass Bridge that connects to Bainbridge Island. Follow the coastal road to Old Man House Park and the grave of Chief Sealth, the wise and welcoming Suquamish chief for whom Seattle is named. From behind the painted twin pillars standing vigil at his grave, you can see across Port Madison Bay to his namesake city. One block downhill, as you rejoin Suquamish Way NE, stop to admire the four totems, which guard plaques memorializing tribal members who served in the armed forces.

Climb inland from Suquamish and head north back to Kingston along Miller Bay Road NE, a busy thoroughfare with an intermittent cycling shoulder. End your ride in the comfortable bike lane on the last leg into Kingston, past two schools serving the expanding town.

Route Connections: Connect to Bainbridge Island via the Agate Pass Bridge to loop the island (Tour 31), visit its southern end (Tour 32), or just head to the Bainbridge ferry (Tour 34); ride north to Point No Point (Tour 35); or continue west to Port Townsend (Tour 37).

MILEAGE LOG

0.0 Exit ferry dock onto Kingston Rd.

0.5 Stay right to continue out of Kingston west on SR 104.

4.2 Stay right on SR 104 to continue to Port Gamble.

7.9 Arrive at Port Gamble.

8.2 Highway curves, but continue straight for 1 block to town center (restrooms) and Salsbury Point Park.

8.7 Return to SR 104 to continue.

9.5 Arrive at intersection where SR 104 continues west over Hood Canal Bridge; stay straight on SR 3. Caution: traffic at highway speeds, but good shoulder.

12.6 Left onto Big Valley Rd. N. Caution: busy crossing.

17.7 Right onto Bond Rd. NE.

17.9 Cross SR 305 at stoplight. Caution: busy crossing.

18.4 Left onto Front St. NE at Y with NW Lindvig Wy.

19.2 Right at intersection with Jensen Wy. NE to continue on Front St. NE into downtown Poulsbo.

19.3 Arrive at Waterfront Park (restrooms). To continue, return to Front St., which becomes Anderson Pkwy. as it leaves town.

19.4 Right onto Fjord Dr. NE, which becomes Lemolo Shore Dr. NE and, briefly, Peterson Wy. NE.

22.7 Cross SR 305, after which the road becomes NE Totten Rd. Caution: busy crossing.

25.0 Left onto Suquamish Wy. NE at Y where Totten ends.

25.8 Left onto Division Ave. NE.

25.9 Right onto NE South St.

26.0 Left into cemetery containing Chief Sealth's grave. Depart cemetery by turning left back onto South St.

26.1 Left onto Suquamish Wy. in 1 block.

26.2 Stay on Suquamish as it curves left and becomes Augusta Ave. NE, which becomes Miller Bay Rd. NE.

31.1 Right onto NE West Kingston Rd.

32.7 Left at Y to continue on NE West Kingston into town.

33.3 Right onto Central Ave.

33.4 Left at parking by ferry dock to end tour.

37 Kingston to Port Townsend

DIFFICULTY: challenging
TIME: allow 5 hours
DISTANCE: 41 miles
ELEVATION GAIN: 1880 feet

Getting There: From I-5, take exit 177, Edmonds, and proceed west on SR 104. Continue on SR 104, which becomes Edmonds Wy. Follow signs to parking at Washington State Ferries dock, or choose day parking at fringes of downtown Edmonds and cycle to ferry.

GPS Coordinates: N47 48 46 W122 23 00
Transit: Community Transit 110, 116, 130, 196, 416

Many cyclists who want to experience multiday trips set their sights on Port Townsend, and no wonder. This 41-mile, one-way route is the perfect one-day ride with your saddlebags loaded. After a relaxing overnight, you can strike out toward Sequim, Port Angeles, and the Olympic Peninsula coast, or you can hop the short ferry ride to Whidbey Island and cycle north from Coupeville toward Deception Pass and the San Juan Islands. Or stay and play in the area, exploring Jefferson County's quiet roads, small towns, old forts, and connected islands, perhaps getting off your bike to do a little kayaking or beachcombing. Are you starting to plan your cycling vacation?

Begin the trip on the ferry from Edmonds to Kingston. After the glut of motorized vehicles has been disgorged and roared away, cycle up the main highway toward the Hood Canal Bridge. Take a rest break at Salsbury Point Park, on the northeast corner of the bridge, and spend a bit of time considering this amazing structure. At 1.2 miles, it's the third-longest floating bridge in the world and the longest one that spans salt water. And consider this: it has to float with the tides.

It's had a bit of a sketchy history since it opened in 1961. Amid winds gusting up to 120 miles per hour on February 13, 1979, the western half of the bridge sank. It was rebuilt and reopened in 1982, and the eastern half was rebuilt beginning in 2003 and reopened in 2009.

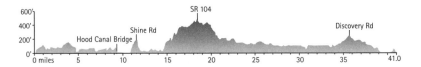

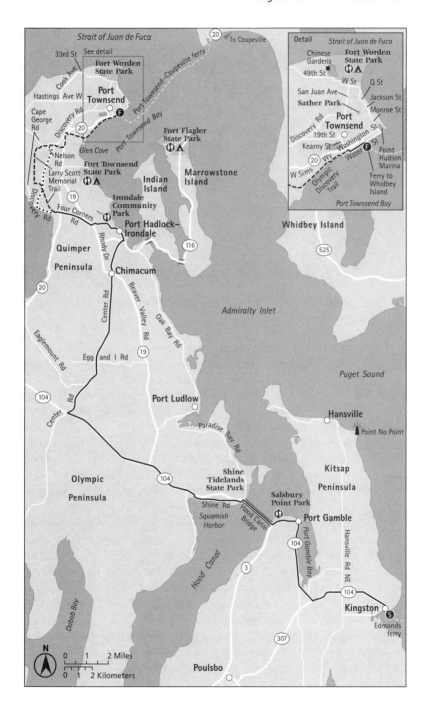

Strait of Juan de Fuca

20 To Coupeville

33rd St   See detail

Cook Ave   Fort Worden
State Park

Hastings Ave W

Port
Townsend

Cape
George
Rd

Discovery Rd

20

F

Port Townsend-Coupeville ferry

Port Townsend Bay

Glen Cove

Nelson
Rd

Larry Scott   Fort Townsend
Memorial   State Park
Trail

Four Corners
Rd

Discovery Rd

19

Irondale
Community
Park

Fort Flagler
State Park

Indian
Island

Marrowstone
Island

Port Hadlock–
Irondale

Quimper

Peninsula

20

Center Rd

Rhody Dr

Chimacum

Beaver Valley Rd

Oak Bay Rd

116

Whidbey Island

525

Admiralty Inlet

Eaglemount Rd

Egg and I Rd

19

Puget Sound

104

Center Rd

Port Ludlow

Paradise Bay Rd

Hansville

Point No Point

Olympic

Peninsula

104

Shine
Tidelands
State Park

Shine Rd

Squamish
Harbor

Hood Canal Bridge

Kitsap

Peninsula

Salsbury
Point Park

Port Gamble

104

Hansville Rd NE

Hood Canal

Dabob Bay

3

Port Gamble Bay

104

Kingston

S

Edmonds
ferry

307

N

0   1   2 Miles
0   1   2 Kilometers

Poulsbo

Detail   Strait of Juan de Fuca

Chinese
Gardens   Fort Worden
State Park

49th St

W St   Q St

San Juan Ave

Sather Park

Jackson St

Monroe St

Discovery Rd

Port
Townsend

19th St

St

Kearny St

Washington St

F

20 Wy

Water St

Point
Hudson
Marina

W Sims

Olympic
Discovery
Trail

Ferry to
Whidbey
Island

Port Townsend Bay

A hard-packed gravel path along Port Townsend Bay leads from the town to the paper mill.

Heading across this big floating bridge used to be a cyclist's nightmare, but no more. Recent renovations have delivered a wide cycling lane with smooth ramps and asphalt decking on the movable parts of this bridge, which has a retractable pontoon draw span that opens to a 600-foot gap. US Navy nuclear submarines sail through Hood Canal from their port at Bangor, 4 miles south of the bridge.

Ride across the incredible structure, then make a long climb to Center Road, which heads north for Port Townsend through farm valleys and a welcoming oasis at Chimacum. The farm stand there is outfitted like a luxury natural-foods market, concentrating on locally produced items, of course.

The last section of the ride is on an excellent set of ever-improving trails. Pass through Port Hadlock and by the county airport, then cross State Route 20 onto Discovery Road and shortly join the Larry Scott Memorial Trail. Most of the trail is unpaved but usable for road bikes, with a hard-packed, fine-grained surface that is smoother than some chip-sealed roads. You can stay on Discovery Road if desired during very wet times; it will add negligible mileage.

Approaching town, join the Olympic Discovery Trail, which announces itself by the odor of the Port Townsend Paper Mill at Glen Cove. Once past that, dodge ambling pedestrians as you skirt Port Townsend Bay, then enter town through the marina. A short ride on the end of busy State Route 20 delivers you to the Victorian-styled brick buildings of downtown Port Townsend and the ferry dock.

To see the town, cycle to the end of Water Street and climb Monroe and Jackson streets to Fort Worden State Park. Head south out of the park along the quiet streets of the upper town, with views down to the water and many picturesque Victorian homes, some remodeled as bed-and-breakfasts. Drop down on Discovery Road to head south out of town to Old Fort Townsend State Park, a mile from town.

If you're staying another day, take a round-trip out to Fort Flagler State Park. Ride south to Port Hadlock and take State Route 116 to Indian and Marrowstone islands. The park is at the northern tip of long Marrowstone Island. Round-trip from Port Townsend is approximately 40 miles, depending on the route. At Fort Flagler, you'll see the remains of gun batteries that were placed there to ward off a seagoing attack. Along with batteries at Fort Worden and Fort Casey—across Admiralty Inlet on Whidbey Island—Fort Flagler was a key element of nautical defense for Puget Sound.

Whether you intend to journey on or not, spend some time enjoying the pub-and-festival culture of Port Townsend, an outdoorsy place that is very welcoming to cyclists.

Route Connections: From this tour's start, you can loop north to Point No Point (Tour 35) or south to the Bainbridge ferry (Tour 34, in reverse), or on the return you can complete the loop through Poulsbo and Suquamish (Tour 36). From this tour's end point, you can take the Port Townsend ferry to Whidbey Island for the central Whidbey rides (Tours 40 and 41), the north Whidbey ride (Tour 42), or the south Whidbey rides toward the Clinton ferry (Tours 38 and 39).

MILEAGE LOG

0.0 Exit Kingston ferry dock onto Kingston Rd.

0.5 Stay right to continue out of Kingston west on SR 104.

4.2 Stay right on SR 104 to continue north to Port Gamble.

7.9 Arrive at Port Gamble.

8.7 Pass Wheeler St. NE, which heads to Salsbury Point Park (restrooms) in 0.25 mile.

9.1 Right onto Hood Canal Bridge.

10.9 Left onto Shine Rd. Caution: fast traffic.

12.1 Pass public beach access on road to left.

13.0 Left onto SR 104 as Shine Rd. ends. Caution: fast traffic.

15.8 Cross intersection with SR 19/Beaver Valley Rd. toward Chimacum. Caution: careful crossing right-turn lane.

20.5   Right at sign for Chimacum and Quilcene. At bottom of ramp, left onto Center Rd.

23.2   Cross Egg and I Rd.

27.3   Arrive at Chimacum, cross SR 19/Beaver Valley Rd., and continue straight on Chimacum Rd.

28.9   Straight at stoplight onto Irondale Rd.

30.0   Curve left to stay on Irondale at 4th Ave.

30.2   Pass Irondale Community Park on left (restrooms).

30.8   Right onto Rhody Dr./SR 19.

31.0   Left onto Four Corners Rd. Caution: fast traffic as you merge to left-turn lane.

32.3   Cross SR 20. Road becomes Discovery Rd.

32.7   Right onto Larry Scott Memorial Trail. Caution: trail is unpaved but hard-packed surface; if extremely wet, continue on Discovery Rd.

34.0   Cross Discovery Rd. and continue on trail.

34.3   Exit trail onto gravel road; in 100 yards, rejoin trail on left.

36.3   Pass trailhead on left at Cape George Rd.

37.4   Curve left to go under SR 20, then curve left again, following signs to Port Townsend. Trail also signed as Olympic Discovery Trail.

37.8   Curve right to stay on trail when approaching road crossing at intersection of SR 20 and Mill Rd.

38.2   Cross Mill Rd. and continue on trail.

38.8   Cross Thomas St. and continue on trail.

39.8   Arrive at Port Townsend's shipyard.

39.9   Exit trail at its end onto Boat St. Continue forward and curve left with road, then right at Port Townsend Brewery.

40.0   Right onto SR 20/W. Sims Wy.

41.0   Arrive at Port Townsend ferry dock to end tour.

Opposite: *Cyclists exit the ferry onto Shaw Island.*

THE ISLANDS

38 South Whidbey Island: Freeland and Langley

DIFFICULTY: challenging
TIME: allow 4.5 hours
DISTANCE: 34.1 miles
ELEVATION GAIN: 2425 feet

Getting There: From I-5 take exit 189, SR 526, and proceed west. Continue on to SR 525, Mukilteo Speedway, to Mukilteo ferry dock. Paid parking at ferry terminal.

GPS Coordinates: N47 56 57 W122 18 16
Transit: Community Transit 113, 417, 880

The easiest way to Puget Sound's islands is by bike, as you zip by long lines of car traffic and are ushered first on and off the ferryboats like royalty. At least you might feel royal when you head to such coveted destinations as Whidbey Island atop your shiny two-wheeler. Leave the car behind to sample Whidbey's pleasures on an afternoon ride around the rolling hills of the island's south end. Pop into two small towns, explore a pebbly beach, and find many a quiet side road lined with tall trees or offering views of salt water and mountain peaks.

From the Clinton ferry dock, proceed clockwise around the island's southern bulge, first climbing inland to traverse to the western shore. Ride north along Bayview Road, meeting up with busy State Route 525, which, linked with State Route 20 in the island's north end, comprise the island's arterial highways. Across this intersection, next to the Bayview Farmers Market, is a bike shop, if needed.

After a brief west stint on the busy highway, turn off onto a side road into Freeland, passing the intriguingly named Earth Sanctuary park on the right. A side trip across the highway and south toward Useless Bay would take you to the popular pebbled beach at Double Bluff County Park, where views of Seattle are in the distance and the Kitsap Peninsula's Foulweather Bluff is in the foreground, just across the shipping lanes.

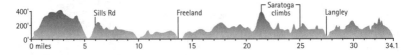

Cyclists enjoy the picturesque shops of Langley.

Turn north into Freeland, the shopping center for the southern island. Skirt the downtown, stopping at the roadside grocery and coffee shop for provisions, then head to the protected town park to commune with the gulls amid the salty air of Holmes Harbor. Travel the shady roads north to the round Rocky Point, where a couple of truly challenging climbs await. Finally, gain views of Saratoga Passage and Camano Island as you travel south toward Langley.

Word of warning: When you reach Langley, you will probably want to linger. You may even check around for a bed for the night (good luck). You'll definitely find plenty to enjoy in this artistic, friendly community. Check out the extensive general store, galleries with local artwork, sidewalk sculptures, and historic eating and drinking establishments. Bear in mind that you still have a few miles to go to finish the tour. If you do plan ahead and stay in Langley for the night

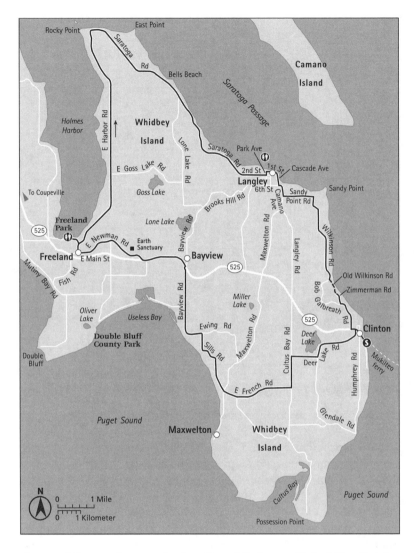

Rocky Point

East Point

Saratoga Rd

Bells Beach

Camano Island

Saratoga Passage

Holmes Harbor

E Harbor Rd

Whidbey Island

Lone Lake Rd

Saratoga Rd

Park Ave

E Goss Lake Rd

2nd St   1st St   Cascade Ave

To Coupeville

Goss Lake

Langley

6th St   Sandy   Sandy Point

Brooks Hill Rd

Camano Ave

Sandy Point Rd

525 Freeland Park

Lone Lake

E Newman Rd

Earth Sanctuary

Maxwelton Rd

Langley Rd

Wilkinson Rd

Freeland   E Main St

Bayview

Bayview Rd

Old Wilkinson Rd

Zimmerman Rd

Mutiny Bay Rd

Fish Rd

525

Miller Lake

Bob Galbreath Rd

Oliver Lake

Useless Bay

Double Bluff County Park

Bayview Rd

Ewing Rd

Maxwelton Rd

Cultus Bay Rd

525

Deer Lake

Clinton

Mukilteo ferry

Double Bluff

Sills Rd

Deer Lake Rd

Humphrey Rd

Puget Sound

E French Rd

Maxwelton

Whidbey Island

Glendale Rd

N   0   1 Mile

0   1 Kilometer

Cultus Bay

Puget Sound

Possession Point

at one of the area's many bed-and-breakfasts, you'll find live theater, an old movie house, and many wonderful restaurants at which to cap the day.

The route back to the ferry takes you past an elaborately fenced vineyard before veering off the main road to the old Wilkinson Road, now closed to car traffic. It's a cool, quiet side lane. Upon returning to Clinton, sink your toes into the sandy beach next to the ferry dock while waiting for the boat.

Route Connections: Reach the Mukilteo ferry via the Interurban Trail (Tour 50). Ride the ferry connector (Tour 42) to reach the Coupeville ride (Tour 40) and continue north up the island to Oak Harbor (Tour 41) and Deception Pass (Tour 42).

MILEAGE LOG

0.0 Depart ferry dock onto SR 525.

0.6 Left onto Deer Lake Rd.

1.5 Right to stay on Deer Lake at intersection with Holst Rd.

2.3 Left onto Cultus Bay Rd. Caution: fast traffic.

3.1 Right onto E. French Rd.

5.1 Straight at stop sign onto Sills Rd.

6.1 Left onto Ewing Rd., which curves left, then right to become Bayview Rd.

9.2 Left onto SR 525 at stoplight. Caution: busy highway, but wide shoulder for riding.

10.5 Right onto E. Newman Rd.

11.1 Right onto E. Main St. in Freeland.

11.4 Right onto E. Harbor Rd., which curves left and becomes Layton Rd.

12.5 Right onto E. Harbor Rd. In 1 block, left onto Stewart Rd.

13.0 Arrive at Freeland Park (restrooms, water, picnic area). Retrace route to E. Harbor Rd.

13.3 Left onto E. Harbor Rd.

14.8 Pass E. Goss Lake Rd. on right.

18.8 Arrive at Rocky Point, where road becomes Saratoga Rd. and curves right.

22.2 Pass Bells Beach on left.

26.1 Arrive at Langley as Saratoga becomes 2nd St.

26.2 Left onto Park Ave.

26.3 Right onto 1st St. Arrive at viewpoint park (restrooms), shops, restaurants. Continue east along 1st St., which becomes Cascade Ave.

27.5 Left onto Camano Ave.

27.9 Left on Sandy Point Rd.

29.5 Right onto Wilkinson Rd.

31.9 Left onto signed bike route, past trail gate.

32.2 Forward onto old Wilkinson Rd. as exiting bike trail.

32.3 Continue through another trail gate onto Zimmerman Rd.

32.6 Left to return to new Wilkinson Rd., which becomes Bob Galbreath Rd., then S. Hinman Dr.

33.5 Left onto SR 525 into Clinton.

34.1 Arrive at ferry dock to end tour.

39 Whidbey Ferries: Coupeville to Clinton

DIFFICULTY: moderate
TIME: allow 3.5 hours
DISTANCE: 34.9 miles
ELEVATION GAIN: 2326 feet

Getting There: To reach the Coupeville ferry, either take the Mukilteo ferry (Tour 50), then from Clinton take SR 525 north to SR 20 north, or from I-5 take exit 230, SR 20, and follow SR 20 west to Deception Pass Bridge, then south to Coupeville. Turn south on S. Engle Rd.; ferry is ahead in 4.6 miles. Free day parking near dock.

GPS Coordinates: N48 09 34 W122 40 22
Transit: Island Transit 1, 6; no Sunday service

The sign reads "Whidbey Scenic Isle Way," drawing you away from the Coupeville ferry terminal and along the water. Above to the left is Fort Casey, symbolically protecting the waterway. The salty tang of Admiralty Bay reaches your nose as you begin the trek from one Whidbey ferry to the other, starting at midisland and heading south for its lowest tip. This tour's snaking route takes you down two-thirds of Whidbey, a good portion of the fourth-longest island in the contiguous United States.

The Coupeville ferry, formerly known as the Keystone run, shuttles people across Admiralty Inlet, with the Victorian buildings of Port Townsend so close you can nearly see the mortar between the red bricks. Heading south on Whidbey, you're skirting the edge of Ebey's Landing National Historical Reserve, an appellation designated entirely across the island here, from Penn Cove north of Coupeville down to the seaside road under your wheels. The reserve includes two state parks made from the old Forts Casey and Ebey and plenty of pleasant, flat riding (see Tours 40 and 41).

As you exit the reserve onto the busier roads of Whidbey's narrow waist, Crockett Lake is on your left, bordered by historic structures from the first settlers. The first community you reach is Admiral's Cove, with

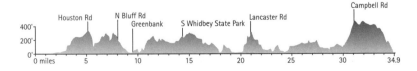

Greenbank Farm in midisland is a great place to stop for a picnic.
Mount Baker is visible to the northeast.

tidy rows of houses facing the view, along roads named for famous naval leaders (Halsey, Nimitz, Michler, Russell, Rickover—collect them all!).

There's no way to avoid a bit of the main road, State Route 525, as you head down-island, because there just aren't many connecting side roads here. If you're carrying a load or you're in a hurry (I hope you're not), you could make a beeline to the other ferry on the highway. It has a wide shoulder and gentler hills and is the most direct route. But it's loud, the traffic is fast, and there's no shade cover from trees. And the best scenery is on the back roads.

After a mile and a half on the main drag, carefully cross the highway to the rolling hills of tree-lined North Bluff Road, enjoying the views of Saratoga Passage and finally passing by a stunning cove and farm valley before reaching Greenbank. Make a stop here at picturesque Greenbank Farm, which has been converted to a community locus, with shops, a café, community gardens, a farmers market, and regular events.

From Greenbank Farm, it's back across State Route 525, this time heading south on South Smugglers Cove Road, which climbs to flat, wooded scenery on a road with a comfortable shoulder. It's the ideal biking side road, with only local traffic and even a rest stop along the way. At 14 miles, South Whidbey Island State Park offers restrooms, water, and hiker-biker campsites right inside its gates. If you're inclined to stay, you'll find trails through old-growth forests and tidelands for crabbing and clamming on a saltwater beach.

Evocative road names like Smugglers Cove may get your imagination whirring along with your chain-powered drivetrain. Did the

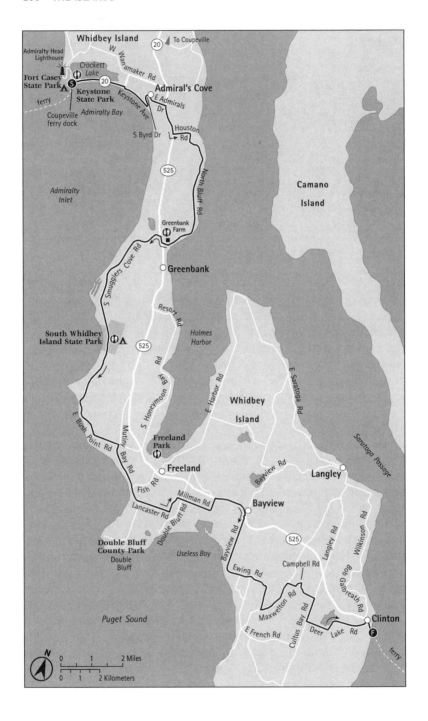

Whidbey Island

To Coupeville

Admiralty Head Lighthouse

W Wanamaker Rd

Crockett Lake

Fort Casey State Park

Keystone State Park

Admiral's Cove

E Admirals Dr

Keystone Ave

Coupeville ferry dock

Admiralty Bay

S Byrd Dr

Houston Rd

525

Admiralty Inlet

North Bluff Rd

Camano Island

Greenbank Farm

S Smugglers Cove Rd

Greenbank

Resort Rd

Holmes Harbor

South Whidbey Island State Park

525

S Honeymoon Bay Rd

Whidbey Island

E Harbor Rd

E Saratoga Rd

Saratoga Passage

E Bush Point Rd

Mutiny Bay Rd

Freeland Park

Freeland

Bayview Rd

Langley

Fish Rd

Lancaster Rd

Millman Rd

Double Bluff Rd

Bayview

Bayview Rd

525

Langley Rd

Wilkinson Rd

Bob Galbreath Rd

Double Bluff County Park

Double Bluff

Useless Bay

Ewing Rd

Campbell Rd

Maxwelton Rd

Cultus Bay Rd

Deer Lake Rd

Clinton

Puget Sound

E French Rd

ferry

N

0   1   2 Miles

0   1   2 Kilometers

smugglers rebel at Mutiny Bay, just south of here? Perhaps they threw their overlords off the precipice at the end of Double Bluff Road. You'll find many such fanciful, unique names as you bicycle the back roads of Puget Sound, and hopefully you'll never encounter "Shopping Mall Access Road."

Hilly Mutiny Bay Road drops to a bayside community, then crosses Fish Road, which connects to the town of Freeland in a half mile. But stay on Mutiny Bay, which becomes Lancaster, and as it gives way to Millman Road, you cross aforementioned Double Bluff. A 2-mile side trip here would take you to a small park with big views. On a clear day, you'd spy Seattle's skyscrapers and Mount Rainier beyond.

A brief, necessary spin down State Route 525 takes you to the turn at Bayview, which features a bike shop next to the farmers market site on the north side of the highway. You turn south for the last leg of this tour. Bayview Road doesn't disappoint, with a stunning Useless Bay scene. Farm views and intermittent shoulders greet you on the next few turns as you ride Ewing, Maxwelton, Campbell, Cultus Bay, and Deer Lake roads on the last 10 miles into Clinton and the short ferry ride to Mukilteo.

Route Connections: Loop central Whidbey from Fort Casey (Tour 40), or turn north on Fish Road into Freeland to connect with the south Whidbey loop (Tour 38).

MILEAGE LOG

0.0 From Coupeville ferry dock, turn right onto SR 20, which becomes W. Wanamaker Rd.

1.7 Right onto Keystone Ave.

2.3 Enter community of Admiral's Cove.

2.7 Curve left around cove as road ends.

3.0 Continue straight up the hill onto S. Byrd Dr.

3.1 Curve right onto E. Admirals Dr.

3.8 Right onto SR 525.

4.8 Left onto Houston Rd. Caution: highway-speed traffic.

5.3 Road becomes North Bluff Rd.

9.4 Right onto Wann Rd., and in 0.1 mile arrive at Greenbank Farm (restrooms).

9.7 Right onto SR 525.

9.9 Left onto S. Smugglers Cove Rd. Caution: highway-speed traffic.

14.3 Pass South Whidbey Island State Park (restrooms, water, hiker-biker campsites).

16.9 Continue forward as road becomes E. Bush Point Rd.

18.5   Right onto Mutiny Bay Rd.

20.0   Stay right at intersection with Fish Rd. (for 0.5-mile detour to rest stop in Freeland, left onto Fish Rd.).

20.5   Continue forward as road becomes Lancaster Rd.

22.2   Cross Double Bluff Rd. (for 2-mile detour to county park, right onto Double Bluff Rd.) as road becomes Millman Rd.

23.2   Curve left at intersection with Useless Bay Rd.

23.6   Right onto SR 525.

24.8   Right onto Bayview Rd.

27.1   Straight onto Ewing Rd as main road curves to right and becomes Sills Rd.

28.8   Left onto Maxwelton Rd.

30.1   Right onto Campbell Rd.

31.3   Right onto Cultus Bay Rd.

32.0   Left onto Deer Lake Rd.

32.8   Left to stay on Deer Lake Rd.

34.3   Right onto SR 525 in Clinton.

34.9   Arrive at Clinton ferry dock to end tour.

40 Central Whidbey Island: Coupeville and Fort Casey

DIFFICULTY: easy
TIME: allow 1.5 hours
DISTANCE: 12.7 miles
ELEVATION GAIN: 506 feet

Getting There: To reach Coupeville, either take the Mukilteo ferry (see Tour 38 or Tour 50), then from Clinton take SR 525 north to SR 20 north, or from I-5 take exit 230, SR 20, and follow SR 20 west to Deception Pass Bridge, then south to Coupeville. Turn north onto NW Broadway Ave., then right onto NW Coveland St. in 0.6 mile. Coupeville Town Park is on the left.

GPS Coordinates: N48 13 14 W122 41 27

Transit: Island Transit 1, 6; no Sunday service

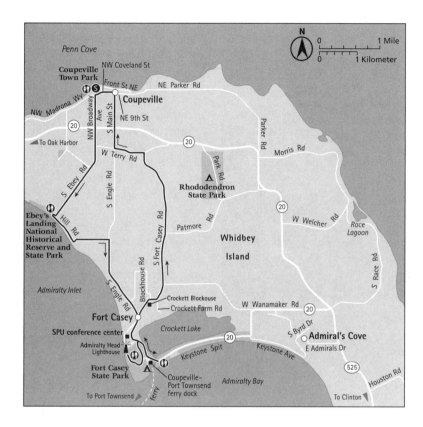

The long crescent of Whidbey Island is most pleasing to cyclists in its center section, from Penn Cove to Admiralty Bay. Here you'll find historic towns, scenic coastline roads, old military installations, and flat, open riding. Nowhere do all these elements come together as nicely as in this Coupeville and Fort Casey loop.

Begin the tour from the Coupeville Town Park. Its free, shady parking is just two blocks from the town's waterfront shops and the island historical museum. Save exploring the town center for last, unless you intend to picnic at Fort Casey State Park, the ride's halfway point. If that's the case, stop at the shops on Front Street or Main before beginning the ride. Snacks also can be purchased at the Coupeville–Port Townsend ferry landing, a quarter mile from the state park.

Head south out of town on NW Broadway Avenue, taking care when crossing busy State Route 20 to exit town south toward Fort Casey. If traffic is especially heavy, detour a couple blocks east to the signal at Main Street. Across the highway, Broadway becomes South Ebey Road,

Picturesque Admiralty Head Lighthouse at Fort Casey

which loops around and drops down briefly along the coast, where you'll find a nice beach and walking trails up to viewpoints at Ebey's Landing National Historical Reserve and State Park. Continue by climbing aptly named Hill Road, then drop down to the entrance to Fort Casey State Park and the ferry dock beyond.

The old fort offers plentiful scenic areas and picnic spots. The military fortifications—cement bunkers and grassy, covered tunnels dating from the late 19th century—are well worth exploration. Two 10-inch "disappearing" guns are on display atop the battlements, aiming toward the placid shipping lanes of Admiralty Inlet. Nearby, the simple, elegant Admiralty Head Lighthouse provides a high vantage point over the area. The fort's old barracks and administration buildings have been converted into a conference center operated by Seattle Pacific University. Exiting the fort, look for the well-preserved Crockett Blockhouse, a wooden relic by the edge of the road that looks out over the Crockett Farm and Admiralty Bay.

The road back north to Coupeville offers a look at the other side of this flat farm valley, heading back into town via the long Main Street. (Or you can extend the tour by continuing east on West Wanamaker Road and crossing State Route 20 to ride the east edge of the island along Race Road, which leads north, then loop back to Coupeville on Morris and Parker roads.) Cross the highway again and head into the main part of this historic town.

Spend some time exploring Coupeville, Washington's second-oldest town. Its history is clearly on display with the restored homes and buildings that line its few streets. Nautical touches reveal that it was once the home of sea captains. Learn more by picking through the exhibits at the Island County Historical Society Museum, adjacent to which is the Alexander Blockhouse, a protective enclosure dating from the mid-1800s.

End the tour by riding along picturesque Front Street, walking out to the Harbor Store on the Coupeville Wharf, or kicking back at one of the welcoming establishments overlooking famous Penn Cove. For a slight extension, continue west out of Coupeville on NW Madrona Way, a winding waterfront road that overlooks the Penn Cove mussel-farm rafts.

Route Connections: Use the ferry connector (Tour 39) to reach the south Whidbey ride (Tour 38); ride west 3.3 miles on NW Madrona Way from Coupeville to reach State Route 20, which connects to Oak Harbor for rides to Fort Ebey (Tour 41) and the San Juan Islands ferry (Tour 42).

MILEAGE LOG

0.0 From Coupeville Town Park (restrooms), right onto NW Coveland St.

0.1 Left onto NW Broadway Ave.

0.2 Cross NW Madrona Wy.

0.6 Cross SR 20. Caution: busy road. Continue south as Broadway becomes S. Ebey Rd.

0.9 As main road curves at Y at W. Terry Rd., right to stay on S. Ebey Rd.

2.3 Reach Ebey's Landing National Historical Reserve and State Park (restrooms), where road curves left at beach to become Hill Rd.

3.4 Right onto S. Engle Rd.

4.8 Stay right at intersection with Fort Casey Rd.

5.3 Arrive at entrance to Fort Casey State Park. Continue forward to ferry dock.

5.7 Arrive at Coupeville–Port Townsend ferry dock. Reverse route.

6.2 Left into Fort Casey.

6.8 Arrive at main parking and picnic area (restrooms). Right to lighthouse.

6.9 Arrive at Admiralty Head Lighthouse. Reverse route to exit park.

7.5 Left onto Engle Rd.

8.0 Right at intersection onto S. Fort Casey Rd.

8.4 Pass Crockett Blockhouse.

10.9 Left onto W. Terry Rd.

11.4 Right onto S. Main St. S.

11.7 Cross SR 20 at signal.

12.3 Left onto Front St. NE.

12.4 Left onto Alexander St. NW as Front St. ends. Museum on right.

12.5 Right onto NW Coveland St.

12.6 Right at Y to stay on NW Coveland St.

12.7 Arrive at Coupeville Town Park to end tour.

41 Central Whidbey Island: Oak Harbor and Fort Ebey

DIFFICULTY: easy
TIME: allow 3 hours
DISTANCE: 19.3 miles
ELEVATION GAIN: 1309 feet

Getting There: To reach Oak Harbor, either take the Mukilteo ferry (see Tour 38 or Tour 50), then from Clinton take SR 525 north to SR 20 north, or from I-5 take exit 230, SR 20, and follow SR 20 west to Deception Pass Bridge, then south to Oak Harbor. Reach intersection of SR 20 and W. Pioneer Wy. From the south, turn right on SW Beeksma Dr.; from the north, go straight ahead (south) on SW Beeksma Dr. Go 0.2 mile to parking area at Windjammer Park.

GPS Coordinates: N48 17 02 W122 39 26
Transit: Island Transit 1, 6; no Sunday service

A tour out of bustling Oak Harbor is replete with coastal views. In fact, you get a look at beaches along both sides of Whidbey Island. Although the city of Oak Harbor itself is not included in this tour, the island's largest town deserves some exploring. It's home to a US Navy air base, and you can still see influences of the Dutch people who were the first colonists in the area in the 1850s. A beach walk curves around the harbor from Windjammer Park, adjacent to a developing downtown.

Start at Windjammer Park (formerly City Beach Park) at the south edge of town, easily found just two blocks off State Route 20. If you're planning a picnic, stop for provisions at the shopping district along West Pioneer Way before leaving town. Except for water and restrooms at Fort Ebey, there are no services on this rural ride.

The tour departs Oak Harbor fairly quickly, climbing along Fort Nugent Road and then cutting across prime farmland. At the intersection with Zylstra Road, the Hummingbird Farm and its popular display gardens invite a walk-through. Continue to the island's west coast, where a southbound ride rewards cyclists with stunning views of the Olympics beyond the verdant valleys and glittering Strait of Juan de Fuca.

A group of Oak Harbor friends cycles around Penn Cove.

At nearly 10 miles, arrive at Fort Ebey State Park, the smaller and more recent of the two former military battlements strategically placed on Whidbey to defend the entry to Puget Sound. Fort Casey, a few miles to the south, offers more extensive relics of its defenses—which date to the 1890s—as well as a picturesque lighthouse and extensive open areas for picnicking, kite-flying, and views (Tour 40).

But Fort Ebey, which was made a military installation during World War II, has its own charms. Hiking and mountain-biking trails snake through the wooded hillsides and to the freshwater Lake Pondilla, and a dirt trail at the end of the road leads to a bicycles-only camping area. Both parks are part of Ebey's Landing National Historical Preserve, managed by the National Park Service.

After a picnic and exploration at the park, return toward Oak Harbor by traveling east to State Route 20. Turn north onto the island's busy "main drag" just south of NW Madrona Way, the scenic 3.3-mile ride along Penn Cove to Coupeville (Tour 40). Exit State Route 20 to ride the east edge of the island along much-less-traveled Penn Cove Road, which becomes North Scenic Heights Road, to finish the ride.

This section of the route offers shortcuts available only to those on two wheels. Your first opportunity to join Penn Cove Road comes just

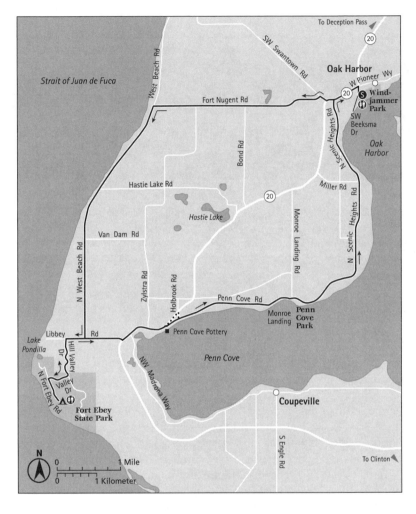

as State Route 20 rounds the bay and departs the coastline. There, at the imposing Penn Cove Pottery building, you can slip through a break in the parking lot barriers and drop down to the end of Penn Cove Road, a couple of feet below the parking grade. A ride along the water takes you by Monroe Landing and Penn Cove Park, where you could stop and dip your fingers in the water. Then, at the intersection of North Scenic Heights and Miller roads, a sign warns of a dead end. Don't believe it. The road, which skirts a bluff right by the water, was closed to vehicle traffic, but bikes are allowed to traverse the barriers and continue, rewarded with great views of Oak Harbor and snowy

Mount Baker beyond. Such traffic revisions make for quiet, pleasurable riding, enhancing an already excellent central Whidbey excursion.

Route Connections: For more scenic island viewing, you could visit north Whidbey by cycling north to Deception Pass (Tour 42) and stop for a hike and tour of its state park and stunning bridge. Or turn south at NW Madrona Way to connect with the Coupeville ride (Tour 40), or ride south all the way to the Clinton ferry (Tours 38 and 39).

MILEAGE LOG

0.0 Exit parking at Windjammer (City Beach) Park (restrooms) onto SW Beeksma Dr. north toward SR 20.

0.1 Left onto SR 20 at light. Caution: busy intersection.

0.7 Right onto SW Swantown Ave.

0.8 Left onto Fort Nugent Rd.

3.5 Left on N. West Beach Rd.

7.4 Right onto Libbey Rd.

7.6 Left onto Hill Valley Dr.

8.3 Right into park.

8.6 Left onto N. Fort Ebey Rd. to beach overlook and trails. Gun battery relic on the left.

9.2 Arrive at parking (restrooms). Retrace route to exit park.

10.3 Left at park exit to return to Libbey Rd.

10.5 Curve right and stay on main road to retrace route.

10.9 Right onto Libbey Rd.

11.8 Left onto SR 20.

12.0 Pass NW Madrona Wy.

12.6 Right into parking at Penn Cove Pottery; proceed through barrier to join Penn Cove Rd. Alternate route: Ride to mile 13.5, turn right onto Holbrook Rd., then left onto Penn Cove Rd. in 1 block.

14.5 Arrive at Monroe Landing, beach and historic marker. Continue forward on Penn Cove Rd.

14.9 Pass Penn Cove Park.

14.9 Road becomes N. Scenic Heights Rd.

17.4 Continue forward at intersection with Miller Rd., ignoring sign saying "dead end no outlet." Bike access available to continue on N. Scenic Heights Rd. into town.

17.7 Traverse street closure barrier.

18.8 Right onto SR 20 into town.

19.2 Right onto SW Beeksma Dr.

19.3 Arrive at parking at Windjammer Park to end tour.

42 North Whidbey Island: Deception Pass and San Juan Islands Ferry

DIFFICULTY: challenging
TIME: allow 6 hours
DISTANCE: 47.4 miles
ELEVATION GAIN: 2795 feet

Getting There: To reach Oak Harbor, either take the Mukilteo ferry (Tour 38 or Tour 50), then from Clinton take SR 525 north to SR 20 north, or from I-5 take exit 230, SR 20, and follow SR 20 west to Deception Pass Bridge, then south to Oak Harbor. Reach intersection of SR 20 and W. Pioneer Wy. From the south, turn right on SW Beeksma Dr.; from the north, go straight ahead (south) on SW Beeksma Dr. Go 0.2 mile to parking area at Windjammer Park.

 GPS Coordinates: N48 17 02 W122 39 26
 Transit: Island Transit 411; also 2, 3, 6; no Sunday service

In these parts, a true getaway by bike often involves a ferryboat ride, and the most desirable watery route to reach a biking vacation aims for the San Juan Islands. Many people drive to Anacortes with their bikes on the car, then park and ride onto the ferry, but what if you wanted to strike out from home and just ride there? It's often said that the journey is as important as the destination. This loop ride offers a key link in the plan to bike to the ferry, but it also makes a nice day outing.

The ride begins in Oak Harbor, Whidbey Island's biggest town. This navy air town has all the services, from chain supermarkets to an aviation-themed microbrewery, so it's easy to stock up on provisions if you want to picnic en route. Depart from its downtown park and head north, meeting up with the island's main highway, State Route 20, just north of town. You'll pass the entrance to the US Navy's Naval Air Station Whidbey Island and will probably hear or see the streaking jets throughout the ride. Although highway traffic is fast, the shoulder is good and the climbs are gentler than those on some back roads, which is an especially important consideration if you're loaded down with luggage for a San Juan Islands vacation. Don't worry; you'll get plenty of chances to tackle hills on this ride.

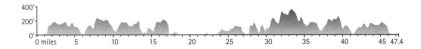

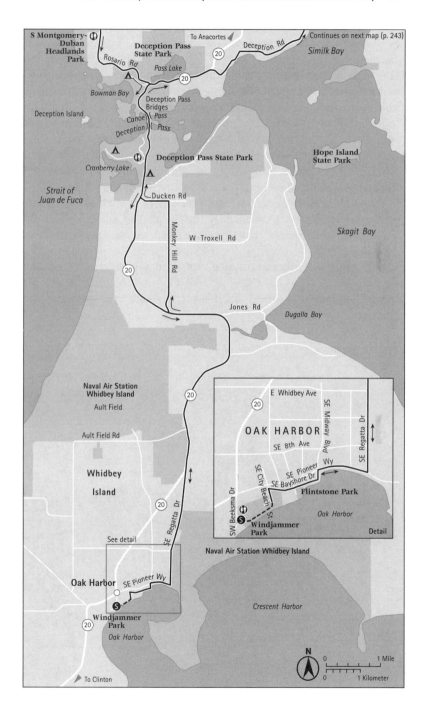

S Montgomery-
Duban
Headlands
Park

To Anacortes

Continues on next map (p. 243)

Deception Rd

Deception Pass
State Park

20

Rosario Rd

Pass Lake

Similk Bay

20

Bowman Bay

Deception Pass
Bridges

Deception Island

Canoe
Pass

Pass

Deception

Pass

Cranberry Lake

Deception Pass State Park

Hope Island
State Park

Strait of
Juan de Fuca

Ducken Rd

Monkey Hill Rd

W Troxell Rd

Skagit Bay

20

Jones Rd

Dugalla Bay

Naval Air Station
Whidbey Island

Ault Field

20

E Whidbey Ave

20

SE Midway Blvd

SE Regatta Dr

Ault Field Rd

OAK HARBOR

SE 8th Ave

Whidbey

Island

20

SW Becksma Dr

SE City Beach St

SE Pioneer Wy

SE Bayshore Dr

Flintstone Park

Oak Harbor

See detail

SE Regatta Dr

Windjammer
Park

Detail

Naval Air Station Whidbey Island

Oak Harbor

SE Pioneer Wy

Crescent Harbor

20

Windjammer
Park

Oak Harbor

N

0   1 Mile

0   1 Kilometer

To Clinton

A brief climb off the main road onto Monkey Hill Road will test your quads a bit, but once you're up there, the rolling hills, quiet road, and farm scenery are worth it. Rejoin the highway just south of Deception Pass State Park. If you've been riding all the way from home or started from down the island at the Mukilteo or Coupeville ferry, this park would be a great place to stop and camp (bike-in sites at the south park entrance or at Cranberry Lake). This is the most-visited park in the state (and the pass road sees 20,000 cars a day), so plan ahead and grab a campsite early. It's a fairly short ride into Anacortes from here, but why not take your time? The trail will be there tomorrow.

The highlight of Deception Pass State Park is a thrilling, mercifully short ride over the bridge. Actually, it's two spans, with a little hump of rock between them. These historic bridges don't have a shoulder, and their walkways are barely wide enough for today's average American's girth, so stay on the road, take over the lane, and just barrel on through. Think of it this way: you are doing the drivers a favor, making them slow down to a speed where they can enjoy the scenery.

The Thompson Trestle conveys cyclists into Anacortes across inner Fidalgo Bay.

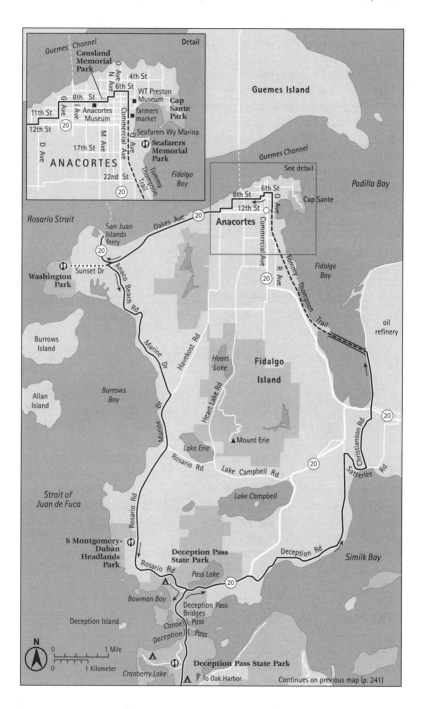

Detail

Guemes Channel

Causland
Memorial
Park

4th St
6th St
WT Preston
Museum
8th St
N Ave
O Ave

Cap
Sante
Park

Anacortes
Museum

farmers
market

11th St
G Ave
I Ave

Commercial Ave

Seafarers Wy Marina

12th St
M Ave

Seafarers
Memorial
Park

17th St
D Ave

ANACORTES

22nd St
Tommy Thompson Trail

Fidalgo
Bay

(20)

Guemes Island

Guemes Channel

See detail

Padilla Bay

Rosario Strait

Oakes Ave (20)

San Juan
Islands
ferry

8th St   6th St
O Ave

12th St

Anacortes

Commercial Ave

Cap Sante

(20)

Washington
Park

Sunset Dr

Anaco Beach Rd

R Ave

(20)

Fidalgo
Bay

Tommy Thompson Trail

oil
refinery

Burrows
Island

Marine Dr

Havekost Rd

Heart
Lake

Fidalgo

Island

Allan
Island

Burrows
Bay

Heart Lake Rd

(20)

Mount Erie

Christianson Rd

Satterlee Rd

Strait of
Juan de Fuca

Marine Dr

Lake Erie

Rosario Rd

Lake Campbell Rd

(20)

Rosario Rd

Lake Campbell

S Montgomery-
Duban
Headlands
Park

Rosario Rd

Deception Pass
State Park

Pass Lake

Deception Rd

Similk Bay

Bowman Bay

(20)

Deception Pass
Bridges

Deception Island

Canoe Pass

Deception l Pass

N

0   1 Mile
0   1 Kilometer

Cranberry Lake

Deception Pass State Park

To Oak Harbor

Continues on previous map (p. 241)

There's a great viewpoint on the right side of the south bridge, so pull over for a look (and let the gas guzzlers roar by). Gawk at the bridge's green spiderweb superstructure and roiling waters below, then regain serenity by lifting your gaze to the forested bluffs and islands beyond.

Heading toward Anacortes, you must endure a few twists in the road with scant shoulder. Steel yourself for the plentiful RVs and boat-pulling pickups, as well as the commercial trucks, that frequent this desirable road, the only access to Whidbey that does not involve a ferry. In less than 2 miles you are on low-traffic side roads that take you all the way to Anacortes, where you connect to a great trail into town.

A ride along Similk Bay, with its views toward Mount Baker and the Cascades, takes you back to State Route 20, but you need only cross it at a stoplight and cycle past the big oil refinery to get to the Tommy Thompson Trail, a bike-ped trestle that cuts diagonally through Fidalgo Bay and connects to a trail into town.

Exit the trail in old downtown and cross Commercial Street, with its two bike shops to the right. Ride through Anacortes on low-traffic residential streets, then pedal the bike lane along Oakes Avenue, with views of Guemes and Cypress islands, to reach the ferry dock. If you're making it a day ride (or if you have a lot of time before the next ferry), consider a short side trip down Sunset Drive to Washington Park, which offers a loop trail and beach.

Head back to Whidbey by making a loop around the outer edge of Fidalgo Island. The first leg takes you through stunning bayside neighborhoods that look west along Burrows Bay, and then you turn inland a bit and ride south through the countryside. You're never far from the water's edge, and peekaboo views appear. This stretch includes a fair bit of climbing. The last 2 miles to rejoin State Route 20 contain some enjoyable downhill cruises.

Yes, you must endure State Route 20 again as you climb to cross the bridge. Continue south on the highway's generous shoulder, enduring the traffic noise, back to Oak Harbor.

Route Connections: Ride west from the starting point to Fort Ebey (Tour 41) or east from Christianson Road to La Conner (Tour 49).

MILEAGE LOG

0.0   From Windjammer Park (restrooms) parking area, ride north along waterfront trail.

0.4   Left onto SE City Beach St. to exit park trail. In 1 block, right onto SE Bayshore Dr., which becomes SE Midway Blvd.

0.9   Right onto SE Pioneer Wy.

1.2 Left on SE Regatta Dr.

3.3 Merge onto SR 20 northbound. Caution: traffic.

4.0 Pass Ault Field Rd., entrance to Naval Air Station Whidbey Island.

7.4 Right onto Monkey Hill Rd.

7.7 Left at intersection with Henni Rd. to stay on Monkey Hill.

9.5 Road curves left and becomes Ducken Rd.

10.0 Right onto SR 20.

10.2 Pass entrance to Deception Pass State Park (restrooms, water, camping); grocery-deli on right in 0.25 mile.

11.3 Cross Deception Pass Bridge.

13.3 Right onto Deception Rd.

13.6 Veer left to stay on Deception Rd.

14.1 Right on Gibralter Rd.

16.9 Right onto Satterlee Rd.

17.5 Left onto Christianson Rd.

18.4 Curve left to stay on Christianson.

18.6 Cross SR 20 at stoplight onto March Point Rd. Caution: oil refinery traffic.

19.6 Left onto Tommy Thompson Trail.

21.6 Trail enters industrial marina area.

22.7 Pass Seafarer's Way marina (restrooms) and Seafarers Memorial Park.

23.0 Pass Saturday farmers market.

23.3 Left onto 6th St. In 1 block, cross Commercial Ave.

23.4 Left onto O Ave., then in 1 block, right onto 7th St., then left onto N Ave.

23.5 Right onto 8th St. at Causland Memorial Park.

24.0 Left onto G Ave.

24.2 Right onto 11th St.

24.4 Left onto D Ave., then in 1 block, right onto SR 20, which is 12th St. and becomes Oakes Ave.

26.7 Right on a spur down to the San Juan Islands ferry.

27.3 Arrive at ferry dock. Retrace route to depart uphill.

28.0 Right onto Sunriser's Ln. for a steep 100 yards, then right onto Sunset Dr. (Detour to Washington Park and restrooms by continuing on Sunset Dr.) In ½ block, left onto Anaco Beach Rd.

29.1 Curve uphill to stay on Anaco Beach Rd., which becomes Marine Dr.

31.0 Right to stay on Marine Dr.

32.0 Keep right at Y to stay on Marine, which becomes Rosario Rd.

33.6 Pass S. Montgomery-Duban Headlands Park (restrooms).

35.3 Right onto SR 20; cross Deception Pass Bridge.

37.3 Pass entrance to Deception Pass State Park (restrooms, water, camping).
37.5 Pass Ducken Rd.
40.0 Pass Monkey Hill Rd.
43.9 Left into turning lane onto SE Regatta Dr. Caution: fast traffic.
44.4 Right at Y to stay on Regatta.
46.1 Right onto SE Pioneer Wy.
46.5 Left onto SE Midway Blvd. which becomes SE Bayshore Dr.
47.0 Left onto SE City Beach St. to enter park trail. In 1 block, right at street end onto waterfront trail in Windjammer Park (restrooms).
47.4 Arrive at parking to end tour.

43 Lopez Island

DIFFICULTY: moderate
TIME: allow 4.5 hours
DISTANCE: 34.2 miles
ELEVATION GAIN: 1865 feet

Getting There: Take I-5 north to exit 230, SR 20; turn left at exit onto SR 20 west to Anacortes. Right onto Commercial Ave., then left onto 12th St., following signs for Washington State Ferries. Paid parking at ferry terminal.

GPS Coordinates: N48 30 23 W122 40 42
Transit: Skagit Transit 410; no Sunday service

If you're looking for a bike-friendly island ride on quiet roads, Lopez is your mecca. Amiable locals wave from the few cars that pass you along the mostly gentle terrain. This loop explores the island's shoreline parks and mostly avoids Center Road, which handles the bulk of car traffic. Although the route loops to and from the ferry, an overnight stay is suggested to really enjoy the island; easy camping locations exist, as well as a number of bed-and-breakfast accommodations.

After the inevitable hill climb from the ferry dock, pass the entrance to Odlin County Park. Continue south to Lopez Village, the only town on

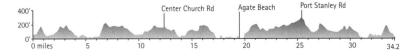

Bicycle recycling, Lopez Island style

the island. In a few short blocks, it contains two grocery stores, a bike shop, a bakery, espresso stands, and a few cafés, two of which are open in the evening. Near the village is picturesque Lopez Island Winery, whose wines are available in the shops. Purchase the makings of a picnic lunch here, as additional stops for provisions are few and far between.

Watch for blue herons standing sentinel in the shallows of Fisherman Bay as you exit the village and head south for Shark Reef. Cycle along protected Fisherman Bay. To the right is Otis Perkins County Park, which offers beachcombing and a great view of the village.

An option for a lunch break is at Shark Reef Sanctuary, reached via a quarter-mile walk through the woods, ducking branches and stepping over tree roots. At the south end of the trail, seals are often visible on the rocky shore. Just across the channel is San Juan Island.

Next, venture inland a bit to visit the picturesque Center Church, whose white steeple overlooks the Lopez Union Cemetery and an expansive agricultural valley. The church and cemetery date from the 1880s. At the intersection of Mud Bay Road and MacKaye Harbor Road is Islandale, which has a small grocery and deli, with restrooms. Three miles south is tiny Agate Beach County Park, another option for a lunch break, about halfway through the tour.

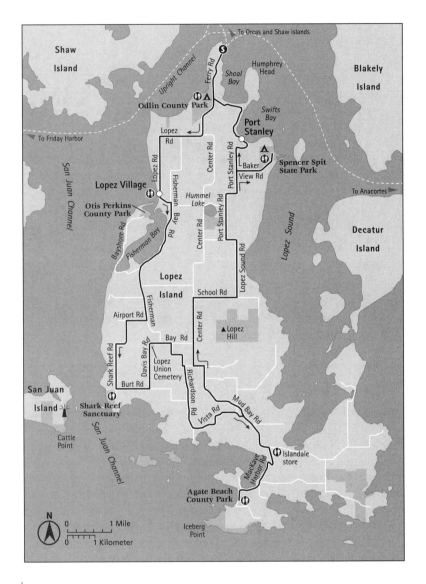

After your visit to the island's southern tip, turn north and cycle through the middle of the island, heading for its east shore via quiet Port Stanley Road, where alder trees meet overhead to create a quiet, shady lane.

Finally, detour slightly east to Spencer Spit State Park, a popular camp spot for kayakers and bikers. It has restrooms and a historic log cabin. Both Odlin and Spencer Spit are easily attainable destinations for camping, although reservations must be made well ahead. Return to the ferry by looping around Swifts and Shoal bays, fronted by a small community of shore homes.

Route Connections: Ride the interisland ferries to Orcas (Tour 44), San Juan (Tours 45 and 46), and Shaw (Tour 47) islands.

MILEAGE LOG

0.0 From ferry dock, head south on Ferry Rd.

1.1 Cross Port Stanley Rd. and pass entrance to Odlin County Park (restrooms, camping).

2.1 Curve right at intersection with Center Rd. onto Fisherman Bay Rd.

2.6 Right onto Military Rd., which becomes Lopez Rd.

4.4 Arrive at Lopez Village.

4.7 Right onto Fisherman Bay Rd. to depart town center.

6.4 Pass Bayshore Rd., which goes to Otis Perkins County Park.

7.5 Right onto Airport Rd.

8.7 Left onto Shark Reef Rd.

9.8 Arrive at Shark Reef Sanctuary. Depart by returning on Shark Reef Rd. to Burt Rd.

10.0 Right onto Burt Rd.

10.8 Left onto Davis Bay Rd.

11.6 Arrive at Center Church and Lopez Union Cemetery.

12.0 Right onto Fisherman Bay Rd.

12.3 Right onto Kjargaard Rd.

13.0 Right onto Richardson Rd., which becomes Vista Rd. as it curves east.

15.7 Right onto Mud Bay Rd.

16.8 Right onto MacKaye Harbor Rd. at Islandale store (restrooms, groceries).

18.6 Arrive at Agate Beach County Park (restrooms). Depart by returning north on MacKaye Harbor Rd. to Mud Bay Rd.

20.5 Left onto Mud Bay Rd., which becomes Center Rd.

24.9 Right onto School Rd.

25.8 Left onto Lopez Sound Rd.

27.3 Right onto Port Stanley Rd.

29.1 Right onto Baker View Rd.

29.9 Arrive at Spencer Spit State Park (restrooms, camping). Depart by returning on Baker View Rd. to Port Stanley Rd.

30.7 Right onto Port Stanley Rd.

33.1 Right onto Ferry Rd.

34.2 Arrive at ferry dock to end tour.

44 Orcas Island

DIFFICULTY: moderate
TIME: allow 3 hours
DISTANCE: 21.8 miles
ELEVATION GAIN: 1615 feet

Getting There: Take I-5 north to exit 230, SR 20; turn left at exit onto SR 20 west to Anacortes. Right onto Commercial Ave., then left onto 12th St., following signs for Washington State Ferries. Paid parking at ferry terminal.

GPS Coordinates: N48 30 23 W122 40 42
Transit: Skagit Transit 410, no Sunday service

Orcas Island is a conundrum shaped like a horseshoe. On one hand, it provides some of the most beautiful, challenging terrain in the San Juans and some wonderful places to shop, eat, and sleep. On the other hand, that tough terrain is made even more so by narrow, winding roads, most of which do not have shoulders, and by drivers who are not as welcoming or tolerant as are those on the other San Juan islands. It's a combination of factors that, in the end, makes Orcas an island that should be visited only by experienced cyclists who are pretty fit. This tour route provides access to the island's easier half, the west, and leaves you at a jumping-off point if you want to tackle the more challenging east side.

As with all ferry departures, cyclists should pull over as soon as they're clear of the ferry and let the cars depart. It's safer and more efficient, and you breathe a lot less car exhaust. That's especially true on these islands, which invariably have a steep hill to climb as you leave the ferry dock. The small cluster of buildings around the Orcas ferry dock includes a hotel, a grocery, and a couple of eateries, the only services available until you reach Eastsound, the tour's destination. But it's just 12 miles to Eastsound, and there are great lunch and picnic choices there, so riders should just fill their water bottles in Orcas and climb that first hill. Once the ferry has emptied, the traffic is generally pretty light, although this route makes liberal use of the island's main road.

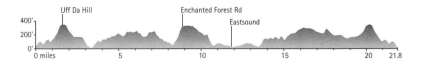

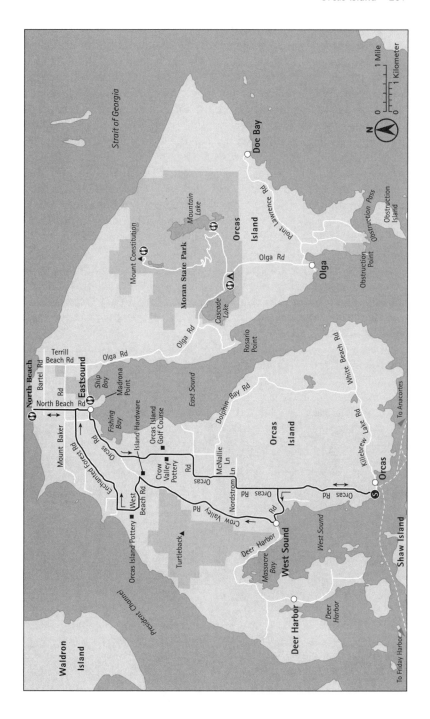

Depart the main road at the top of the first big hill, fittingly named by some wag as "Uff Da Hill" (note the sign naming the small lane at the top of the hill as Uff Da Hill Road). Loosely translated from the Norwegian, another name for the long climb would be #$*^!$% Hill. You'll see a couple more of these hills, but first you enjoy a quiet road that takes you west through picturesque West Sound and then north to rolling hills and beautiful scenery on the west side of Crow Valley.

The valley holds working farms flanked by forests and two pottery studios. On the way north, visit Orcas Island Pottery in its stunning setting at the end of a wooded lane above West Beach. The outbound route continues north to meet the cunningly named Enchanted Forest Road (which greets you with up to a 10 percent grade in a half-mile climb at 8.3 miles—another "uff da" experience you may find yourself walking up).

If you're staying the night, book a place in or near Eastsound, which is at the top of the horseshoe, and make the island's main town your home base for other rides. Its dozen blocks contain a great variety of eateries, a well-stocked market, and shops representing the plentiful local artisans.

A delightful jaunt out of Eastsound takes you a mile north to touch the waters on the north side of the island. Ride up North Beach Road to its end, where sits a small beachfront park. Across the pebbled beach

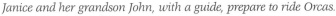

Janice and her grandson John, with a guide, prepare to ride Orcas.

and blue water can be seen Patos, Sucia, and Matia islands. Another great picnic spot, adjacent to downtown Eastsound, is the Madrona Point Preserve, just east around the bay from Main Street.

The adventurous could depart Eastsound up another Viking-vexing hill away from Crescent Beach Drive, then down Olga Road toward Moran State Park on the far side of the island (not charted in this tour, but obvious on a map). The 5.5 miles to the park's entrance, just beyond Rosario Road, are pretty much one big climb, but if the spirit is willing, the shoulder is (mostly) generous. The biggest climb, of course, comes within the park, if you ascend nearly 2000 vertical feet to the top of Mount Constitution in another 5 miles. You can visit Cascade Lake and Mountain Lake along the way or make one of those bracing, beautiful spots your camping destination. Hardy souls wanting to complete the island circuit can ride 2 more hilly miles south from the park entrance to the burg of Olga and 3 similar miles farther to Doe Bay Resort, which has much-anticipated hot tubs and accommodations ranging from camping to hostel beds to yurts.

For this tour, return from Eastsound via the main road, which takes you by Crow Valley Pottery, the oldest occupied building on the island, dating from 1866, which is now a potter's studio. The main road, although containing more traffic, has a shoulder suitable for use part of the way, and of course you get to take your revenge on Uff Da Hill in a screaming ride back down to the ferry dock.

Route Connections: Ride the interisland ferries to Lopez (Tour 43), San Juan (Tours 45 and 46), and Shaw (Tour 47) islands.

MILEAGE LOG

0.0 Depart ferry dock up Orcas Rd.

2.5 Left onto Pinneo Rd., which becomes Deer Harbor Rd.

3.5 Right onto Crow Valley Rd. just beyond West Sound.

7.0 Left at Island Hardware onto West Beach Rd.

8.0 Pass lane to Orcas Island Pottery, a 0.5-mile round-trip detour.

8.3 Right onto Enchanted Forest Rd.

10.7 Enter Eastsound, crossing Lover's Ln. at a stop sign.

10.9 Left at T onto North Beach Rd.

11.9 Arrive at North Beach (restrooms). Reverse route to return to Eastsound.

12.9 At intersection with Enchanted Forest Rd., continue south into town.

13.3 Arrive at Main St. in center of town (restrooms). Turn right on Main St. to begin return route.

13.5 Left onto Orcas Rd. to depart Eastsound.

14.7 Bear left at clearly marked Y to stay on Orcas Rd.

15.7 Arrive at Crow Valley Pottery on west side of road, just beyond golf course entrance.

16.5 Continue south on Orcas Rd. as it curves right at triangular intersection, then left, then right and left again.

21.8 Arrive at ferry dock to end tour.

45 San Juan Island: Lime Kiln and Roche Harbor

DIFFICULTY: moderate
TIME: allow 4 hours
DISTANCE: 31.8 miles
ELEVATION GAIN: 2059 feet

Getting There: Take I-5 north to exit 230, SR 20; turn left at exit onto SR 20 west to Anacortes. Right onto Commercial Ave., then left onto 12th St., following signs for Washington State Ferries. Paid parking at ferry terminal.

GPS Coordinates: N48 30 23 W122 40 42
Transit: Skagit Transit 410; no Sunday service

Ah, for a bike and the island life . . . you don't need much more motivation than that for an enjoyable trip to San Juan Island. Although the riding is more challenging than it is on Lopez, it's less so than on Orcas, making it the perfect middle ground for a few days of exploration. In this chapter are two San Juan Island tours—this one encompasses most of the island and the other (Tour 46) picks up its southeast corner—but a quick look at the map shows that you can easily depart from either of these directions to discover your own path. Or combine them for a complete circuit.

Each tour is a loop from Friday Harbor, the county seat and largest town in the islands. This loop, the larger of the two, heads west from

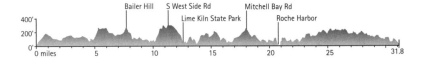

Rolling hills, cattle, and few cars are found on San Juan Island.

town on San Juan Valley Road, with open views of farms and ranches. Turning south, you encounter Pelindaba Lavender Farm, which fills one side of a small valley with rows of the fragrant herb. Picturesque farm buildings and equipment, a gift shop with lavender lemonade and cookies, and a self-guided walking tour make this a great break. Restrooms are available here, and you'll probably find your panniers scented with the purple flowers for the rest of the ride. The farm has a lavender festival in late July and operates a downtown Friday Harbor store, if you want to load up on lotions and soaps as gifts but don't want to lug them up the island's hills.

Speaking of which, the next leg takes you to the most beautiful views on any of the island tours, as you head for the island's west side. Turning west, you crest Bailer Hill Road at Edwards Point and burst upon the expanse of Haro Strait far below. West Side Road then snakes its way north, with continuous views along an open expanse of road until you reach Lime Kiln State Park, also known as Whale Watch Park. Exploration here is a must. You may or may not see orca acrobatics in the waters of Deadman Bay, but you will enjoy a picturesque light-house, a rocky shoreline, and the unique lime kilns, which were used to cook limestone into lime, a lucrative business when the island was

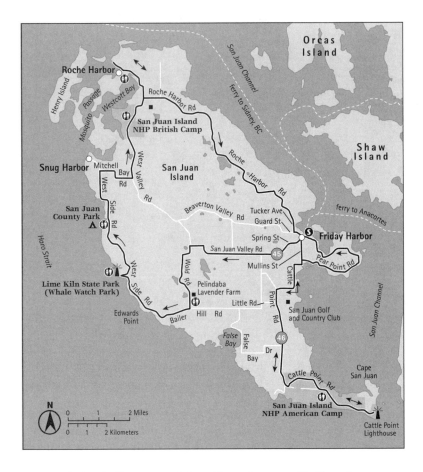

first settled. A hulking stone kiln still perches on a bluff, and remnants of the operation can be seen throughout the park. Restrooms and water with a high sodium content are available at the parking area of this popular park.

Continuing north, you can drop down to the water at San Juan County Park or take a short side trip into Snug Harbor on a steep gravel road before turning east, then north again to head for British Camp and Roche Harbor.

The San Juan Island National Historical Park British Camp is one of two sites on the island that commemorate the Pig War, which began in 1859 when an American settler on the island killed a British settler's pig. Get the full story of the ensuing 12-year standoff between American and British soldiers at this park or the American Camp, which is visited on Tour 46. Today the British Camp flies a mammoth Union Jack above a small formal garden and restored blockhouse, and a walk along the brief trails reveals great views from Mount Young, a cemetery, and other relics.

Roche Harbor offers a delightful final stop on this loop tour. A bustling harbor for big yachts is presided over by the Hotel de Haro, built in 1886 by the founder of the settlement, who also was the owner of the lime mining company. Open-air cafés serve up sandwiches and fish-and-chips in an idyllic waterfront setting. The town has been expanding, and rows of brightly painted townhomes line the road down to the old hotel. At the town's entrance is the Westcott Bay Institute Sculpture Garden, which offers self-guided tours of more than 100 sculptures in natural settings, supported by modest donations requested of visitors.

Ride southeast on Roche Harbor Road. Although it's the island's busiest drive, it offers a good shoulder for safe cycling back to Friday Harbor.

Route Connections: Connect to the shorter San Juan Island loop (Tour 46); ride the interisland ferries to Lopez (Tour 43), Orcas (Tour 44), and Shaw (Tour 47) islands.

MILEAGE LOG

0.0 Right off ferry dock onto Front St., then left in 1 block onto Spring St., heading west.

0.8 Spring St. becomes San Juan Valley Rd. as you leave town.

4.4 Left onto Wold Rd.

6.2 Arrive at Pelindaba Lavender Farm (restrooms).

6.8 Right onto Bailer Hill Rd., which becomes West Side Rd.

9.9 Left into Lime Kiln State Park.

10.1 Arrive at parking area in park (restrooms).

10.2 Left onto West Side Rd. when leaving park.

12.6 Left into San Juan County Park (restrooms). Retrace route to depart park.

14.7 Curve right onto Mitchell Bay Rd. (turn left here for a detour to Snug Harbor).

16.0 Left onto West Valley Rd.

17.8 Left into San Juan Island National Historical Park at British Camp.

18.2 Arrive at British Camp parking lot (restrooms). Retrace route to depart park.

18.6 Left onto West Valley Rd. when leaving park.

19.7 Left onto Roche Harbor Rd.

21.3 Arrive at town of Roche Harbor.

21.4 Take first right to hotel and harbor (restrooms).

21.6 Forward at end of parking onto Reuben Memorial Dr.
21.7 Left onto Roche Harbor Rd. to depart town.
22.4 Right into parking at Westcott Bay Institute Sculpture Garden.
      Depart park by making right onto Roche Harbor Rd.
28.0 Pass San Juan Vineyard tasting room in an 1896 schoolhouse.
31.0 At Friday Harbor town limits, road becomes Tucker Ave.
31.3 Left onto Guard St.
31.7 Left onto Spring St.
31.8 Arrive at ferry dock to end tour.

46 San Juan Island: Cattle Point

DIFFICULTY: moderate
TIME: allow 3 hours
DISTANCE: 26 miles
ELEVATION GAIN: 1486 feet

Getting There: Take I-5 north to exit 230, SR 20; turn left at exit onto SR 20 west to Anacortes. Right onto Commercial Ave., then left onto 12th St., following signs for Washington State Ferries. Paid parking at ferry terminal.

GPS Coordinates: N48 30 23 W122 40 42
Transit: Skagit Transit 410; no Sunday service

This shorter, less hilly tour of southeast San Juan Island offers a mellower form of entertainment. Although fewer points of interest are found along its 26-mile route and there is no glittering marina socked away at the far end, there are similarities. You'll find plentiful water views, a historical park, and a lighthouse. On clear days, you'll also be treated to views of stunning snowcapped peaks. This tour provides a wonderful opportunity to while away an afternoon, perhaps with a snack stop or relaxation at one of the beaches in American Camp. Restrooms and water are available at the park's visitor center, but no other services are to be found along the route.

Depart Friday Harbor through its southern neighborhood and enjoy the well-kept, Victorian-style homes on Argyle Road. Skirt the

Cattle Point Lighthouse

fairgrounds, airport, and golf course as you pedal south. A side trip west to False Bay, via Little Road, Bailer Hill Road, and False Bay Drive (partly unpaved), gains views south toward the Olympic Peninsula.

At 6 miles from town you arrive at San Juan Island National Historical Park American Camp. The visitor center provides details of the American-British boundary dispute that led to this military camp being occupied between 1859 and 1872. (Visit British Camp, on the other end of the island, by riding Tour 45.) A packed-gravel road through the windswept grasses of the park provides wonderful views of the Strait of Juan de Fuca to the south. A lower foot trail goes to the beach. There are also two beaches on the northern side of this narrow spit occupied by the park, and they provide worthwhile short hikes or picnic spots.

One interesting site high on this overlook is Robert's Redoubt. This "redoubt" was an earthen fortification dug to contain the large cannons the Americans planned to use to blast British ships out of the bay below. Although a naval standoff took place during the Pig War, only once was a gun fired from this redoubt, and that was to salute the camp's commander. The redoubt is named for Second Lieutenant

Henry M. Robert, who supervised its construction and went on to later, greater fame as the author of *Robert's Rules of Order*—clearly a good person to have in charge of a standoff.

After exploring the park, venture farther south to the end of Cattle Point Road. You'll enjoy a long, gradual hill that provides stunning views of the Cattle Point Lighthouse and land masses beyond; Lopez Island is just to the east. A clear day will treat you to more wondrous mountain views, as Mount Rainier looms above the verdant lands to the south and Mount Baker is visible above the islands to the east.

This lighthouse, as with the one at Lime Kiln State Park on the other San Juan tour, must be visited on foot. Until 2004 a horn sounded every 30 seconds from this lighthouse to aid navigation through the San Juan Channel. Just up the road is a rocky overlook with an interpretive area that includes a small building where a military radioman was stationed to listen for the navigational call "QTE," which in the language of the mariner means "where am I?" You won't need directional aids on your ride, however, because the road dead-ends at a private marina, forcing you to loop back and return to the park and, ultimately, to Friday Harbor, via Cattle Point Road.

As you near town, detour east onto Pear Point Road, which skirts North Bay past a gravel pit and through pastoral scenes before curving back around, above a shipyard and through a dense section of town overlooking Brown Island. The route drops you into downtown just two blocks from the ferry.

Route Connections: Connect to the longer San Juan Island loop (Tour 45); ride the interisland ferries to Lopez (Tour 43), Orcas (Tour 44), and Shaw (Tour 47) islands.

MILEAGE LOG

0.0 Right off ferry dock onto Front St., then left in 1 block onto Spring St., heading west.

0.2 Left onto Argyle Rd.

1.3 Left onto Cattle Point Rd.

3.1 Pass Little Rd. on right.

4.6 Pass False Bay Dr. on right.

6.2 Right into San Juan Island National Historical Park American Camp at driveway beyond sign.

6.5 Arrive at visitor center (restrooms). Ride through American Camp on gravel road at east end of parking lot.

7.7 Right onto Cattle Point Rd. at end of park road.

9.9 Arrive at path to lighthouse (no bikes allowed on path).

10.1 Arrive at Cattle Point Interpretive Area.

10.8 Reach end of road at Cape San Juan private dock. Retrace route to return to Cattle Point Rd.

16.0 Pass entrance to American Camp visitor center. At all intersections, stay on Cattle Point Rd.

20.9 Right onto Pear Point Rd.

21.5 Pass gravel pit, where road is unpaved for 0.3 mile.

23.2 Road becomes Turn Point Rd.

24.6 Pass Shipyard Harbor.

25.4 Right at Y onto Warbass Wy.

25.8 Right onto Harrison St.

25.9 Right onto East St.

26.0 Arrive at ferry dock to end tour.

47 Shaw Island

DIFFICULTY: easy
TIME: allow 2 hours
DISTANCE: 13.4 miles
ELEVATION GAIN: 886 feet

Getting There: Take I-5 north to exit 230, SR 20; turn left at exit onto SR 20 west to Anacortes. Right onto Commercial Ave., then left onto 12th St., following signs for Washington State Ferries. Paid parking at ferry terminal.

GPS Coordinates: N48 30 23 W122 40 42
Transit: Skagit Transit 410; no Sunday service

A leisurely spin around the smallest of the four San Juan islands served by the state ferries holds some quiet revelations. Walk the grounds of the school if it's closed; you may see the alphabet spelled out in pieces of driftwood, mounted in rows on an exterior wall. Riding the main road, where a car goes by every 15 minutes or so, you may startle a deer bounding off into the opposite ditch, hind hooves kicking soil onto the road in its haste.

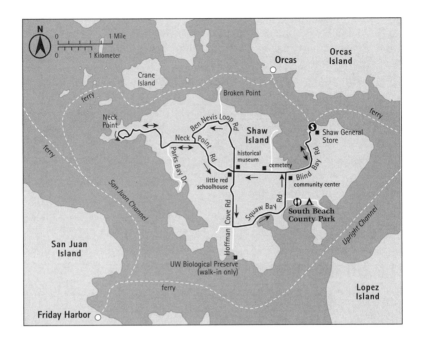

Those delightful moments are a fitting way to end a visit to the San Juan islands, and this tour can be easily managed in the middle of a day returning to Anacortes, or plan for it to be an easy day trip out and back from a multiple-day stay on another island. Shaw is 7.7 square miles of mostly wooded land snuggled between Lopez, Orcas, and San Juan islands. Its ferry dock is visible from the Orcas dock, and the other islands seem so close you feel you can almost touch them. Take an early-morning boat from San Juan or Orcas to be on Shaw's quiet roads by midmorning, and you can easily complete the island ride and be somewhere else by lunch. Or take the day, pack a picnic, and spend the afternoon on the beach at Shaw's one public resting spot: South Beach County Park.

The only road from the ferry, Blind Bay Road, leads south, then west past the cemetery to an intersection with the island's main side roads. Here you'll find the small public library and even smaller historical museum. Across the road sits the well-kept school, its meticulous red-and-white paint job masking its age; it is the oldest continually operating school in the state. A comfortable playground and newer classrooms centered around a courtyard behind the classic old "little red schoolhouse" complete a picture of an educational haven. No wonder it's on the National Register of Historic Places.

Head north from the main road onto Ben Nevis Loop Road, which reaches nearly the west edge of the island. Complete the cross-island ride by taking Neck Point Road all the way to its end, even though the views are mostly of trees and a few houses on the road end's cul-de-sac. Head back east to the school intersection, this time heading south on the other side road, Hoffman Cove Road. This takes you past the University of Washington Biological Preserve, where walk-in viewing is allowed. Continue along Squaw Bay Road east past South Beach to the county park, which has pit toilets, water, camping, and a curving stretch of sandy beach. Lopez can be seen across Upright Channel, in which sailboats often ply the waters.

From the county park it's a quick 2 miles north back to the ferry. At the dock, shop the only commercial establishment on the island: visit the Shaw General Store, open on Sundays during the summer.

Route Connections: Ride the interisland ferries to Lopez (Tour 43), Orcas (Tour 44), and San Juan (Tours 45 and 46) islands.

The well-kept Little Red Schoolhouse

MILEAGE LOG

0.0 Depart ferry dock onto Blind Bay Rd.

1.3 Pass community center at intersection with Squaw Bay Rd.

2.2 Arrive at 4-way intersection; school, library, and historical museum. Turn right onto Ben Nevis Loop Rd.

4.2 Right onto Neck Point Rd.

4.7 Stay right at Y with Parks Bay Dr.

5.6 Stay left at Y at Harbor Wy.

5.8 Stay right at Y at Sylvan Circle.

5.9 Stay left at Y with Cameron Rd. to stay on Sylvan Circle.

6.3 Right onto Neck Point Rd.; retrace route.

8.0 Right onto Ben Nevis Loop Rd.

9.0 Right onto Hoffman Cove Rd. at 4-way intersection with school-house.

10.0 Left onto Squaw Bay Rd. (continue straight for side trip to UW Biological Preserve).

11.2 Right onto unpaved road signed for camping.

11.4 Arrive at South Beach County Park (restrooms). Retrace route to depart park.

11.7 Right onto Squaw Bay Rd.

12.1 Right on Blind Bay Rd.

13.4 Arrive at ferry dock to end tour.

Opposite: *Tulips bloom at the Roozengaarde display garden.*

48 Skagit Flats and Tulip Fields

DIFFICULTY: moderate
TIME: allow 4 hours
DISTANCE: 35.7 miles
ELEVATION GAIN: 227 feet

Getting There: Take I-5 to Mount Vernon; depart at exit 226, Kincaid St./SR 536. Left at stoplight onto Kincaid. Cross railroad tracks, then right onto S. 3rd St. Road curves left and turns into Division St. Continue 2 blocks, cross bridge, then first left onto N. Front St. into Edgewater Park.

GPS Coordinates: N48 25 05 W122 20 31

Transit: Skagit Transit 90X county connector to Everett; 204, 205, 206, 207

Here's a tour for those longing for the open road—the flat, open road. It's 35 miles of farm roads, punctuated by a visit to the small tourist town of La Conner. Former Midwestern farm kids will feel at home, and city dwellers will definitely know they're not in urbanity any more.

Skagit Flats has much to offer beyond tulips. Although the spring flowers are the most colorful example of Northwest farming, they're only a part of Skagit Valley agriculture. Farmers post signs along the roads listing their crops, from wheat to berries to seed crop for spinach, beets, and cabbage. Riding along the fields provides a connection with those farms and our amazing abundance of healthy food. That's why on this tour, perhaps more than any other, slow your pedaling a bit when you see a farmer out working in the fields and raise a hand in appreciation. You most certainly will get a friendly wave in return.

Park at convenient Edgewater Park, just across the river from downtown Mount Vernon. It's free, easy to find, and very accessible to Interstate 5. Bike across the rusty bridge and cycle through the town's homey business district, then in a few minutes you're south of town, riding along a dike that protects the residences from the annual rising of the Skagit River.

As you ride south, the Cascades loom to the east. A quick right over the bridge at Conway puts you on Fir Island, actually a riverine delta where the fertile sponginess of the soil is evident in the abundant rows

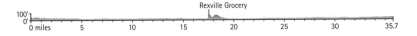

Rexville Grocery

100'
0'
0 miles   5   10   15   20   25   30   35.7

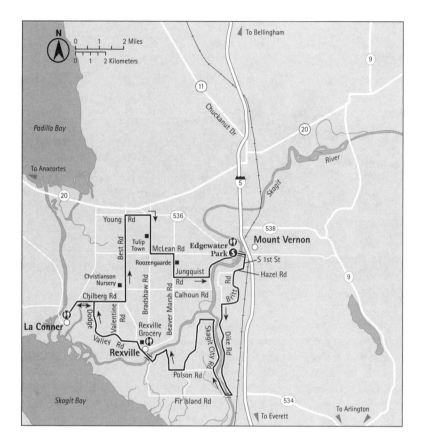

of crops. Ride north along the other side of the dike on Skagit City Road to circumnavigate the northern edges of the island. This is the most secluded, verdant segment of the ride. Look for many varieties of birds, keeping an eye open for hawks and eagles that are known to soar the thermals and perch in the trees along the river.

Exit the island on Best Road via a busy bridge with no shoulder. Coast off the bridge into the waiting arms of the Rexville Grocery, with its jaunty promise of "Foods Galore." Adjacent to this well-stocked grocery-deli is the Rexville Farmers Market, bursting every Saturday in summer with local vegetables, baked goods, smoked fish, and other delicacies.

(If you'd like to get to a tour of the tulips more quickly, skip the Fir Island portion of the ride and head straight west on McLean Road from the start. You can easily navigate the grid of roads and follow your own path through this wide-open country, simply meeting up with a familiar road should you stray.)

Cyclists enjoy the tulip fields in spring.

Next stop on this route is La Conner, a sophisticated small town. Head west into town on Chilberg Road, idling alongside the inevitable tourist traffic past the town's many curio shops and antique stores. Highlights include the glass and sculpture of the Museum of Northwest Art on South First Street. There are plenty of places for a coffee or snack stop.

Refreshed and feeling fully like a tourist, head toward the tulip fields. Take care to note intersection signs that warn "crossing traffic does not stop." Nor does it slow down. But most of the busy roads in this area have wide, clean shoulders, so ride north with confidence. Along the way you'll pass Christianson Nursery and, in season, plenty of colorful tulip fields. But the real tulip show is yet to come, at Tulip Town, one of the area's two major show gardens. As you wheel by the long lines of cars inching toward the paid parking, you'll feel quite superior and free.

After a visit, shake off the tulip-color dizziness and get back on the road heading south. For comparison, stop at Roozengaarde, the other tulip haven. This one boasts a larger windmill and outdoor show gardens with swaths of tulips in every color, stripe, and crinkle style. (Note: both tulip farms charge a small entrance fee.) Wheel out of there, again heading south, making the first left to head back to Mount Vernon. At the edge of the valley, ride north along the dike once again to head back to Edgewater Park.

Route Connections: Loop northwest to Anacortes at La Conner (Tour 49).

MILEAGE LOG

0.0 Right out of Edgewater Park's (restrooms) parking lot onto S. Ball St.

0.1 Right onto sidewalk on Division St. to cross bridge into downtown Mount Vernon.

0.4 Right onto S. 1st St., which becomes Cleveland St.

1.0 Right onto W. Hazel St.

1.4 Hazel curves left and becomes Britt Rd.

3.5 Left onto Dike Rd. as Britt Rd. ends.

7.4 Right onto Fir Island Rd.; cross over bridge onto Fir Island.

7.7 Right onto Skagit City Rd. immediately after bridge. It turns west, then south to become Dry Slough Rd.

12.6 At stop sign, cross Moore Rd. to continue south on Dry Slough Rd.

13.8 Right onto Polson Rd.

15.3 Left onto Moore Rd.

16.1 Right onto Best Rd.; cross over bridge to leave Fir Island. Caution: no bike lane or shoulder on bridge.

16.7 Arrive at Rexville Grocery (restrooms).

17.1 Left onto Dodge Valley Rd. Caution: busy stretch of road; traffic can be fast.

18.0 Left at Y at Valentine Rd.

20.2 Left onto Chilberg Rd. Caution: highway speeds; cross traffic does not stop.

21.0 Continue west through roundabout into La Conner.

21.4 Arrive at La Conner town center (restrooms). Retrace route to depart La Conner.

21.8 Continue east at roundabout on Chilberg Rd.

24.3 Left onto Best Rd.; pass Christianson Nursery (restrooms) on left.

27.3 Right onto Young Rd.

28.3 Merge onto SR 536 at stop sign, then turn right onto Bradshaw Rd. Caution: busy highway; traffic can be fast.

28.6 Arrive at Tulip Town display gardens.

29.9 Left onto McLean Rd.

30.8 Right onto Beaver Marsh Rd.

31.3 Arrive at Roozengaarde tulip display gardens.

31.8 Left onto Jungquist Rd.

33.4 Left onto Penn Rd.

34.4 Right onto McLean Rd.

35.4 Left onto S. Wall St.

35.5 Right onto W. Division St. at light.

35.6 Right onto S. Ball St. to return to Edgewater Park and end tour.

49 La Conner to Anacortes

DIFFICULTY: challenging
TIME: allow 5 hours
DISTANCE: 38.8 miles
ELEVATION GAIN: 2075 feet

Getting There: Take I-5 to Conway; depart at exit 221, SR 536. Left onto Pioneer Hwy., then quickly right onto Fir Island Rd. Left onto Best Rd., left onto Dodge Valley Rd., and left onto Chilberg Rd. to arrive at La Conner. Left onto Maple Ave., right onto Caledonia St., and right onto 3rd St. to reach public parking at 10.9 miles from I-5.

GPS Coordinates N48 23 16 W122 29 50
Transit 90X county connector to Everett; 615

If you get up to Skagit County only for the tulip tour or when you're heading to the San Juan Islands, you're missing out. There are some great rides around the county, visiting its small towns, waterfront roads, and islands. This tour, exploring Fidalgo Island, combines all those elements.

Start in La Conner, on the southwest corner of the county's mainland. The tour immediately heads out of this small tourism-heavy town, but plan some time either before or after your ride to explore it. It's an artistic place, and many galleries and artisan shops line the downtown streets. The Museum of Northwest Art showcases the work of many modern artists, including famous ones who lived, visited, and worked in La Conner. The town is also connected to the area's agricultural bounty, so you can eat and drink well here. The county's historical museum is in town, and through parks, plaques, and preserved historic structures, there's plenty of grist for the historian's mill as well.

Departing town on this ride, you pass by one of those historical spots. Pioneer Park sits at water's edge and pays homage to the town's namesake, Louisa A. Conner, whose husband, John, started a trading post here in the 1860s and bought the deed to the town's original land. Pass over the arcing red Rainbow Bridge, which is on a national historic registry, and enter the Swinomish Indian Tribal Community. The Swinomish, original settlers on this land, are still a large presence.

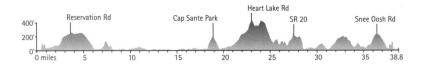

The bridge is your gateway to Fidalgo Island, which you'll be on for the entire tour. Ride north up Reservation Road until you nearly reach busy State Route 20, the highway that connects Interstate 5 to Anacortes and the San Juan Islands ferry terminal. Parallel the highway and soon cross under it to pass the Swinomish Casino and Lodge, then head west and north to circumnavigate March Point, a large thumb separating Padilla Bay to the east from Fidalgo Bay, which laps at the shore of downtown Anacortes.

March Point is a bit of a conundrum. Look left on much of this 5-mile loop and you'll see industry, as the point is mostly covered with two large oil refineries. But look right, or cast your gaze upward, and it's a different story. The road runs right along the coastline, so you get great views of the bay and the islands. Overhead, herons head to a nearby rookery, and many other birds, including eagles, can be spotted.

Depart the point by taking the trail on a trestle that cuts through Fidalgo Bay. Called the Tommy Thompson Trail, it's been renovated as a bike-ped gem. The trail continues along the shore into downtown Anacortes.

And now, about halfway through the tour, take some time to enjoy another great town. At about 15,000 people, Anacortes is much larger than La Conner, and its downtown Commercial Avenue hosts a number of cafés and shops. A picturesque marina is protected by a hook-shaped outcropping of land capped by Cap Sante Park. Ride to the tip of the park for a fabulous lookout that gives you great views on nearly all points of the compass.

Cycling through Anacortes, you'll find quiet, designated bike routes. Pass Causland Park, and stop to admire its stonework. It was built in

Cap Sante Park, near downtown Anacortes, offers a 360-degree view of the town, the bay, and Guemes Island.

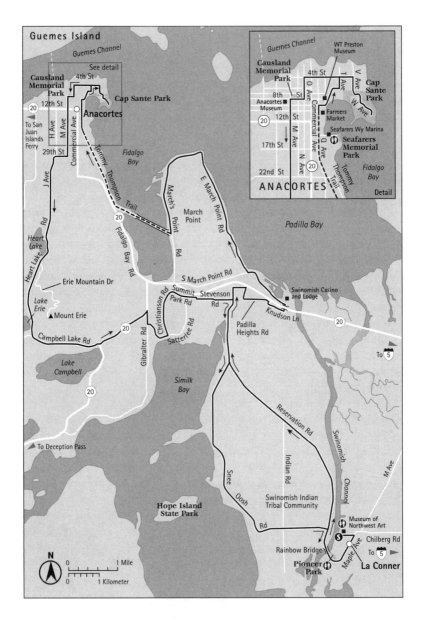

the 1920s by a World War I veteran, Louis Lapage, who needed to exorcise his demons from that terrible war. The meticulous, intricate laying of colored stones in whimsical patterns must have been soothing to his psyche, and it is a great legacy for the town.

Depart Anacortes south through the center of Fidalgo Island. (If you want to circle its perimeter and/or head to the San Juan Islands Ferry, see Tour 42, which brings you up from Oak Harbor on Whidbey Island through Deception Pass to the ferry dock.)

The center of Fidalgo Island's main mass gets rural, hilly, and wooded, but you won't see just trees. You pass by a few lakes, the most scenic being Lake Erie, on your right at about 25 miles. On your left is Mount Erie, which another cycling author, Mike McQuaide (see Recommended Resources), called the "leg shredder." He points out that its 1273 feet, 900 of which are gained in just 1.5 miles from this road, earns it that nickname and another one: "the house of pain." But if you're feeling frisky at this juncture, take a detour and climb its steep paved road. I hear the view is great, and I'm sure coming down is simply thrilling.

Climbers scale the bare rock face of Erie, which can be seen on the left as you turn here and head east. Another scenic view soon comes up on the right: Lake Campbell. You can see a small wooded island in the center, giving Campbell the unusual situation of being a lake on an island with an island in its lake. Ponder that brainteaser as you pick up busy State Route 20 northbound for a bit, then enjoy a number of small side roads around Similk Bay and through the reservation to head back to La Conner.

Route Connections: From La Conner, head northeast to tour the Skagit Flats (Tour 48). From the middle of this ride, at State Route 20 near Campbell Lake, you could head south to Oak Harbor (Tour 42). Also, the Skagit Valley is only a few miles from the north terminus of the Centennial Trail (Tour 51), which heads north to the Skagit Valley line from Snohomish; ride north and west on State Route 9 and State Route 534 to intersect Interstate 5 at Conway in 8 miles, and, after crossing under the freeway, side roads can be taken to get to La Conner and the rest of the valley.

MILEAGE LOG

0.0 Left out of street parking onto 3rd St. In 100 yards, left onto Caledonia St.

0.3 Right onto Maple Ave.

0.6 Pass Pioneer Park (restrooms).

0.7 Cross Rainbow Bridge in car lane, not narrow sidewalk. Road continues as Reservation Rd.

2.8 Pass Indian Rd.

5.4 Pass Snee Oosh Rd.

6.9 Right onto Padilla Heights Rd. Gear down for short, steep climb.

8.0   Right onto Long John Dr.

8.5   Cycle three-fourths of the way around roundabout. Follow signs to Casino Rd. In 1 block, after passing under SR 20, proceed forward on Casino Rd. around second roundabout.

9.0   Right onto E. March Point Rd. Follow Bike Route 10 signs.

9.7   Right onto March's Point Rd.

14.3 Right onto Tommy Thompson Trail.

16.3 Pass Anacortes shipyard.

18.0 Right onto 9th St. In 1 block, soft left onto Market St., which becomes 6th St. Pass marina (restrooms) on right.

18.4 Left onto T Ave.

18.5 Right onto 4th St.

18.6 Right onto V Ave. as road comes to a T.

19.1 Arrive at Cap Sante Park and lookout. Retrace route to depart park.

19.6 Left onto 4th St.

20.1 Left onto O Ave.

20.3 Right onto 8th St. Pass Causland Memorial Park.

20.4 Left onto M Ave.

21.6 Right onto 29th St.

21.9 Straight at J Ave. onto bike lane facing the one-way street. J Ave. becomes I Ave., then Heart Lake Rd.

23.5 Pass Heart Lake.

23.8 Pass Erie Mountain Dr.

25.4 Pass Lake Erie.

25.5 Left onto Campbell Lake Rd. at intersection with Rosario Rd.

25.9 Pass Lake Campbell.

27.0 Left onto SR 20. Caution: traffic.

28.2 Right onto Gibralter Rd.

28.4 Left on Satterlee Rd.

29.0 Left onto Christianson Rd.

29.9 Bear right onto Summit Park Rd. at Y with Christianson.

30.4 Right onto Thompson Rd., then in 50 yards, left on Stevenson Rd.

31.2 Right onto Reservation Rd.

32.4 Right onto Snee Oosh Rd.

37.7 Right onto Reservation Rd.

38.1 Cross Rainbow Bridge. Road becomes Maple Ave.

38.6 Left on Caledonia St.

38.8 Right on 3rd St.; arrive at street parking to end tour.

Opposite: *A ferry docks next to the waterfront park in Edmonds.*
(Photo by L. J. McAllister)

SNOHOMISH COUNTY

50 Interurban Trail and Mukilteo

DIFFICULTY: challenging
TIME: allow 5 hours
DISTANCE: 44.3 miles
ELEVATION GAIN: 2109 feet

Getting There: From I-5, take exit 178, Mountlake Terrace/236th St. SW. Turn left onto 236th St. SW, which becomes Lakeview Dr. Turn left into parking at Ballinger Park.

GPS Coordinates: N47 47 07 W122 19 33
Transit: Community Transit 113, 417, 880

Patching together a bike route through urban and suburban neighborhoods, not to mention crossing city lines into different jurisdictions, is a long, arduous process. So it's no surprise that the north section of the Interurban Trail, which runs from Shoreline to Everett, has been a patchwork project. Just a few years ago, this 20-plus-mile route (nearly 45 if you make it a round-trip) was a meandering amalgam of streets, trail segments, sidewalks, even parking lots. But today, it includes fairly long stretches of trail, new overpasses over some of the busiest roads, and well-signed connections. As you ride north, offer silent thanks to the project managers and planners who have made this happen.

The former streetcar route is a fairly safe and interesting connection to the Mukilteo ferry terminal, for those interested in a Whidbey Island excursion (see Tours 38–42). Along the way, you spin by two malls, travel along both sides of Interstate 5, and explore some nice Everett residential neighborhoods.

Start at the south end of the trail, which currently is close to the Snohomish County line, or ride up from Green Lake using the Edmonds route (see Tour 5) to connect with the trail. On the first leg, which bisects Mountlake Terrace and Lynnwood, you ride behind office parks and along busy retail corridors. Cross over Interstate 5 and ride a tree-lined corridor that heads briefly toward Martha Lake and then crosses back to the west side of the interstate as you enter Everett, using a

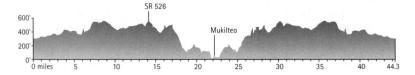

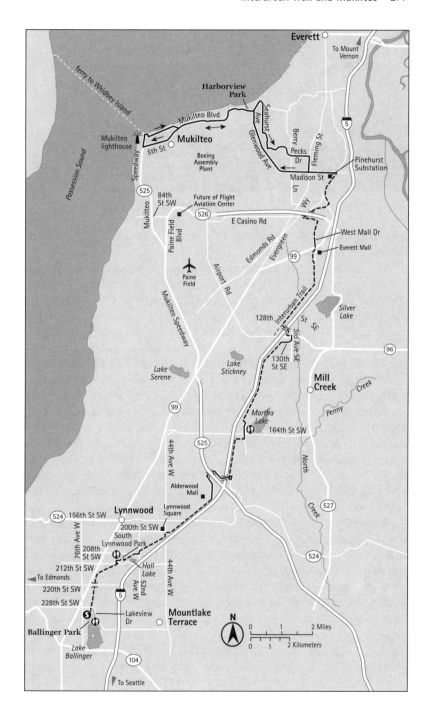

Everett

To Mount
Vernon

5

To Whidbey Island

Ferry to Whidbey Island

Harborview
Park

Mukilteo Blvd

Seahurst Ave

Glenwood Ave

Berry

Fleming St

Mukilteo
lighthouse

5th St

Mukilteo

Pecks
Dr

Pinehurst
Substation

Possession Sound

Speedway

Boeing
Assembly
Plant

Madison St

525

84th
St SW

Future of Flight
Aviation Center

Mukilteo

Paine Field Blvd

526

E Casino Rd

West Mall Dr

Edmonds Rd

Evergreen

99

Everett Mall

Paine
Field

Airport Rd

Interurban Trail

Silver
Lake

96

Mukilteo Speedway

128th

St SE

3rd Ave SE

Lake
Serene

Lake
Stickney

130th
St SE

Mill
Creek

Creek

Penny

99

Martha
Lake

164th St SW

North

525

44th Ave W

Alderwood
Mall

527

Creek

524

156th St SW

Lynnwood

Lynnwood
Square

524

200th St SW

76th Ave W

208th
St SW

South
Lynnwood Park

44th Ave W

212th St SW

Hall
Lake

To Edmonds

220th St SW

52nd Ave W

5

228th St SW

Lakeview
Dr

Mountlake
Terrace

N

0   1   2 Miles

Ballinger Park

Lake
Ballinger

104

0   1   2 Kilometers

To Seattle

Mukilteo Lighthouse and a Washington State ferry

recently created bike-pedestrian Interstate 5 overpass that was one of the biggest hurdles for planners to surmount.

Stay with the trail until south Everett, then head northwest on streets toward Mukilteo Boulevard, a wide, winding road with excellent bike lanes. Endure the traffic to get to Mukilteo, and you won't be disappointed. The ferry-side burg hosts a small collection of shops and cafés, and a picturesque lighthouse sits adjacent to the ferry dock.

If you're feeling adventurous, extend the ride by continuing south out of Mukilteo on the Mukilteo Speedway to a left turn at 84th Street SW that will take you to Paine Field Boulevard and Boeing's Future of Flight Aviation Center. You're greeted by a shining, luxurious company museum that is the starting point for tours of the world's largest building by volume, the company's jet assembly plant. If you're taking this detour, which adds a half-dozen miles on a busy road with a bike lane, I recommend retracing your steps to the ferry dock and rejoining the tour route for the remainder of the return ride, because the busy highways south of Paine Field carry heavy traffic and do not connect well to the Interurban Trail.

Besides, it's a good challenge to try to hit all your marks when returning via the snaky Interurban route. You no longer need a treasure map to navigate your way, but you might feel like you've conquered one of the most circuitous urban routes in the region.

Route Connections: Ride south on the Interurban Trail to Green Lake (Tour 5), or take the Mukilteo ferry to loop south Whidbey Island (Tour 38) or ride to the Coupeville ferry (Tour 39 in reverse), and then on to Coupeville, Oak Harbor, and Deception Pass (Tours 40, 41 and 42). Or turn east on Madison Street in Mukilteo, then north on Broadway to 52nd Street SE and right to pass under Interstate 5 onto Lowell Road to connect to the Snohomish to Everett ride (Tour 52).

MILEAGE LOG

0.0 Left out of parking at Ballinger Park (restrooms) onto Lakeview Dr.

0.3 Right onto Interurban Trail.

0.8 Proceed through underpass at 220th St. SW.

1.6 Left onto 212th St. SW as trail ends, then first right, onto 63rd Ave. W.

1.7 Right onto 211th St. SW.

1.9 Right into South Lynnwood Park (restrooms) between playfield and tennis courts to rejoin trail.

2.4 Jog left as trail ends at 54th Ave. W., then right onto 208th St. SW to continue in bike lane.

2.8 Left onto 52nd Ave. W. briefly, then right onto trail.

3.3 Left onto near sidewalk on 44th Ave. W.

5.0 Stay left at Y to trail end, then ride briefly on Alderwood Mall frontage street to rejoin trail.

5.4 Merge into bike lane along 26th Ave. W.

5.5 Right onto Maple Rd. to go under SR 525, then over I-5.

6.1 Right onto Butternut Rd., then right in 1 block to rejoin trail.

7.3 Left to continue on 13th Ave. W.

7.9 Left onto trail about 1 block north of 164th St. SW, at Martha Lake park (restrooms). Caution: busy road.

10.1 Left onto 130th St. SE.

10.6 Left onto trail at northwest corner of 128th St. SW. Caution: heavy traffic.

10.9 Cross I-5 on bike-pedestrian overpass.

11.0 Right onto trail when exiting overpass.

12.6 Left off trail onto 100th Pl. SE.

12.7 Left onto trail at 100th St. SE.

13.0 Right along SE Everett Mall Wy. Cross street at light, then turn north to continue in bike lane on West Mall Dr.

13.3 Rejoin trail at end of street.

13.7 Left onto 84th St. as trail ends; parallel SR 526.

14.1 Right onto 7th Ave. SE, follow trail signs; curve right again at E. Casino Rd., stay on near sidewalk.

14.3 Right onto trail again after passing under SR 526.

15.0 Cross Beverly Blvd. onto sidewalk, then turn left next to Beverly Park Substation to rejoin trail.

15.6 Left onto Wetmore Ave. as trail ends at Pinehurst Substation.

15.7 Left onto Madison St., which curves north and becomes Glenwood Ave.

18.5 Left onto Mukilteo Blvd., which becomes 5th St.

21.5 Right onto Mukilteo Speedway to waterfront.

21.8 Left onto Front St. to lighthouse and ferry dock. Return from lighthouse, cross Mukilteo Speedway, and continue east on Front St.

22.0 Right onto Mukilteo Speedway.

22.1 Left onto 2nd St.

22.2 Left onto Mukilteo Ln.

23.0 Left onto W. Mukilteo Blvd. to depart town.

25.4 Right onto Seahurst Ave. Caution: steep climb first block.

26.1 Seahurst becomes 52nd St. SW, then 51st Pl. SW, then back to Seahurst.

26.5 Left onto Brookridge Blvd., which becomes Pecks Dr. at Beverly Ln.

27.7 Right onto Fleming St.

28.1 Left onto Madison St. Caution: busy street.

28.7 Right onto Wetmore to rejoin trail.

28.9 Right onto trail at Pinehurst Substation.

29.3 Cross street to right at Beverly Park Substation to rejoin trail.

30.1 Right off trail back onto E. Casino Rd.

30.2 Stay on near sidewalk under SR 526, then left onto 7th Ave. for 1 block, then left into bike lane on 84th.

31.0 Right onto trail as road ends at SE Everett Mall Wy.

31.3 Cross SE Everett Mall Wy., then right onto south sidewalk on West Mall Dr.

31.6 Rejoin trail on left as road curves right.

33.3 Left onto overpass to cross I-5.

33.9 Right onto 3rd Ave. SE and cross 128th St. SW; 3rd curves right to become 130th St. SE.

34.2 Right onto trail as road curves left.

36.5 Right onto Meadow Rd. as trail ends. Meadow becomes 13th Ave. W.

37.0 Right onto trail.

38.1 Left onto Butternut Rd. as trail ends.

38.2 Left onto Maple Rd. Cross over I-5, then under SR 525.

38.9 Merge into left lane for left onto 26th Ave. W. Caution: busy intersection.

39.3 Rejoin trail as road curves right.

41.0 Cross over 44th Ave. W. on bike-pedestrian overpass.

41.8 Left onto 52nd Ave., then right onto trail.

41.9 Exit trail into bike lane on 208th St. SW, then left at 54th Ave. W. to rejoin trail.

42.4 Left out of South Lynnwood Park onto 61st, which curves right to become 211th St. SW.

42.6 Left onto 63rd Ave. W.

42.7 Left onto 212th St. SW, then cross street to rejoin trail.

43.5 Cross 220th St. SW, then right on sidewalk briefly, then left on trail.

44.0 Left onto 228th St. SW.

44.3 Return to parking at Ballinger Park to end tour.

51 Centennial Trail

DIFFICULTY: challenging
TIME: allow 6.5 hours
DISTANCE: 65.6 miles
ELEVATION GAIN: 1131 feet

Getting There: From I-5 in Everett, travel east on US 2 toward Wenatchee. Take third exit off US 2 into Snohomish. Turn right onto 92nd St. SE, which becomes 2nd St. Park at corner of 2nd St. and Lincoln Ave.

GPS Coordinates: N47 56 31 W122 04 33

Transit: Community Transit 424 from Seattle; 270 or 275 from Everett

This is a flat, relaxing ride, mostly in the country, on a trail that's been much expanded recently to create a great link between the towns of Snohomish, Lake Stevens, and Arlington. If you start your tour in Snohomish and loop the entire distance, you'll put in 65 miles (a "metric century" in cycling lingo), which is quite a challenge for many people, even on a flat trail. But the nice thing about this linear rail-trail is that you can pick it up from various trailheads and just ride a section or two, based on your available time and energy level. There are toilets (but not water) at all the trailheads.

A bridle trail parallels the bike and pedestrian trail, mostly set a few feet away on a dirt path in the adjacent ditch. However, equestrians do join the trail at bridges and other crossings, and it's a good idea to leave plenty of space and approach at a moderate speed. At one point, Snohomish County was the dairy capital of the state, but today the closest you'll get to livestock near the trail will be seeing well-groomed, well-behaved horses. As with many communities in the Interstate 5 corridor, the towns along this trail are sprawling into the rural landscape. If that process continues, the Centennial Trail will become another two-wheel commuter link.

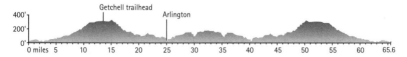

A heritage dairy barn, dating to 1908, marks the north terminus of the Centennial Trail.

Head north out of Snohomish from a new downtown trailhead that includes parking and a small park with a playground. You're just a few blocks from the town's welcoming old center, with its cafés and shops. Public restrooms are available at the corner of First Street and Avenue B in the heart of downtown. As you leave Snohomish, the trail runs close to the Pilchuck River.

There are seasonal services and water at Machias Station, another few miles ahead at the Machias trailhead. During summer, the converted rail depot hosts a snack shop and bicycle rentals. With picnic tables and a covered shelter, it's a nice place to stop and a great meeting point.

Next you skirt the edge of the town of Lake Stevens (detour at the 20th Street trailhead for a side trip to its town center) and pick up the newer section of the trail, notable for the lack of tree roots that can heave the asphalt under your tires (a common affliction of older trails). At about 12 miles you reach Lake Cassidy, on the eastern edge of Marysville, which has trail access to a dock and wetland interpretive area. There are picnic tables here as well. Not far beyond are restrooms at the Getchell trailhead.

The trail continues north through denser tree cover, and as it nears Arlington, you begin to get views west through the valley. You do make a bit of a climb over the entire course of the trail, but it's so gradual you might not notice it until you cross Quilceda Creek and coast down to the Armar Road trailhead, which is the last stop before Arlington.

The trail continues along 67th Avenue NE (also known as Armar Road) for 1 mile before shifting to a 12-foot-wide sidewalk at 172nd St. NE that takes you into town. To cycle through Arlington, turn right at Cemetery Road, which is also 204th Street NE, and ride two blocks to the well-equipped Haagen's Supermarket to sample its deli selections and facilities. Continue 4 miles on city streets into Arlington, using a short bike lane through downtown that parallels the main street and connects to riverside parks.

The trail used to end at Haller Park, on the north end of Arlington. The park abuts the Stillaguamish River confluence, where the north and south forks meet. From the renovated rail-to-trail bridge above the park, you get a stunning view of the confluence and often see people fishing from the banks or the shallows.

But Snohomish County pushed out of Arlington in recent years to extend the trail, and in 2013 the last section opened, which takes you on a quiet, woodsy ride all the way north to the Skagit County line. Now it's Skagit's turn to take us even farther north!

Three miles north of Arlington, a trailhead has opened at the tiny community of Bryant. The well-equipped general store here would be a good stop for picnic provisions, because in another 4 miles you reach the end of the trail, in a small valley dotted with homes along the eastern ridge. At the north terminus there's a picturesque red barn that dates to 1904, flanked by picnic tables, a large parking area, and a portable toilet. The trail connects with State Route 9, which is less busy here than farther south, but it's still a highway with scant shoulders.

However, to complete your Centennial Trail ride, from the North trailhead turn your wheels south. On the return, after some mild rolling hills north of Arlington and a steady climb from Armar Road, you begin to notice a downhill slope, and you might find yourself coasting along or really picking up speed. The trail has a posted speed limit of 15 miles per hour, which is mostly a concern on the busy sections or where you reach a crossing with cars, pedestrians, and horses. When you arrive back in Snohomish, marvel at your smooth return cruise on this recreational trail that offers a quite pleasant, and lengthy, country ride.

Route Connections: Ride south from Snohomish to Woodinville (Tour 19). From the Centennial Trail, turn west at the Pilchuck trailhead to ride to Everett (Tour 52), or continue southeast at Snohomish to Monroe (Tour 53). From the Centennial Trail's north terminus, ride north on State Route 9 and in 2 miles, at Lake McMurray, ride west on State Route 534 6 more miles to Conway, then north on Fir Island to connect to the Skagit Flats ride (Tour 48).

MILEAGE LOG

0.0 North on trail from downtown Snohomish street parking (restrooms 1 block away).

0.9 Cross 10th St. and Maple Ave.

2.1 Arrive at Pilchuck trailhead (restrooms).

5.3 Arrive at Machias trailhead (restrooms, water available).

7.9 Arrive at 20th St. trailhead (restrooms) in the town of Lake Stevens.

12.0 Arrive at Lake Cassidy Wetlands Park (picnic area, dock).

12.9 Arrive at Getchell trailhead (restrooms).

13.7 Cross under SR 9 on trail.

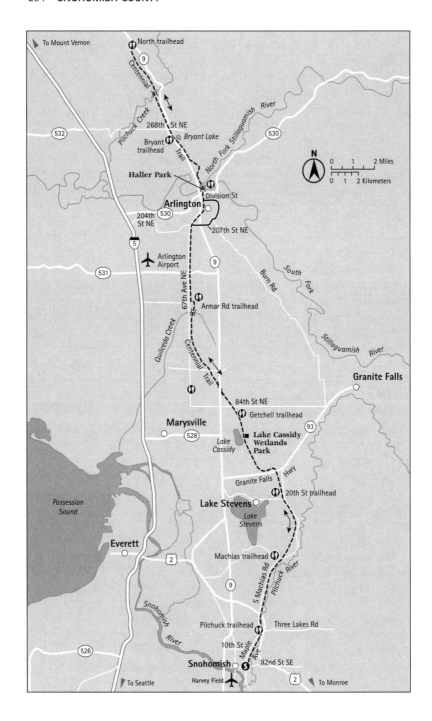

19.1 Arrive at Armar Rd. trailhead (restrooms).
20.2 Cross 172nd St. onto sidewalk bike path on east side of road.
22.6 Right onto 204th St. NE, which crosses SR 9, then curves left to become 207th St. NE.
23.8 Left onto Stillaguamish Ave.
24.5 Left onto 3rd St.
25.0 Right onto downtown Arlington trail just past Olympic Ave.
26.3 Arrive at Haller Park (restrooms, water).
28.8 Pass Bryant Lake.
29.5 Arrive at Bryant trailhead (restrooms); general store nearby.
29.6 Cross SR 9 on trail. Caution: traffic.
31.0 Cross bridge over Pilchuck Creek.
33.7 Arrive at North trailhead (restrooms). Reverse route to return.
37.9 Arrive at Bryant trailhead (restrooms) and general store.
41.1 Pass Haller Park (restrooms, water).
42.0 As trail ends, slight right onto Lebanon St. In 100 yards, left onto 67th Ave. NE.
42.9 Cross 204th St. NE to rejoin trail adjacent to 67th Ave. NE.
46.3 Pass Armar Rd. trailhead (restrooms).
52.3 Pass Getchell trailhead (restrooms).
53.4 Pass Lake Cassidy picnic area.
54.3 Pass town of Lake Stevens and 20th St. trailhead (restrooms).
60.3 Pass Machias trailhead (restrooms, water available).
63.5 Pass Pilchuck trailhead (restrooms).
65.6 Arrive at downtown Snohomish street parking to end tour.

52 Snohomish to Everett

DIFFICULTY: moderate
TIME: allow 2.5 hours
DISTANCE: 21.8 miles
ELEVATION GAIN: 793 feet

Getting There: From I-5 in Everett, travel east on US 2 toward Wenatchee. Take third exit off US 2 into Snohomish. Turn right onto 92nd St. SE, then right onto Pine Ave. Turn right onto Maple Ave., which becomes S. Machias Rd. Pilchuck trailhead is on the right in approximately 2 miles.

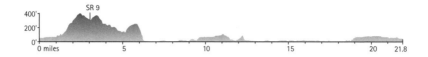

GPS Coordinates: N47 56 31 W122 04 33

Transit: Community Transit 424 from Seattle; 270 or 275 from Everett (2 miles from start)

Central Snohomish County is a region where the rural areas are giving way to suburbs, although north and east of Bothell, Mill Creek, and Everett, you can still see open land and wildlife. Finding them is the goal of this tour, which includes rolling hills but also a stretch of moderate rural highway along the verdant Snohomish River valley.

The tour begins north of the Snohomish town center, then skirts Ebey Slough, downtown Everett, and the winding river. Coming back through Snohomish provides a lunch or snack visit to the town's touristy main street, from where you can connect to other tours if the spirit moves you (see Route Connections below). Because of this tour's fairly modest length, there's plenty of time for exploration or relaxation along the way.

Begin at the Centennial Trail's Pilchuck trailhead just north of Snohomish. Ride a bit north, then turn west and cross the valley. The route takes you on a climb, then across busy State Route 9, before dropping back down onto the flats of Ebey Slough, at the point where US 2 comes across on a trestle from Everett and splits with State Route 204 to Lake Stevens. This is a tricky interface with a major highway, but cyclists ride under the ramps where the roads diverge. Choosing the road not taken by either highway allows avoidance of most of the commotion.

Lowell–Snohomish River Road is a comfortable link between Everett and Snohomish.

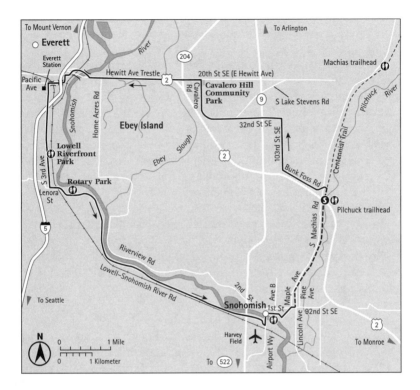

Ride west along the north edge of the slough, hard up against the highway on one side, viewing a raised set of pipelines on the other. Halfway through the slough, you curve south into Ebey Island a bit, and you can further explore this farm-centric floodplain by making a detour south on Home Acres Road. That route would take you quickly back to Snohomish via Riverview Road, but to see a bit of Everett, this tour follows the signed bike route to the north, up onto the protected pedestrian–bike lane bridge that joins US 2 over the Snohomish River. Drop into downtown Everett, riding past the combined train and bus transit center called Everett Station.

A few blocks north and west is the Everett Events Center, with its distinctive masts and wires looking like a frigate without sails. From here you could continue northwest to Everett's waterfront, west to Mukilteo, or north to the bike paths of Smith Island. But this tour continues south and east along the river. A relaxing break can be had at Lowell Riverfront Park as you cross from the city streets to Lowell–Snohomish River Road. Continue back to Snohomish along this relatively quiet road, which is regularly used by cyclists doing time-trials on their fast bikes.

As you cross the bridge into downtown Snohomish, you'll find a visitor information center. There's also a short, scenic riverfront trail that connects two small parks. On busy First Street, the town's true touristy nature is revealed: six blocks jammed with eateries, tea shops, and antiques, plus a couple of gourmet coffee shops, and at the intersection with Avenue B, restrooms. Visitors line up at the ice cream shop, which also carries a vast array of collectibles, such as all things Coca-Cola or Betty Boop. Another popular stop is the Pie Company, which sells sandwiches and dessert pies, whole or by the slice. Exit stage right and head north up Maple to connect with the Centennial Trail at Second and Lincoln, finishing the tour by cycling on the trail back to the Pilchuck trailhead.

Route Connections: From Lowell–Snohomish River Road, connect to the Mukilteo ride (Tour 50) by cycling up 52nd Street SE, then south on Broadway and west on Madison Street. From Snohomish, ride south to Woodinville (Tour 19), north on the Centennial Trail (Tour 51), or southeast to Monroe (Tour 53).

MILEAGE LOG

0.0 From Pilchuck trailhead (restrooms), ride north on Centennial Trail.

0.7 Left off trail onto Ritchey Rd. Cross S. Machias Rd. and proceed west across valley. Climbing out of valley, Ritchey becomes Bunk Foss Rd.

1.8 Right onto 103rd St. SE.

2.9 Left onto 32nd St. SE.

3.3 Cross SR 9. Caution: busy intersection, highway speeds.

3.7 As 32nd St. SE curves right, it becomes 91st Ave. SE.

3.8 Left onto S. Lake Stevens Rd., which curves north and becomes Cavalero Rd.

5.5 Left onto 20th St. SE, also called E. Hewitt Ave.

5.9 Merge into left lane and stay on 20th when approaching ramps to US 2 north, which exits to right, and US 2 south, which exits to left.

6.0 At stop sign, cross SR 204 onto a marked bike lane on left side of 20th. Note: at this point, 20th becomes an eastbound one-way, and cyclists ride against traffic in a wide bike lane on this little-used road.

7.2 Left onto 51st Ave. SE toward Home Acres Rd.

7.9 Right onto bike path as road curves left and becomes Home Acres Rd. Follow bike path up and along US 2 over Snohomish River.

8.8 Left onto Hewitt Ave. at base of trestle.

8.9 Right onto Chestnut St., which becomes Pacific Ave. and goes under I-5, then rises on a bridge over railroad tracks.

9.6 Left on Smith Ave. as you come off west side of bridge. Everett Station (restrooms) immediately on left.

10.7 Right onto Lowell-Larimer Rd. at stop sign at 38th St. It becomes S. 3rd Ave.

11.5 At Lowell Park (restrooms), road curves and becomes S. 2nd Ave.

12.2 Left on Lenora St. Road curves right at railroad tracks and becomes Lowell–Snohomish River Rd.

12.3 Pass Rotary Park (restrooms) on your left.

18.6 Left onto Airport Wy.

18.8 Right onto 1st St. into downtown Snohomish. At Avenue B, restrooms on right.

19.5 Left onto Maple Ave. after 1st St. curves right.

19.7 Right onto 2nd St. In ½ block, left onto Centennial Trail.

20.6 Cross 10th St. and Maple Ave.

21.8 Arrive at Pilchuck trailhead to end tour.

53 Snohomish to Monroe

DIFFICULTY: moderate
TIME: allow 3 hours
DISTANCE: 30.9 miles
ELEVATION GAIN: 815 feet

Getting There: From I-5 in Everett, travel east on US 2 toward Wenatchee. Take third exit off US 2 into Snohomish. Turn right onto 92nd St. SE, then right onto Pine Ave. Turn right onto Maple Ave., which becomes S. Machias Rd. Pilchuck trailhead is on the right in approximately 2 miles.

GPS Coordinates: N47 56 31 W122 04 33

Transit: Community Transit 424 from Seattle; 270 or 275 from Everett (2 miles from start)

Many routes will take you through the farm communities of Snohomish County, and this one is an introduction to the communities and major roads that can lead to much more exploration. Begin this tour on the

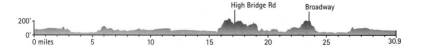

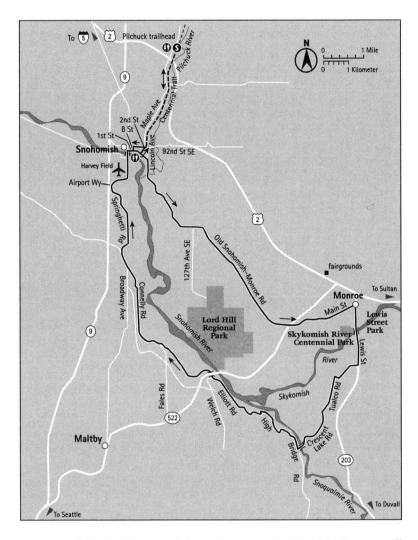

Centennial Trail, riding south into downtown Snohomish. Here you'll find an information center and a town center tailor-made for visitors.

Head down the trail to downtown Snohomish, then east along First to Lincoln, which takes you out of town, past soccer fields and into grazing fields. The route uses Old Snohomish–Monroe Road, which has relatively light traffic except at peak hours, due to the presence of US Highway 2 just beyond the valley to the north. But much of this road does not have a shoulder and there are plenty of curves, so caution is warranted. Watch for the curious blue "Fish Crossing" signs, which lead to musing on the presence of evolution continuing in the valley.

Climbing out of the Snoqualmie River valley on Crescent Lake Road

About halfway between Snohomish and Monroe is the turnoff to Lord Hill Regional Park, a 2-mile climb south of the road. The heavily wooded park, which borders the Snohomish River, offers hiking, horse, and mountain-biking trails but not much for road cyclists. The valley, however, is a beautiful ride, and you rise up a bit along the edge of the foothills to get a look at Monroe on the approach.

Enter Monroe at a roundabout and cycle down Main Street, a long, wide, quiet lane leading to the town center. Ride past schools and the Washington State Reformatory. Just to the north, at the intersection of US 2 and State Route 522, sits the sprawling fairgrounds where the Evergreen State Fair is held every summer. There is also much commercial development along US 2.

Downtown Monroe, a four-block radius around the junction of Lewis Street and Main, includes a couple cafés, a bakery, antique shops, and a bike store, which is on the south side of Main one block before Lewis. Exit the homey town center by turning right on Lewis and heading south. Cross the Skykomish River and continue south for a bit on busy State Route 203 to a right turn at Tualco Road. This begins the loop back to Snohomish, through a flat, verdant river valley fed by both the Skykomish and the Snoqualmie. Tualco Road stands up well as an idyllic setting for river-valley farming, and you cycle by a great variety of market crops, from corn to raspberries.

Cross the Snoqualmie and climb out of the valley via High Bridge Road, entering a section of rolling hills. The road winds through more picturesque farm- and ranchland before dropping back down to the Snohomish River valley. As you turn north onto Connelly, then Broadway for a quick descent to the valley, be mindful of a right turn onto Springhetti that comes quickly. Development along State Route 9 has stretched north into this bluff above the Snoqualmie River valley, and traffic can be an issue as you skirt the edge of it. The final leg is again a flat farm-road route back into town.

Route Connections: From Snohomish, ride south to Woodinville (Tour 19) or north on the Centennial Trail (Tour 51) and link up at the Pilchuck trailhead to head west to Everett (Tour 52). From Monroe, ride east to Sultan (Tour 54).

MILEAGE LOG

0.0 From Pilchuck trailhead (restrooms), ride south on Centennial Trail into Snohomish.

2.1 Right onto 2nd St.

2.5 Left onto Avenue B.

2.6 Left onto 1st St. (restrooms).

3.0 Right onto Lincoln Ave.

6.4 Pass entrance to Lord Hill Regional Park on right.

9.4 Cross under intersection with SR 522; stay in right lane and go halfway around the roundabout to continue onto Main St.

10.5 Arrive in downtown Monroe.

11.4 Right onto Lewis St., which is also SR 203.

11.8 Pass Lewis Street Park (restrooms) on the left.

13.0 Right onto Tualco Rd.

13.9 Curve left and stay on Tualco Rd. at intersection with Tualco Loop Rd.

14.9 Curve left onto Crescent Lake Rd.

16.3 At T after crossing Snoqualmie River, right onto High Bridge Rd. Caution: winding road with no shoulders climbing out of valley.

19.9 At Y with Welch Rd., stay right as High Bridge becomes Elliott Rd., then cross under SR 522.

21.9 Continue on Elliott at intersection with Fales Rd.

22.4 Right onto Connelly Rd.

24.4 Right onto Broadway Ave.

24.9 Right onto Springhetti Rd. Caution: be prepared for turns on this steep downhill segment.

26.9 Right onto Airport Wy.

28.0 Cross bridge into downtown Snohomish.

28.2 Right onto 1st St.; restrooms at Avenue B.

28.6 Left onto Maple Ave.

28.8 Right onto 2nd St. In ½ block, left onto Centennial Trail.

30.9 Arrive back at Pilchuck trailhead to end tour.

54 Monroe to Sultan

~~~~~~

DIFFICULTY: moderate
TIME: allow 2.5 hours
DISTANCE: 24.7 miles
ELEVATION GAIN: 965 feet

Getting There: From SR 522, travel east toward Monroe and take the W. Main St. exit. Follow sign to City Center/W. Main St. around the roundabout. Turn right onto Lewis St. at 1.7 miles. Turn left into parking just beyond Lewis Street Park entrance at 2.2 miles. From US 2, travel east toward Stevens Pass and turn right on Lewis St. in Monroe, proceeding to parking at Lewis Street Park at 0.7 mile.
GPS Coordinates: N47 50 54 W121 58 15
Transit: Community Transit 270 or 275 from Everett

There is a point where communities along US 2 shake off the atmosphere of suburban Snohomish County and settle down into "mountain time," and you might feel that shift on a quick tour of the foothills between Monroe and Sultan. Exploring the side roads that roughly parallel the Stevens Pass Highway, you will find an abundance of scenic views: snow-capped mountains, rushing rivers, tree-lined lanes, and pastoral valleys.

Start the loop in Monroe. Settled in the 1860s because of its rich farmland, the area is best known today for hosting a state reformatory (read: prison) and the Evergreen State Fair; I'm not aware of any connection between the two, although the draw of the Midway could have lured me into juvenile delinquency as a kid. Monroe is also the last shopping metropolis for people heading across Stevens Pass, so a crowded strip of businesses line the highway on the edge of town. This tour mostly avoids that mess, crossing the highway at a stoplight when you're heading out of town.

Begin at Lewis Street Park, which sits beside the Skykomish River on the south edge of town; two other parks are adjacent with riverfront access. The Skykomish and its sister from the south, the Snoqualmie,

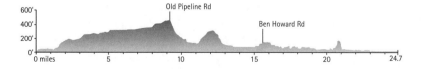

join forces and become the Snohomish River southwest of Monroe. The Snohomish empties into Puget Sound at Everett. Lewis Street Park has an interpretive trail through riverside wetlands, plus picnic areas and restrooms.

Head northeast out of Monroe into the Woods Creek Valley along Old Owen Road, where bedroom communities are reaching farther into the countryside. A view of the Cascades' jagged peaks makes it easy to see why high parts of the valley would be coveted for homes. For a bit of variety, swing north along Woods Lake Road, then loop back south along Reiner Road, which follows the Sultan River down into Sultan. These quiet lanes expose the desirable side of country life being sought a few yards off a main road: the whinny of horses, odors of wood smoke and freshly cut hay, and a casual wave from a neighborly farmer.

After climbing out of the river valley, drop down back onto Old Owen Road and then to US 2 at the edge of Sultan. Take a break and explore this small town: Have coffee at the renowned bakery, check out the barbecue joint or art gallery on Main Street, or kick back at Sportsman Park. Then cross the highway onto Mann Road (311th Avenue SE) and turn onto Ben Howard Road, which heads west to Monroe. Cross a series of bridges that span the sloughs and tributaries of the Skykomish.

The undulations of Ben Howard Road seem to be beloved by motorcycle riders, as they will be by you. Along its 10-mile stretch you're very likely to encounter that other style of biker: the noisy one who makes the scene with gasoline. The road parallels the Skykomish and

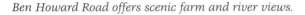

Ben Howard Road offers scenic farm and river views.

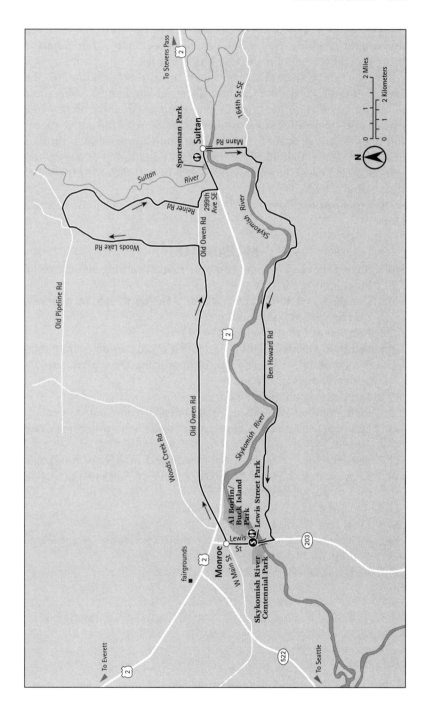

opens onto ranching valleys but also offers a couple of hill climbs to bring that crisp mountain air deep into the lungs.

At the end, Ben Howard Road meets up with State Route 203, the Duvall–Monroe Road. Join this busy thoroughfare briefly as you cross the Skykomish. Mind the bridge, as it—like most country bridges of a certain age—makes no allowance for cyclists. Slowing the impatient car traffic by pedaling across a bridge makes one appreciate the niceties of modern design that allow for the comfort and safety of non-motor-vehicle bridge users. From the bridge, head north back to Lewis Street Park to end the tour.

Route Connections: From Monroe, ride west out to Snohomish (Tour 53).

MILEAGE LOG

0.0 Right out of Lewis Street Park (restrooms) parking onto Lewis St.

0.5 Right onto W. Main St.

0.9 Cross US 2 at stoplight on Main St. On north side of highway, road becomes Old Owen Rd.

1.1 Bear left at Y to stay on Old Owen Rd.

6.6 Left onto Woods Lake Rd. (Note: you could continue straight on Old Owen Rd. to shorten tour by approximately 4 miles and skip one challenging hill climb.)

9.3 Right onto Old Pipeline Rd.

9.7 Right onto Reiner Road at Y. Caution: sharp downhill curve.

13.1 Left onto Old Owen Rd. at stop sign. Road curves to become 299th Ave. SE.

13.7 Left onto US 2 at stoplight; Sportsman Park on right before signal.

13.8 Arrive at Sultan. Visit the bakery or cafés (restrooms) or stop at the city park for a break.

14.5 Right onto Mann Rd. to begin return.

15.4 Right onto Ben Howard Rd.

24.2 Right onto SR 203/Lewis St. to go north into Monroe. Caution: no shoulder or bike lane on bridge.

24.7 Arrive at Lewis Street Park to end tour.

Opposite: *Mount Rainier looms over the Foothills Trail.*

PIERCE COUNTY

55 Downtown Tacoma, Point Defiance, and the Narrows

DIFFICULTY: moderate
TIME: allow 3 hours
DISTANCE: 23.8 miles
ELEVATION GAIN: 1069 feet

Getting There: From I-5 take exit 133, Tacoma Dome; follow "City Center" off-ramp, then make first right onto E. 26th St. at light. In 0.1 mile, turn left onto E. D St., then right onto E. 25th St. to arrive at Freighthouse Square. Parking on street and in adjacent park-and-ride lot.
   GPS Coordinates: N47 14 23 W122 25 42
   Transit: Pierce Transit 41, 42, 400, 500, 501

A tour through Tacoma can include many interesting sights and stops, from art to parks to waterfronts to wonderful neighborhoods. Why not combine them all into one ride and make a day of it?

Begin at Freighthouse Square, the old-is-new transit center area tucked near the Tacoma Dome just southeast of downtown. It's got great freeway access and cheap or free parking, and the transit stop makes it ideal for tourists not using a car to visit Tacoma.

The downtown Tacoma area is experiencing a renaissance, visible in the first leg of this tour. Travel carefully through a busy traffic corridor before reaching the renovated Union Station and federal courthouse, Tacoma Art Museum, and Washington State History Museum. This handsome strip sits just above the waterfront digs of the Museum of Glass, which you reach by looping down onto Dock Street. The modern building, with its glass funnel angling skyward like a postindustrial factory smokestack, provides a welcome connection to the picturesque Thea Foss Waterway and its marina.

Cycle along the promenade, past the museum at the Foss Waterway Seaport and Thea's Park, then climb up to ride a safe, although not generous, sidewalk along the fast-moving Schuster Parkway. Skirt the city along the shore of Commencement Bay, cranes and freighters off your starboard bow. Climb briefly into the Old Town neighborhood before

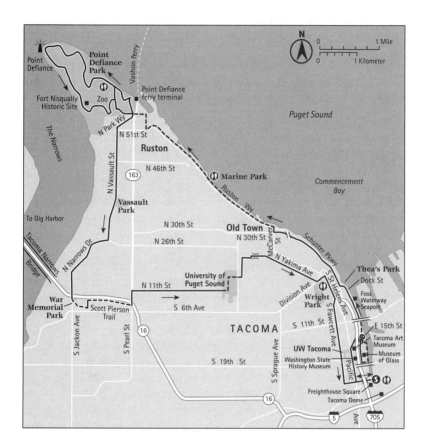

dropping down to the park trail alongside Ruston Way. Here you'll find sculptures, an old fireboat, fishing piers, and the remains of an old mill, along with plenty of people on a nice afternoon.

At the far end of Ruston Way, ride through the developing Point Ruston area. In 2013, a new park was opened, with aquatic tiled-and-painted scenes at intervals along its path, and a temporary trail from the waterfront to Point Defiance Park was created, with plans for a permanent trail through a new hillside park to enhance the connection to the breakwater marina and ferry terminal to Vashon Island. Climb the trail to enter the Ruston neighborhood, then reward yourself with a treat at the old-fashioned soda fountain in Don's Ruston Market (two blocks up Pearl, then left on 51st Street) before heading into Point Defiance Park.

Point Defiance makes a great midway stop, with many attractions along its 5-mile-long road: a Chinese garden and pagoda; sandy Owen Beach; viewpoints to Vashon Island and Gig Harbor; historic displays at

Recently expanded trails in the Ruston area connect the waterfront to Point Defiance Park.

restored Fort Nisqually; a logging museum; and picnic areas in the towering, moss-covered forest. The big attraction, of course, is the Point Defiance Zoo and Aquarium. The polar bears are sometimes visible from the road.

Exit the park and head south toward the impressive twin spires of the recently expanded Tacoma Narrows Bridge. The route takes you over the broad hill of northwest Tacoma, then drops into the neighborhood adjacent to the suspension bridge, where you get great views of the magnificent structure. The new bridge includes a safe, grade-separated bicycle trail (to ride it, see Tour 56). Across from the trail's entrance is the relocated War Memorial Park, whose shaded benches provide a nice break area.

Head back east through quiet Tacoma neighborhoods to finish the tour. The route travels through the University of Puget Sound campus for a glimpse of college life. Continue on over the car-free Yakima Bridge and through the neighborhood of stately old homes and apartment blocks on North Yakima Avenue. Skirt the edge of Wright Park and end the tour by riding along a relatively quiet street above downtown Tacoma. Drop down one of the steep cross streets to get a closer look at the city's commercial center, or stay above the busy downtown streets and enjoy the view on your way back to Freighthouse Square.

Route Connections: From Tacoma Narrows Bridge, ride north to Gig Harbor (Tour 56).

MILEAGE LOG

0.0 From Freighthouse Square (restrooms), left onto E. 25th St.

0.2 Right onto Pacific Ave. Pass Washington State History Museum.

1.1 Right onto Hood St. at Tacoma Art Museum.

1.2 Right onto S. 15th St. and curved overpass.

1.4 Left onto Dock St.

1.6 Left at pedestrian entrance to Museum of Glass, then right on promenade to end of walkway at Thea Foss Waterway; reverse route to ride promenade north past Foss Waterway Seaport.

2.3 Switch to street as promenade ends.

2.7 At Thea's Park, left to climb overpass and leave waterfront. In 100 yards, cross Schuster Pkwy. at light and turn right onto far side sidewalk, a pedestrian-bike trail.

4.0 Cross under overpass to turn left onto Schuster as trail ends. Schuster becomes N. 30th St. as you enter Old Town.

4.3 Right onto McCarver St.

4.4 Cross Ruston Wy. and turn left onto waterfront trail, which passes through Marine Park (restrooms).

6.6 Cross intersection with N. 49th St. and in 100 yards turn right onto the Point Ruston trail.

7.1 At end of park, trail turns uphill toward Point Defiance Park.

7.5 Cross marina parking lot on right edge, then cross left onto Ferry Rd.

7.7 Right into Point Defiance Park onto Five Mile Drive. Caution: busy 5-way intersection, with ferry traffic.

7.9 Arrive at main park picnic area (restrooms).

8.0 Take middle fork at stop sign with Owen Beach Rd.

11.3 Right into short loop through Fort Nisqually Historic Site.

11.7 Return to Five Mile Drive; take short loop through logging museum displays on the right if desired.

12.5 Soft right onto N. Park Wy. when exiting Point Defiance Park.

12.8 N. Park Wy. becomes N. Vassault St., then N. Narrows Dr.

14.7 Right to stay on N. Narrows Dr. at N. 26th St.

15.9 Continue forward as N. Narrows Dr. becomes N. Jackson Ave.

16.0 Arrive at Tacoma Narrows Bridge. Forward through intersection at off-ramps (to ride 1-mile bike trail across bridge, turn right on south side of intersection). Left onto east sidewalk to enter War Memorial Park and proceed through it. Caution: busy freeway exit; use pedestrian walking signal.

16.3 Left to exit park onto Skyline Dr.

16.5 In 2 blocks, as Skyline ends, cross N. 9th St. onto Scott Pierson Trail on sidewalk above SR 16.

17.2 Left onto S. Pearl St.

17.4 Right on N. 11th St.

18.9 Cross N. Union Ave. into University of Puget Sound campus.

19.0 Left onto path into University of Puget Sound campus to right of sports field. Right at Benefactor Plaza, then left around Wheelock Student Center.

19.4 Right onto 15th St. to exit campus.

19.5 Left onto Cedar St.

19.8 Right onto 22nd St.

20.0 Jog left at street end for 1 block, then right, and cross intersection onto N. Yakima Ave. Continue forward past barriers onto pedestrian- and bike-only Yakima Bridge.

20.2 Continue forward on Yakima Ave.

21.2 Left onto Division Ave.; Wright Park (restrooms) to south.

21.4 Right on S. St. Helens Ave.

21.8 Angle right onto Baker St. In one block, cross S. 7th St. to a soft left onto Fawcett Ave.

23.2 Left onto E. 25th St.

23.8 Arrive at Freighthouse Square to end tour.

56 Gig Harbor and Fox Island

DIFFICULTY: challenging
TIME: allow 5 hours
DISTANCE: 33.2 miles
ELEVATION GAIN: 2753 feet

Getting There: From I-5 in Tacoma, merge to SR 16 west toward Tacoma Narrows Bridge. Turn off at exit 4, then left onto N. Jackson Ave. and left onto 6th Ave. Parking is ahead on left in 1 block.

GPS Coordinates: N47 15 21 W122 31 58

Transit: Pierce Transit 1, 10, 16

This ride offers a spin across a very big bridge with big views, a visit to a little village and a little park, and a ride across a small, scenic bridge to loop a little island. On the way, there are plenty of climbs along tree-lined roads and not many services.

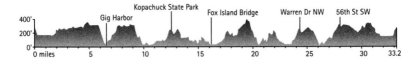

Cyclists spy Fox Island Bridge, with Mount Rainier in the distance.

Start your ride by cycling through the War Memorial Park, whose entrance can be found under a big American flag at the north end of the park-and-ride lot. You can ride either sidewalk downhill through the park to North Jackson Avenue below, but you might want to spend a few minutes now, or at the end of the ride, visiting the park and considering the plaques and statues.

This park was relocated from its previous waterside home when the new Tacoma Narrows Bridge was built. It had been in the shadow of the old bridge, but the new location suits it. Somehow the somber theme of honoring the members of the Armed Forces who fought for our country is enhanced by the sweeping views of the bridges and the Narrows waterway from the park's new sloping hillside location.

The first leg of this ride is the 1.5-mile-long Tacoma Narrows Bridge, which vaults over the Narrows waterway with graceful twin suspension spans. When the second, new bridge opened in 2007, it included a wide, grade-separated bike and pedestrian trail, much needed and now quite beloved. It replaced a narrow pedestrian walkway along the old bridge that was not fit for cycling. The one hazard that remains is this: on windy days, cycling this bridge can be a balance-challenging experience, as the side winds gust over the bridge decking. High barriers on both sides of the trail make it safe, but it can be unnerving.

Coming off the bridge you find another local gem, the Cushman Trail, which takes you north on a near-continuous ride into Gig Harbor.

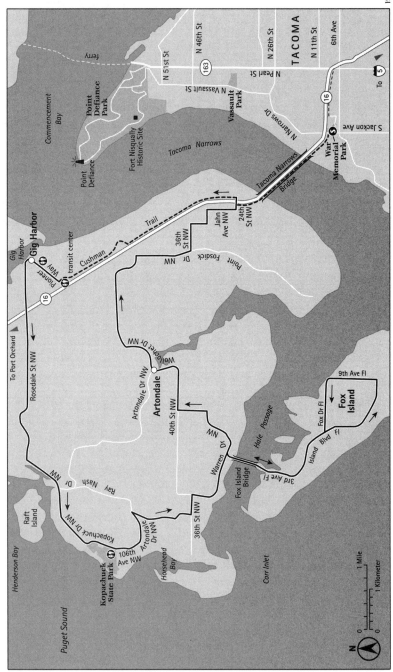

The trail's entrances and turns are well marked, with parking areas at two access points. The trail mostly runs next to State Route 16 but cuts into the trees and is quieter for a time. The asphalt path is smooth and wide, with distances marked in kilometers and miles.

Gig Harbor is a quiet community with a picture-postcard waterfront, at the downhill end of Pioneer Way. You'll find a whole-foods market, a sweet shop, taverns, and a coffee shop. One block to the right are public restrooms at the People's Dock, a pier established in 1890. Here, people were brought to town via steamboat. In the 1920s it served as a dock for a car ferry. Check out the pier's historic former grocery store, now a tavern and restaurant.

Head out of town on three good climbs along Rosedale Street NW. There's a pretty consistent shoulder and low traffic by Seattle standards. On your way to a midride break at Kopachuck State Park, stop at the tiny Island View Market, facing a quiet inlet of Henderson Bay. Prepare yourself for a big climb to the park that follows.

Kopachuck is on the Marine Recreation Trail and Cascadia Marine Trail. From the picnic tables, it's an easy half-mile hike to a pebbly beach under the heavy forest canopy. Restrooms and water are available here.

Continue south, then veer east toward Tacoma and you will be rewarded by views looking south across the water to the mountains. In the foreground, spanning Hale Passage, sits the Fox Island Bridge; behind is Mount Rainier.

Traverse the bridge in the car lane, then make a short loop around quiet, wooded Fox Island just to see it. A detour at the far end of the loop would take you to the local historical museum in a quarter mile. Toward the end of the loop, you'll see the only services: a small park followed by a gas station and espresso stand.

Back on the peninsula, the route takes you back toward Gig Harbor on a couple of improved roads with bike lanes. Pick up the Cushman Trail again to cross the Narrows and conclude the ride.

Route Connections: From Narrows Bridge, connect to downtown Tacoma ride (Tour 55).

MILEAGE LOG

0.0 Depart street parking into War Memorial Park; ride down to bridge.

0.2 Cross N. Jackson Ave. at crosswalk to enter trail on near side of bridge.

2.1 Right at end of Tacoma Narrows Bridge onto 24th St. NW; cross over SR 16.

2.3 Left onto 14th Ave. NW.

2.8 Left onto Cushman Trail.

4.5 Merge onto Olympic Dr. NW. In 1 block, left at stoplight at 56th St. NW, also signed as Hollycroft St.

4.8 Right at **T** onto Soundview Dr. In 1 block, left onto trail.

5.3 Left onto Kimball Dr. as trail ends.

5.6 Pass transit center (restrooms, water).

5.8 Right onto Pioneer Wy.

6.4 Left onto Harborview Dr. on Gig Harbor waterfront. (Right 1 block to People's Dock; restrooms.)

6.5 Left on Rosedale St. NW.

9.7 Left onto Ray Nash Dr. NW.

10.6 Straight onto Kopachuck Dr. NW as Ray Nash goes left at a Y.

12.2 Right onto 56th St. NW; in 1 block, right into Kopachuck State Park.

12.5 Arrive at parking (restrooms). Depart on one-way road out of park.

12.9 Right onto Kopachuck Dr. NW, which becomes 106th Ave. NW, then Artondale Dr. NW.

13.8 Right onto Ray Nash Dr. NW.

14.8 Left onto 36th St. NW.

15.2 Right onto Warren Dr. NW.

15.4 Right onto Fox Island Bridge.

15.9 Continue forward on 3rd Ave. FI (FI is for Fox Island), which becomes Island Blvd. FI, then 6th Ave. FI.

19.8 Left onto 9th Ave. FI, which curves left and becomes Fox Dr. FI.

21.5 Right onto Island Blvd. FI to return to bridge.

23.6 Right off bridge back onto Warren Dr. NW eastbound.

24.6 Left onto 70th Ave. NW.

25.1 Right onto 40th St. NW, also called Horsehead Bay Rd.

25.8 Curve left as road becomes Wollochet Dr. NW, also signed Artondale Dr. NW at Gig Harbor Grange, and then Wollochet–Gig Harbor Rd.

27.0 Right onto Fillmore Dr. NW, which becomes 56th St. NW, then Olympic Dr. NW.

28.9 Right onto Point Fosdick Dr. NW.

29.6 Left at roundabout onto 36th St. NW.

30.0 Right onto 22nd Ave. NW, which curves left and becomes 32nd St. NW, then curves right and becomes Jahn Ave. NW.

31.0 Left onto 24th St. NW; in 100 yards, right onto trail, then onto Narrows Bridge.

33.0 Cross N. Jackson Ave. and back into War Memorial Park.

33.2 Return to parking to end tour.

57 Foothills Trail

DIFFICULTY: easy
TIME: allow 2.5 hours
DISTANCE: 29.8 miles
ELEVATION GAIN: 402 feet

Getting There: From I-5, take exit 142 west on SR 18 to SR 161/ Enchanted Pkwy. southbound, which becomes Meridian Ave. Turn east on SR 167/Valley Freeway to SR 410. Take SR 410 to Valley Ave./ SR 162 exit. Turn right on Valley Ave. and travel 0.4 mile south to right turn onto 80th St. E. Trailhead is on left in 1.3 miles.
  GPS Coordinates: N47 11 03 W122 14 42
  Transit: Pierce Transit 409

A leisurely spin on the Foothills Trail offers a scenic ride through wooded countryside and along a rushing river, skirting small towns and new subdivisions on a trail that gently rises toward the pinnacle of Washington attractions: Mount Rainier. In fact, the trail is a crucial link in getting cyclists to the challenging roads encircling "the Mountain." The route is a popular destination for Tacoma cyclists looking for a laid-back outing. Developers call it the "Foothills Trail Linear Park," but before its rails-to-trails reincarnation, it was known as the Buckley Line, hosting both Northern Pacific freight and a passenger train from Orting to South Prairie, the current southern terminus of the trail.

Begin at the East Puyallup Trailhead, just southeast of the intersection of State Routes 167 and 410. When extensions are created going north, the trail will connect with the in-town trails in Puyallup, and plans call for further connections north to King County's Interurban Trail at Pacific and south toward Mount Rainier. Going down and back on the current trail, from Sumner to South Prairie, offers a scenic no-sweat 30-mile spin.

As with the Sammamish River Trail (Tour 17), you will encounter walkers, children, in-line skaters, and dogs. The Puyallup section runs alongside railroad tracks for 4 miles and crosses the tracks four times.

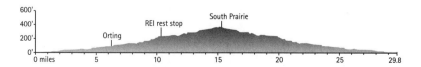

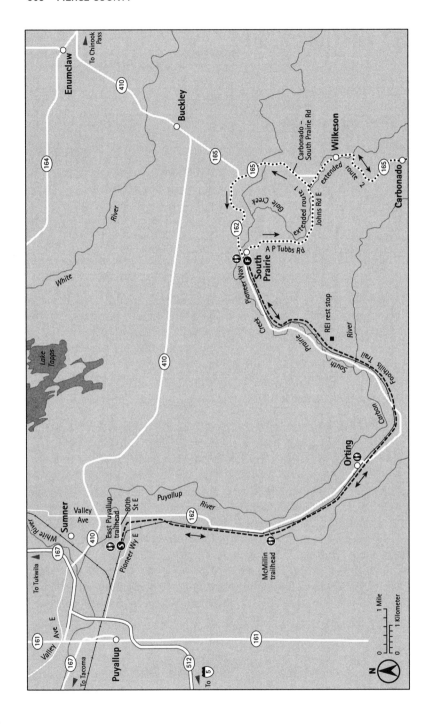

Rural scenes include great views of Mount Rainier.

You may also see people with fishing poles trying their luck in the glacially colored waters of the Puyallup and Carbon rivers, which both parallel the trail for long stretches. People used to the busy urban and suburban trails of King County will enjoy the uncrowded feeling here.

Many cyclists stop along the route at the casual Park Bench Café and Eatery, across the street from the trail in Orting's downtown park. South of Orting, the route becomes more rural. Look for a farm with emus and buffalos, and stop at the REI-sponsored wildlife viewing area in a marsh next to the creek. The trail ends at a small park in South Prairie. Nearby are an espresso stand, gas station, and convenience store.

The tour can be extended via road to points north and south. An additional 7-mile loop onto local roads south of town offers some variety on a jaunt through the wooded countryside. Take SE Third Street on a precipitous climb out of town, where it becomes A. P. Tubbs Road, then Johns Road; make a left on Carbonado–South Prairie Road, then another left onto State Route 165; turn left onto Lower Burnett Road and State Route 162 to return to the park in South Prairie. Or at Carbonado–South Prairie Road, continue straight on Johns Road, then turn south on State Route 165 through Wilkeson to the Carbon River entrance to Mount Rainier National Park, where you could lock up the bikes for a hike on the flood-damaged, now-closed road. A third option is to continue north on State Route 165 toward Buckley, cross the White River, enter King County, and continue north through Enumclaw.

Whether you use the Foothills Trail as an out-and-back ride on its own or as a link in a larger loop, riding south on the trail on a clear day may be enough of a treat for many cyclists, as the mountain's snowy slopes quietly fill the skyline above the trees lining the trail. That view might be the most rewarding bit of tourism possible on two wheels.

Route Connections: As of this writing, there aren't any good connections from this trail—but as trail planners continue their work, look for future connections west into Puyallup and Tacoma (Tour 55) and north to the Interurban Trail (Tour 24).

MILEAGE LOG

0.0 Begin at East Puyallup trailhead (restrooms) and ride south. Caution: railroad tracks; cross at right angles.

4.0 Pass McMillin trailhead (restrooms).

5.8 Enter Orting.

6.5 Trail jogs right briefly as it enters Orting Memorial Park (restrooms).

7.3 Ride by skate park and dirt-bike trail.

11.7 Arrive at REI rest stop at marsh.

14.9 Arrive at South Prairie trailhead (restrooms). Retrace route (or take side trip onto local roads; see description above).

18.1 Pass REI rest stop.

23.3 Pass through Orting (restrooms in park).

25.8 Pass McMillin trailhead (restrooms).

29.8 Arrive at East Puyallup trailhead to end tour.

Opposite: *A whimsical bicycling sculpture at the Monarch Sculpture Park*

58 State Capitol and Central Olympia

DIFFICULTY: easy
TIME: allow 2.5 hours
DISTANCE: 17.2 miles
ELEVATION GAIN: 571 feet

Getting There: Take I-5 to Olympia and exit 103, 2nd Ave., and go through first light. Turn left onto Custer Wy. SW and cross over bridge. Take first right onto side road that takes you onto a lower bridge. Cross that and turn left onto Deschutes Pkwy. Entrance to Tumwater Falls Park is on left.
   GPS Coordinates: N47 00 52 W122 54 19
   Transit: InterCity Transit 43, 44

Here's a short tour with plenty of stops that will give a visitor a great look at our state's capitol city and seat of government. The ride loops from Tumwater Falls Park, famous as the home of the Olympia Brewery; the falls is the culmination of the Deschutes River. This park is one of a series around Capitol Lake that celebrate the area's history and connection to commerce.

Climb up onto the city streets above the park, and quickly cross over from Tumwater east and north into Olympia. Skirt the edge of Watershed Park, the heavily wooded sward that supplied the city's water until the 1950s. The route then intersects with Olympia's extensive trail system. You pass by a green-roof-covered restroom at a trailhead for the Olympia Woodland Trail, then shortly pass an "on-ramp" to the loud but safe Interstate 5 bikeway, which runs in a greenspace next to the big freeway, first on one side then on the other, from the suburbs into downtown. As you make your way north into the city center, look for the many murals painted on the sides of downtown buildings.

Cross busy shopping and dining streets as you pedal west on Legion Way, then turn north toward the city's waterfront on Budd Inlet. Pass Percival Landing Park and arrive at your first stop, the welcoming Olympia Farmers Market. With farm stands under arched barn roofs, live music, playful iron vegetable sculptures, and an array of crafts and food for sale, this is a spot to stroll and browse.

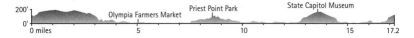

200'
0'
Olympia Farmers Market   Priest Point Park   State Capitol Museum
0 miles   5   10   15   17.2

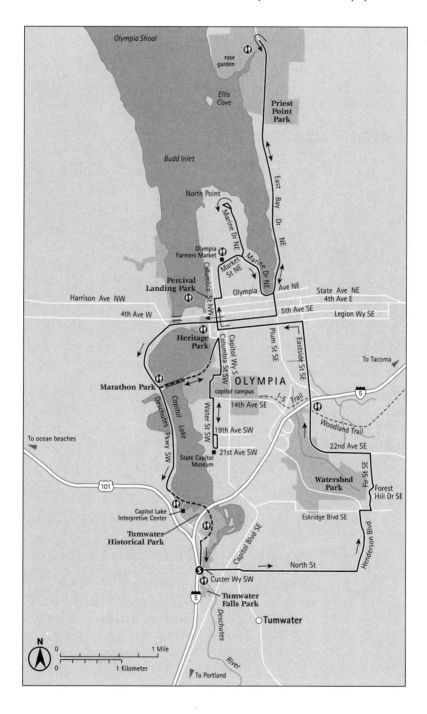

The route intersects with the I-5 Trail, which connects Olympia and Lacey.

Continue exploring the shorelines of the inlet by riding north out Marine Drive to North Point, home to an expansive marina, restaurants, and harborside trails. Then, before riding south to explore the capitol campus, head north out to Priest Point Park. Loop through the park, with its moss-encrusted trees, then stop at the quiet, enclosed rose garden before heading back toward town. The ride south offers a great view of the serene waters of Ellis Cove and the pleasure-boat haven at the south end of the inlet.

Cross back west through downtown on Fifth Avenue to circle around Capitol Lake. A division in the lake's two sections holds a path for hikers and bikers through Marathon Park. The park honors America's first women Olympic marathon runners; Olympia hosted the trials before the 1984 Los Angeles games.

Exit into Heritage Park, whose stately trails skirt the northeast edge of Capitol Lake. From here it's a short climb south to the state government buildings. Tour the grounds to view war memorials, sculptures, and gardens. Ride through in midspring and see an amazing display of cherry blossoms on the trees lining the campus roads. Poke your head into the legislative building, whose grand dome was restored after the 2001 earthquake. Completed in 1928, it was America's last great domed state capitol to be built.

Ride south a few blocks to the State Capitol Museum, in the historic South Capitol neighborhood. Return north through the capitol grounds and back between the lake segments, then ride along the west side of Capitol Lake to return to Marathon Park. As you ride south along the lake's west shore, you leave Deschutes Parkway onto a trail at the south end of the lake and reach Capitol Lake Interpretive Center.

Not far beyond is Tumwater Historical Park, where a plaque notes that this was also the finish line for an overland trading route from Fort Vancouver to Puget Sound. It also marks the end of the settlement route known as the Oregon Trail. If you're there in September, look for salmon in the fish ladders at the adjacent hatchery. In a few short pedal strokes, you arrive back at Tumwater Falls Park to conclude the tour.

Route Connections: Just before passing over Interstate 5 at Eastside Street SE, turn right onto the Woodland Trail at the trailhead to connect to the Chehalis Western Trail (Tour 59).

MILEAGE LOG

0.0 Right out of Tuwmater Falls Park (restrooms) onto Deschutes Pkwy.

0.1 Right to go over falls onto low bridge.

0.2 Right onto Custer Wy. SW. Caution: busy street.

0.5 Merge into center lane to go straight across Cleveland Ave. Custer becomes North St.

1.4 Left onto Henderson Blvd.

1.9 Right onto Eskridge Blvd. SE.

2.0 Left onto Forest Hill Dr. SE.

2.1 At Y, left onto Fir St. SE. Pass Watershed Park.

2.4 Left onto 22nd Ave. SE, which becomes Eastside St. SE after you cross over I-5; just before that, pass Woodland Trail (restrooms) on right, and just after pass I-5 Trail on left.

3.8 Left onto Legion Wy.

4.5 Right onto Columbia St. NW.

4.7 Right onto Olympia Ave. NE as you reach Percival Landing Park (restrooms).

4.8 Left onto Capitol Wy. N.

5.1 Arrive at Olympia Farmers Market (restrooms, services). Continue east on Market St. NE.

5.3 Left on Marine Dr. NE.

5.9 Arrive at North Point, end of Marine Dr. NE. Return south along Marine Dr. NE.

6.5 At intersection with Market St. NE., left to stay on Marine Dr. NE.

6.9 Left onto Olympia Ave. NE.

7.0 Left onto East Bay Dr. NE.

8.5 Right into Priest Point Park.

8.6 Follow "South Exit" signs next to restrooms and rose garden, then merge onto East Bay Dr. NE. to return south to city center, where East Bay becomes Plum St. SE.

10.5 Right onto 5th Ave. SE.

11.0 Arrive at Heritage Park (restrooms) by Capitol Lake.

11.3 Merge into left-turn lane, then turn left onto Deschutes Pkwy. SW.

11.9 Left into Marathon Park (restrooms), in middle of Capitol Lake. Ride or walk packed-gravel path that bisects two parts of lake.

12.2 Stay right to join paved trail on far side of lake.

12.6 Right onto Columbia St. SW. Caution: railroad tracks with bad angle.

12.9 Right onto 11th Ave. SW. In 1 block, left on Water St. SW, which curves right.

13.0 Left onto Cherry Ln. SW. in front of General Administration Building. Follow Cherry to pass state capitol building.

13.1 After road curves left beyond capitol, right at Insurance Building through parking that becomes Water St. SW.

13.5 Water St. curves left and becomes 21st Ave. SW. Pass State Capitol Museum.

13.6 Left onto Columbia St. SW.

13.7 Left onto 19th Ave. SW.

13.8 Right onto Water St. SW.

14.0 Return through capitol grounds.

14.3 Left onto Columbia St. SW to exit capitol campus.

14.6 Cross railroad tracks at Amanda Smith Wy. SW, then left into Heritage Park.

15.0 Left onto trail to return west across lake.

15.2 Left onto Deschutes Pkwy. Caution: angled railroad tracks.

16.1 Left into Capitol Lake Interpretive Center (restrooms). Caution: small sign, easy to miss. Follow waterfront trail under I-5 to Tumwater Historical Park (restrooms).

16.8 At end of parking lot, exit park by taking left branch of Y.

16.9 Left onto Deschutes Pkwy. Caution: freeway on-ramp traffic.

17.2 Left into Tumwater Falls Park to end tour.

59 Chehalis Western and Woodard Bay Trails

SOUTH SECTION
DIFFICULTY: easy
TIME: allow 3 hours
DISTANCE: 28.8 miles
ELEVATION GAIN: 512 feet

NORTH SECTION
DIFFICULTY: easy
TIME: allow 1.5 hours
DISTANCE: 16.5 miles
ELEVATION GAIN: 236 feet

Getting There: Take I-5 to exit 108, Sleater Kinney Rd. SE. Drive 0.8 mile south, turn right onto 14th Ave. SE, then turn left after trestle in 0.3 mile into Chehalis Western trailhead parking at Chambers Lake Park.

GPS Coordinates: N47 02 01 W122 50 23
Transit: InterCity Transit 60, 64

The Olympia area has much to offer touring cyclists. The small city and navigable suburbs are surrounded by tremendous natural beauty, from the Capitol Forest to the inlets of south Puget Sound to the foothills of Mount Rainier. If such a description makes you want to relocate there, use your bike to scout the area for suitable homes. You'll find quiet roads to meander, plenty of rest stops, and striped-and-signed bike lanes on the busier roads, which greatly aid the bike commuter.

Most helpful is a major bike route that bisects Thurston County north to south. The Chehalis Western Trail began—as did so many of our bike trails—as a rail line. Owned by Weyerhaeuser, the line was put into operation in 1926 to bring logs to the sound. The rail line was taken out of operation in the 1980s, and the right-of-way was purchased by the state from the Weyerhaeuser Foundation in 1988. By the mid-2000s, development as a multiuse recreational trail was nearly complete. The 5.8-mile section north of Interstate 5, from the freeway to Woodard Bay, is maintained by the state Department of Natural Resources. The longer south section, whose 14.5 miles run from south of Interstate 5 to an intersection with the Yelm–Tenino Trail (Tour 60), is operated by Thurston County. The two are linked by the I-5 Trail, which crosses Pacific Avenue SE, I-5, and Martin Way East with recently added bike-ped bridges.

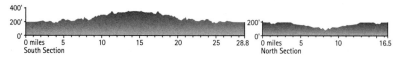

Rural scenes are common along the wide, flat Chehalis Western Trail.

While the northern section is largely a shaded woodland run, the southern portion offers a variety of environments, from suburbs to farmland to river frontage. Because of its easy freeway access, this tour starts at the Chambers Lake trailhead, the northern terminus of the southern section. Cyclists can go down and back on this trail, then add on a trip up to Woodard Bay if more riding is desired. Connections to the Olympia Woodland Trail and I-5 commuter trail, which together can take you nearly to downtown Olympia, and to the aforementioned Yelm–Tenino route, offer variety for those wanting to design their own tours. Linking the southern trail, the commuter trail, and the downtown–state capitol loop (see Tour 58), for example, offers the widest range of Olympia attractions.

Departing from Chambers Lake, the CW's south section bisects residential areas of Olympia and Lacey. By the time you cross 37th Street, homes and golf courses give way to woodland. At the 67th Avenue trailhead, the scenery begins to open up into farms and pastureland, with views of Mount Rainier. Just south of that junction, riders must endure a brief (0.2-mile) section of gravel before popping out onto a road to cross under a railroad trestle and climb a short hill to rejoin the trail. The only other obstacles on the line are barriers at road intersections that one must slow to a near stop to navigate.

An interesting sidelight awaits toward the south end of the trail. The Monarch Sculpture Park sits trailside at mile 12, beckoning visitors with

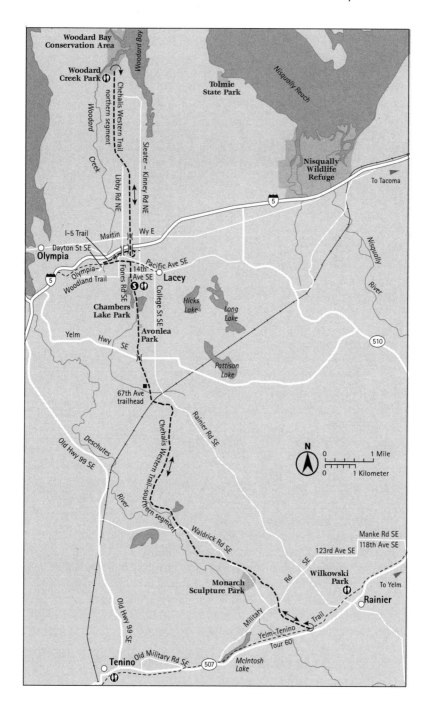

free admission to the grounds. Art in the park includes a whimsical permanent sculpture of a woman and two children wildly balancing atop a small bike. This clearly marked attraction is a good turnaround point or a welcome rest stop if you're going on to the Yelm–Tenino Trail (Tour 60).

Those heading up the northern section encounter the sights and smells of farms and ranches, as well as a well-used equestrian trail that meanders next to the paved route. Small wildlife is in abundance, and a hike out to the muddy flats of Woodard Bay and Henderson Inlet is worth the time at the end of the line. The return can be made more challenging by navigating the hilly local roads, but a map is required for this endeavor.

Taken together, with a lunch stop in the middle, the Chehalis Western represents a nice day's outing. For faster cyclists who want more challenge, add in some of Olympia's other excellent trails. However much ground you plan to cover, these trails make it well worth a trip to Thurston County.

Route Connections: Ride west on the Woodland Trail at the intersection north of Chambers Lake to connect at Eastside Street SE to the State Capitol ride (Tour 58). Connect with the Yelm–Tenino Trail (Tour 60) at the south end of the Chehalis Western Trail.

MILEAGE LOG—SOUTH SECTION

0.0 Right out of parking onto trail.

1.0 Pass Chambers Lake Park (restrooms).

1.7 Pass Avonlea Park.

2.7 Cross Yelm Hwy. SE on trail bridge.

3.3 Pass 67th Avenue trailhead.

4.0 Trail curves left and becomes gravel for 0.2 mile.

4.2 Right onto near-side sidewalk at Rainier Rd. SE to travel under railroad trestle. Merge onto road shoulder.

4.3 Right onto trail just beyond first intersection.

11.9 Pass Monarch Sculpture Park.

14.4 Arrive at intersection with Yelm–Tenino Trail. (Left onto Yelm–Tenino Trail to reach town of Rainier, 2 miles east.) Reverse route to return.

24.5 Left off trail onto Rainier Rd. SE. Caution: busy road.

24.7 Left onto gravel trail section just beyond trestle.

28.8 Arrive at Chambers Lake trailhead to end section.

MILEAGE LOG—NORTH SECTION

0.0 Left out of parking onto trail.

0.4 Left at T onto Olympia Woodland Trail (unmarked).

0.8 Cross Fones Rd. SE and continue on trail.
1.3 Right at first trail intersection onto I-5 Trail.
1.7 Cross Pacific Ave. SE on bike-ped overpass.
2.4 Circle left and up ramp to bike-ped overpass across I-5. Shortly after, cross Martin Wy E. on another bike-ped overpass.
8.0 Left off the trail onto Woodard Bay Rd. NE.
8.2 Right into parking at Woodard Bay trailhead (restrooms). Reverse route to return.
14.0 Arrive at I-5 overpass.
14.1 Right at bottom of ramp onto I-5 Trail.
14.3 Stay right at Y that leads to Lilly Rd. NE and continue next to freeway.
14.8 Arrive at Pacific Ave. overpass.
15.2 Left onto Olympia Woodland Trail.
16.1 Right onto Chehalis Western Trail.
16.5 Arrive at Chambers Lake trailhead to end section.

60 Yelm–Tenino Trail

DIFFICULTY: easy
TIME: allow 3.5 hours
DISTANCE: 27.3 miles
ELEVATION GAIN: 527 feet

Getting There: From I-5 take exit 111, SR 510, and follow SR 510 southeast approximately 13 miles into downtown Yelm. Just prior to first stoplight in Yelm, turn right onto Railroad St. SW in front of Yelm City Hall. Trailhead parking area is 1 block on the left.

GPS Coordinates: N46 56 31 W122 36 29

Transit: InterCity Transit 94

Just a few years ago, Olympia-area cyclists were offered the choice of roads or more roads for their touring pleasure. Not that there's anything wrong with that—the country lanes around our capital city are as inviting and uncrowded as you're likely to find within an hour or so of Seattle.

But then the upside-down T was created. The bottom half of the grand off-road route through Thurston County is the Yelm–Tenino

Trail, which traverses the eastern half of the county and runs through three small towns: Yelm, Rainier, and Tenino. It's an eminently useful and very pleasant amenity.

Begin in Yelm, the most developed of the three modest towns along the route. Situated 13 miles south of Interstate 5 along the Nisqually River, Yelm is a cross between bedroom community and farm town. Park at the trailhead behind the town hall (where restrooms and water are accessible if you visit on a weekday) and quickly depart town heading southwest as the trail winds through expanding neighborhoods. (Note: A 1.1-mile trail segment heads northeast to Canal Road, accessible across Yelm Avenue.)

The east-west trail, acquired by the county from Burlington Northern Railroad in 1993, is 13.5 miles long and quite flat. The first leg out of Yelm runs right alongside State Route 507, which makes for a noisy experience, but it is a great reminder of the benefits of not having to use the highway.

The trail gets away from the road for a quick few miles to the tiny town of Rainier. Ride by modest Wilkowski Park and then through the town center, which has a gas station and market if amenities are desired.

Two miles west of Rainier, the trail intersects with the Chehalis Western Trail (Tour 59), the longer, more scenic north-south route that goes into Lacey and Olympia. An interesting side trip, taken on either direction of this ride, is to detour north onto the CW for a 6-mile round-

trip visit to the Monarch Sculpture Park, whose free grounds, found trailside just north of the Military Road crossing, provide an enjoyable break. The bike-friendly facility has sculptures scattered along winding paths. The ride up and back takes you through the Deschutes River valley, containing ranches and equestrian facilities.

Back on the Yelm–Tenino Trail, cross the Deschutes, then ride along the southern edge of McIntosh Lake before arriving at the end of the line in Tenino City Park. The park provides restrooms

Thurston County's shadiest, quietest trail

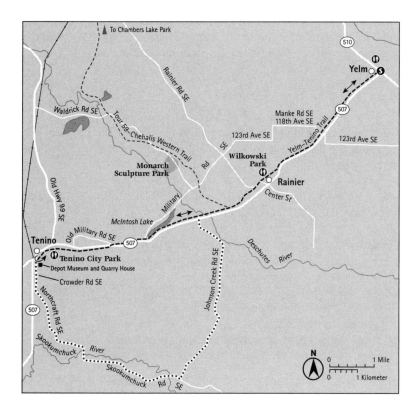

and water, and just beyond the trail's end is the Tenino Depot Museum and Quarry House. The museum houses all manner of old rail memorabilia, while across the parking lot the old house features walls of locally quarried stone. The quarry is now a public swimming pool, bustling on a hot summer day.

Ride into town for a look at the businesses along Sussex Avenue, the main street. Provisions for a park picnic can be found here, or just view the historic Landmark Tavern building at the corner of Howard Street, which dates from 1906.

The return can be made simply by retracing the trail route, making the trip just over 27 miles without the sculpture park detour. For an additional challenge—adding a bit of elevation as well as length— you could head south from Tenino on Crowder Road SE, Northcraft Road SE, Skookumchuck Road SE, and Johnson Creek Road SE to loop around through the Skookumchuck River and Johnson Creek valleys back to the trail near Rainier. It's 14-plus miles of rolling hills on country roads, replacing 5 miles on the trail, which would make the trip about 36 miles total. On the return, look for Mount Rainier's glacial cap peeking over the trees beyond your right handlebar grip.

Route Connections: Connect to the Chehalis Western (Tour 59) on the trail 1 mile west of Rainier.

MILEAGE LOG

0.0 From trailhead parking near Yelm city hall (restrooms), depart onto trail.

2.8 Cross Manke Rd. SE.

5.5 Pass Wilkowski Park and arrive at town of Rainier (restrooms).

7.3 Left at Y with Chehalis Western Trail to stay on Yelm–Tenino Trail.

9.9 Ride along McIntosh Lake.

11.4 Cross SR 507 and rejoin trail. Caution: busy road.

13.4 Arrive at Tenino City Park (restrooms).

13.7 Arrive at Depot Museum and Quarry House, just beyond trail's end. Retrace route (or take side trip on local roads; see above).

16.0 Cross SR 507.

20.0 Pass junction with Chehalis Western Trail.

21.8 Arrive at town of Rainier.

27.3 Arrive at trailhead parking in Yelm to end tour.

RECOMMENDED RESOURCES

Start your research at this book's accompanying website, www.biking pugetsound.com, which contains many links to the resources listed below.

CYCLING CLUBS

Bicycling membership organizations typically offer group rides, socializing, and community events. Some hold classes, maintain trails, negotiate discounts with bike shops, or serve as advocates to governmental entities.

Boeing Employees' Bicycle Club, Seattle; www.bebc-seattle.org. You must be associated with Boeing to be a member but not to participate in their rides.

Capital Bicycle Club, Olympia; www.capitalbicycleclub.org.

Cascade Bicycle Club, Seattle; www.cascade.org. The region's largest club offers free daily rides and sponsors the Chilly Hilly, Seattle to Portland (STP), annual Bike Expo, as well as many other events.

Cyclists of Greater Seattle (COGS); www.cyclistsofgreaterseattle .org. This casual club focuses on fun, friends, and adventure.

Different Spokes, Seattle; www.differentspokes.org. This is a cycling club for the gay, lesbian, bisexual, and transgender communities.

Evergreen Tandem Club, Seattle; www.evergreentandemclub.org. This group promotes the joy of riding tandem in the Puget Sound area.

Marymoor Velodrome Association, Bellevue; http://velodrome. org. This organization promotes track and cyclocross racing and events at the Velodrome.

Mountaineers; www.mountaineers.org. Some local chapters have cycling outings.

Port Townsend Bicycle Association; www.ptbikes.org. This group sponsors the Rhody Tour in early May.

Redmond Cycling Club, Redmond; www.redmondcyclingclub.org. This sponsor of Ride Around Mount Rainier in One Day (RAMROD) has the club slogan "Where hill is not a four-letter word."

Seattle Bicycle Club, Seattle; www.seattlebicycleclub.org. This organization sponsors social rides and a series of short tours around Washington State each summer.

Seattle International Randonneurs; www.seattlerandonneur.org. This club focuses on randonneuring—long-distance, unsupported, noncompetitive cycling.

Skagit Bicycle Club, Mount Vernon; www.skagitbicycleclub.org. This group sponsors the Skagit Spring Classic ride.

Snohomish County BIKES Club, Everett; www.bikesclub.org. This club is the sponsor of the McClinchy Mile ride.

Squeaky Wheels, Bainbridge Island; www.squeakywheels.org. This "bicycling support group" promotes safe biking on Bainbridge Island.

Tacoma Wheelmen's Bicycle Club, Tacoma; www.twbc.org. This organization sponsors the Daffodil Classic ride.

West Sound Cycling Club, Silverdale; www.westsoundcycling. com. This group sponsors the Tour de Kitsap ride.

Whidbey Island Bicycle Club, Coupeville; http://whidbeybicycle club.org. This club promotes recreational riding on the island and advocates on cycling issues.

ADVOCACY ORGANIZATIONS

You can support safety, education, and expansion of bicycle routes or transit amenities for cyclists by joining a group that advocates for the cause.

Bike Works, Seattle; www.bikeworks.org. This Rainier Valley bike shop recycles bikes for youth in its Earn-a-Bike program.

Evergreen Mountain Bike Alliance, Seattle; http://evergreenmtb .org. This organization provides statewide advocacy of backcountry trails.

Foothills Rails-to-Trails Coalition; www.piercecountytrails.org. This group assists in the creation and maintenance of a connected system of nonmotorized trails from Mount Rainier to Puget Sound.

Friends of the Burke-Gilman Trail, Seattle; www.burkegilmantrail .org. This organization supports the completion and maintenance of the granddaddy of Seattle's rail-trails.

Washington Bikes, Seattle; www.wabikes.org. Among its many safety-related activities, Washington Bikes (formerly Bicycle Alliance of Washington) operates the Safe Routes to School program and advocates statewide and at the state legislature for cycling issues.

Woodland Trail Greenway Association, Olympia. www.wood landtrail.org. This group advocates for the rail-trail system in Thurston County.

BIKE MAPS

City

Bellevue: www.chooseyourwaybellevue.org/bike
Burien: www.burienwa.gov/index.aspx?NID = 265
Issaquah: http://gettingaroundissaquah.org/

Kent: http://kentwa.gov/transportation/BikeWalk/
Kirkland: www.kirklandwa.gov/depart/parks/Online_Parks_Guide
La Conner: www.lovelaconner.com/activity-maps-booklets/
Port Townsend: http://ptbikes.org/maps/
Redmond: www.ci.redmond.wa.us/cms/one.aspx?portalId = 169&
pageId = 7398
Renton: http://rentonwa.gov/living/default.aspx?id = 2322
San Juan Island: http://sanjuanislandtrails.org/
Seattle: www.seattle.gov/transportation/bikemaps.htm

County

Island: www.islandcounty.net/publicworks/BikeTours/
King: www.kingcounty.gov/transportation/kcdot/Roads/Bicycling
.aspx
Kitsap: www.kitsapgov.com/pw/bikeplan.htm
Pierce: www.co.pierce.wa.us/index.aspx?NID = 2219
Skagit: www.beactiveskagit.org/maps.cfm
Snohomish: www.communitytransit.org/bikes/#BikeMaps
Thurston: www.trpc.org/maps/pages/BikeMap.aspx

State

A Washington bicycle map showing the average daily traffic of major roads and highways across the state—and highways where bicycles are prohibited—can be ordered through the state Department of Transportation: www.wsdot.wa.gov/bike/statemap.htm.

GUIDEBOOKS OF THE REGION AND BEYOND

Bell, Trudy. *Bicycling with Children.* Seattle: Mountaineers Books, 1999.
A complete how-to guide, from toddlers to teaching to tandems.
Burk, Mia with Joe Kurmaskie. *Joyride: Pedaling toward a Healthier Planet.* 2nd edition. Seattle: Mountaineers Books, 2012. *The behind-the-scenes story of transforming Portland, Oregon, into a premiere bicycling city, told with humor and plenty of examples by an advocate who put in two decades on the effort.*
McQuaide, Mike. *75 Classic Rides Washington: The Best Road Biking Routes.* Seattle: Mountaineers Books, 2012. *This veteran guidebook author offers energetic excursions across the state, probably including every scenic hill climb out there.*
Moore, Jim. *75 Classic Rides Oregon: The Best Road Biking Routes.* Seattle: Mountaineers Books, 2012. *A comprehensive selection of rides, from Portland to the People's Coast to some epic mountain passes.*

Rails-to-Trails Conservancy. *Rail-Trails West: The Official Rails-to-Trails Conservancy Guidebook.* Birmingham, AL: Wilderness Press, 2009. *Looking for scenic rides in California, Arizona, or Nevada? Try these 53 routes charted across the Southwest. Well, there's only one in Nevada.*

Spring, Vicky, and Tom Kirkendall. *Bicycling the Pacific Coast.* 4th edition. Seattle: Mountaineers Books, 2005. *How about a two-wheeled adventure from Vancouver to San Diego? This book tells you how.*

Toyoshima, Tim. *Mountain Bike Emergency Repairs.* Seattle: Mountaineers Books, 1999. *This slim little book is big on practical advice. It identifies hundreds of bike parts and problems and offers a diagnosis, emergency repair, and permanent repair for most gear maladies.*

Wert, Fred. *Washington's Rail-Trails.* Seattle: Mountaineers Books, 2004. *A guide to 48 of the former railroads that can now be enjoyed on foot, by bike, or on horseback.*

Woods, Erin, and Bill Woods. *Bicycling the Backroads of Southwest Washington.* Seattle: Mountaineers Books, 2002. *Forty-six scenic tours from Bremerton to Portland. There's great riding in Grays Harbor and Lewis Counties and other points south.*

Wozniak, Owen. *Biking Portland: 55 Rides from the Willamette Valley to Vancouver.* Seattle: Mountaineers Books, 2012. *Put your bike on the train, and get down there! Or stay a few days for some fun riding after the STP.*

SUGGESTED READING

Note: For training recovery days, injury time-outs, or really nasty winter weather.

Bathurst, Bella. *The Bicycle Book.* New York: Harper Press, 2012. *This engaging British author finds great stories and characters for this tour through the history and lore of the bike.*

Burningham, Lucy, and Ellee Thalheimer. *Hop in the Saddle: A Guide to Portland's Craft Beer Scene, by Bike.* Portland, OR: Action Publications, 2012. *In a size that would fit in your back pocket or seat-post bag, the authors guide you all over the City of Roses for beers by bike.*

Kurmaskie, Joe. *Mud, Sweat, and Gears: A Rowdy Family Bike Adventure Across Canada on Seven Wheels.* Halcottsville, NY: Breakaway Books, 2009. *The "Metal Cowboy" drags his family on yet another bike adventure. Also see his other three crazy adventures in book form.*

Mapes, Jeff. *Pedaling Revolution: How Cyclists Are Changing American Cities.* Corvallis, OR: Oregon State University Press, 2009. *This Oregonian writer and Portland cyclist traces the history of bike advocacy and our growing bike culture.*

Savage, Barbara. *Miles from Nowhere: A Round-the-World Bicycle Adventure.* Seattle: Mountaineers Books, 1985. *Warmly told story of one couple's amazing trip.*

Snyder, Amy. *Hell on Two Wheels: An Astonishing Story of Suffering, Triumph, and the Most Extreme Endurance Race in the World.* Chicago: Triumph Books, 2011. *The most extreme cycling race doesn't involve a yellow jersey, and it's not in some far-flung place you've never heard of. It's from California to Maryland, and this ultradistance race sounds perfectly insane.*

Weir, Willie. *Travels with Willie: Adventure Cyclist.* Seattle: Pineleaf Productions, 2009. "Dream. Pedal. Travel. Repeat." *That was Willie's inscription in my copy, and it pretty well sums up the philosophy of the Adventure Cycling columnist and Seattle-based world biking ambassador. His stories make you want to pedal along on his next excursion.*

INDEX

ABOUT THE AUTHOR

Bill Thorness is a freelance writer and editor based in Seattle. He is the author of four books; in addition to this guidebook, he has written two books on edible gardening and one profiling an auto industry executive. His articles have appeared in many regional publications, including the *Seattle Times*, *Seattle Met*, and *Cascade Courier*, as well as online. He has been a recreational cyclist since the mid-1980s and was a bike commuter into downtown Seattle in the 1990s, where he found that the challenge of traffic can be every bit as sweat-inducing as climbing one of the city's numerous hills. When he's not ditching the computer screen by researching another bike route, he enjoys gardening, hiking, and skiing.

Bill is a member and ride leader for Cascade Bicycle Club and is a supporter of Washington Bikes and the Adventure Cycling Association. Professional affiliations include Society of Professional Journalists and Northwest Independent Editors Guild. He was honored with the 2014 Sustainable Hero award from Sustainable Seattle. See more of Bill's work at www.billthorness.com.

Continue to explore new routes and receive updates to this book by logging on to www.bikingpugetsound.com, which includes a blog, cycling links, and event listings.

Bill Thorness and Susie Thorness (Photo by L. J. McAllister)

recreation · lifestyle · conservation

MOUNTAINEERS BOOKS is a leading publisher of mountaineering literature and guides—including our flagship title, *Mountaineering: The Freedom of the Hills*—as well as adventure narratives, natural history, and general outdoor recreation. Through our two imprints, Skipstone and Braided River, we also publish titles on sustainability and conservation. We are committed to supporting the environmental and educational goals of our organization by providing expert information on human-powered adventure, sustainable practices at home and on the trail, and preservation of wilderness.

The Mountaineers, founded in 1906, is a 501(c)(3) nonprofit outdoor activity and conservation organization whose mission is "to explore, study, preserve, and enjoy the natural beauty of the outdoors." One of the largest such organizations in the United States, it sponsors classes and year-round outdoor activities throughout the Pacific Northwest, including climbing, hiking, backcountry skiing, snowshoeing, bicycling, camping, paddling, and more. The Mountaineers also supports its mission through its publishing division, Mountaineers Books, and promotes environmental education and citizen engagement. For more information, visit The Mountaineers Program Center, 7700 Sand Point Way NE, Seattle, WA 98115-3996; phone 206-521-6001; www.mountaineers.org; or email info@mountaineers.org.

Our publications are made possible through the generosity of donors and through sales of more than 500 titles on outdoor recreation, sustainable lifestyle, and conservation. To donate, purchase books, or learn more, visit us online:

MOUNTAINEERS BOOKS
1001 SW Klickitat Way, Suite 201 • Seattle, WA 98134
800-553-4453 • mbooks@mountaineersbooks.org • www.mountaineersbooks.org

Mountaineers Books is proud to be a corporate sponsor of The Leave No Trace Center for Outdoor Ethics, whose mission is to promote and inspire responsible outdoor recreation through education, research, and partnerships · The Leave No Trace program is focused specifically on human-powered (nonmotorized) recreation · Leave No Trace strives to educate visitors about the nature of their recreational impacts and offers techniques to prevent and minimize such impacts · Leave No Trace is best understood as an educational and ethical program, not as a set of rules and regulations · For more information, visit www.lnt.org, or call 800-332-4100.

OTHER TITLES YOU MIGHT ENJOY FROM MOUNTAINEERS BOOKS

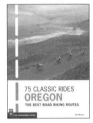

Biking Portland
Owen Wozniak
55 rides around Portland from the
Willamette Valley to Vancouver

**75 Classic Rides Washington:
The Best Road Biking Routes**
Mike McQuaide
A full-color guidebook to the best
cycling routes in Washington—
a biking mecca

**75 Classic Rides Oregon:
The Best Road Biking Routes**
Jim Moore
The "classic" cycle routes for
one of the nation's top biking
destinations—in full-color

**Triathlon Revolution: Training,
Technique, and Inspiration**
Terri Schneider
For both novice and experienced
triathletes, this is the definitive
manual for a multisport lifestyle.

The Healthy Knees Book
Dr. Astrid Pujari and
Nancy Shatz Alton
Details the structure and function
of the knee and explains its
common injuries and chronic pains.